CASENOTE® Legal Briefs®

CIVIL PROCEDURE

Keyed to Courses Using

Yeazell, Schwartz, and Carroll's
Civil Procedure
Eleventh Edition

Authored by: Publisher's Editorial Staff

ASPEN PUBLISHING

To contact Customer Service, e-mail customer.service@aspenpublishing.com, call 1-800-950-5259, or mail correspondence to:

Aspen Publishing
Attn: Order Department
1 Wall Street
Burlington, MA 01803

Printed in the United States of America.

1 2 3 4 5 6 7 8 9 0

ISBN 978-1-5438-5059-8

SUSTAINABLE FORESTRY INITIATIVE Certified Sourcing
www.forests.org
SFI-00756

About Aspen Publishing

Aspen Publishing is a leading provider of educational content and digital learning solutions to law schools in the U.S. and around the world. Aspen provides best-in-class solutions for legal education through authoritative textbooks, written by renowned authors, and breakthrough products such as Connected eBooks, Connected Quizzing, and PracticePerfect.

The Aspen Casebook Series (famously known among law faculty and students as the "red and black" casebooks) encompasses hundreds of highly regarded textbooks in more than eighty disciplines, from large enrollment courses such as Torts and Contracts to emerging electives such as Sustainability and the Law of Policing. Study aids such as the *Examples & Explanations* and the *Emanuel Law Outlines* series, both highly popular collections, help law students master complex subject matter.

Major products, programs, and initiatives include:

- **Connected eBooks** are enhanced digital textbooks and study aids that come with a suite of online content and learning tools designed to maximize student success. Designed in collaboration with hundreds of faculty and students, the Connected eBook is a significant leap forward in the legal education learning tools available to students.

- **Connected Quizzing** is an easy-to-use formative assessment tool that tests law students' understanding and provides timely feedback to improve learning outcomes. Delivered through CasebookConnect.com, the learning platform already used by students to access their Aspen casebooks, Connected Quizzing is simple to implement and integrates seamlessly with law school course curricula.

- **PracticePerfect** is a visually engaging, interactive study aid to explain commonly encountered legal doctrines through easy-to-understand animated videos, illustrative examples, and numerous practice questions. Developed by a team of experts, PracticePerfect is the ideal study companion for today's law students.

- The **Aspen Learning Library** enables law schools to provide their students with access to the most popular study aids on the market across all of their courses. Available through an annual subscription, the online library consists of study aids in e-book, audio, and video formats with full text search, note-taking, and highlighting capabilities.

- Aspen's **Digital Bookshelf** is an institutional-level online education bookshelf, consolidating everything students and professors need to ensure success. This program ensures that every student has access to affordable course materials from day one.

- **Leading Edge** is a community centered on thinking differently about legal education and putting those thoughts into actionable strategies. At the core of the program is the Leading Edge Conference, an annual gathering of legal education thought leaders looking to pool ideas and identify promising directions of exploration.

Format for the Casenote® Legal Brief

Nature of Case: This section identifies the form of action (e.g., breach of contract, negligence, battery), the type of proceeding (e.g., demurrer, appeal from trial court's jury instructions) or the relief sought (e.g., damages, injunction, criminal sanctions).

Palsgraf v. Long Island R.R. Co.

Injured bystander (P) v. Railroad company (D)

N.Y. Ct. App., 248 N.Y. 339, 162 N.E. 99 (1928).

NATURE OF CASE: Appeal from judgment affirming verdict for plaintiff seeking damages for personal injury.

FACT SUMMARY: Helen Palsgraf (P) was injured on R.R.'s (D) train platform when R.R.'s (D) guard helped a passenger aboard a moving train, causing his package to fall on the tracks. The package contained fireworks which exploded, creating a shock that tipped a scale onto Palsgraf (P).

RULE OF LAW

The risk reasonably to be perceived defines the duty to be obeyed.

FACTS: Helen Palsgraf (P) purchased a ticket to Rockaway Beach from R.R. (D) and was waiting on the train platform. As she waited, two men ran to catch a train that was pulling out from the platform. The first man jumped aboard, but the second man, who appeared as if he might fall, was helped aboard by the guard on the train who had kept the door open so they could jump aboard. A guard on the platform also helped by pushing him onto the train. The man was carrying a package wrapped in newspaper. In the process, the man dropped his package, which fell on the tracks. The package contained fireworks and exploded. The shock of the explosion was apparently of great enough strength to tip over some scales at the other end of the platform, which fell on Palsgraf (P) and injured her. A jury awarded her damages, and R.R. (D) appealed.

ISSUE: Does the risk reasonably to be perceived define the duty to be obeyed?

HOLDING AND DECISION: (Cardozo, C.J.) Yes. The risk reasonably to be perceived defines the duty to be obeyed. If there is no foreseeable hazard to the injured party as the result of a seemingly innocent act, the act does not become a tort because it happened to be a wrong as to another. If the wrong was not willful, the plaintiff must show that the act as to her had such great and apparent possibilities of danger as to entitle her to protection. Negligence in the abstract is not enough upon which to base liability. Negligence is a relative concept, evolving out of the common law doctrine of trespass on the case. To establish liability, the defendant must owe a legal duty of reasonable care to the injured party. A cause of action in tort will lie where harm, though unintended, could have been averted or avoided by observance of such a duty. The scope of the duty is limited by the range of danger that a reasonable person could foresee. In this case, there was nothing to suggest from the appearance of the parcel or otherwise that the parcel contained fireworks. The guard could not reasonably have had any warning of a threat to Palsgraf (P), and R.R. (D) therefore cannot be held liable. Judgment is reversed in favor of R.R. (D).

DISSENT: (Andrews, J.) The concept that there is no negligence unless R.R. (D) owes a legal duty to take care as to Palsgraf (P) herself is too narrow. Everyone owes to the world at large the duty of refraining from those acts that may unreasonably threaten the safety of others. If the guard's action was negligent as to those nearby, it was also negligent as to those outside what might be termed the "danger zone." For Palsgraf (P) to recover, R.R.'s (D) negligence must have been the proximate cause of her injury, a question of fact for the jury.

ANALYSIS

The majority defined the limit of the defendant's liability in terms of the danger that a reasonable person in defendant's situation would have perceived. The dissent argued that the limitation should not be placed on liability, but rather on damages. Judge Andrews suggested that only injuries that would not have happened but for R.R.'s (D) negligence should be compensable. Both the majority and dissent recognized the policy-driven need to limit liability for negligent acts, seeking, in the words of Judge Andrews, to define a framework "that will be practical and in keeping with the general understanding of mankind." The Restatement (Second) of Torts has accepted Judge Cardozo's view.

Quicknotes

FORESEEABILITY A reasonable expectation that change is the probable result of certain acts or omissions.

NEGLIGENCE Conduct falling below the standard of care that a reasonable person would demonstrate under similar conditions.

PROXIMATE CAUSE The natural sequence of events without which an injury would not have been sustained.

Party ID: Quick identification of the relationship between the parties.

Fact Summary: This is included to refresh your memory and can be used as a quick reminder of the facts.

Rule of Law: Summarizes the general principle of law that the case illustrates. It may be used for instant recall of the court's holding and for classroom discussion or home review.

Facts: This section contains all relevant facts of the case, including the contentions of the parties and the lower court holdings. It is written in a logical order to give you a clear understanding of the case. The plaintiff and defendant are identified by their proper names throughout and are always labeled with a (P) or (D).

Issue: The issue is a concise question that brings out the essence of the opinion as it relates to the section of the casebook in which the case appears. Both substantive and procedural issues are included if relevant to the decision.

Holding and Decision: This section offers a clear and in-depth discussion of the rule of the case and the court's rationale. It is written in easy-to-understand language and answers the issue presented by applying the law to the facts of the case. When relevant, it includes a thorough discussion of the exceptions to the case as listed by the court, any major cites to the other cases on point, and the names of the judges who wrote the decisions.

Concurrence/Dissent: All concurrences and dissents are briefed whenever they are included by the casebook author.

Analysis: This last paragraph gives you a broad understanding of where the case "fits in" with other cases in the section of the book and with the entire course. It is a hornbook-style discussion indicating whether the case is a majority or minority opinion and comparing the principal case with other cases in the casebook. It may also provide analysis from restatements, uniform codes, and law review articles.

Quicknotes: Conveniently defines legal terms found in the case.

Note to Students

Aspen Publishing is proud to offer *Casenote® Legal Briefs*—continuing thirty years of publishing America's best-selling legal briefs.

Casenote® Legal Briefs are designed to help you save time when briefing assigned cases. Organized under convenient headings, they show you how to abstract the basic facts and holdings from the text of the actual opinions handed down by the courts. Used as part of a rigorous study regimen, they can help you spend more time analyzing and critiquing points of law than on copying bits and pieces of judicial opinions into your notebook or outline.

Casenote® Legal Briefs should never be used as a substitute for assigned casebook readings. They work best when read as a follow-up to reviewing the underlying opinions themselves. Students who try to avoid reading and digesting the judicial opinions in their casebooks or online sources will end up shortchanging themselves in the long run. The ability to absorb, critique, and restate the dynamic and complex elements of case law decisions is crucial to your success in law school and beyond. It cannot be developed vicariously.

In addition to *Casenote® Legal Briefs*, Aspen Publishing offers the following study aids:

- *Casenote® Legal Briefs*
- *Emanuel® Law Outlines*
- Emanuel® *Law in a Flash* Flash Cards
- Emanuel® *CrunchTime®* Series

Each of these series is designed to provide you with easy-to-understand explanations of complex points of law. Each volume offers guidance on the principles of legal analysis and, consulted regularly, will hone your ability to spot relevant issues. We have titles that will help you prepare for class, prepare for your exams, and enhance your general comprehension of the law along the way.

To find out more about our law school tools for success, visit us at *www.AspenPublishing.com* or e-mail us at *customer.service@aspenpublishing.com*. We'll be happy to assist you.

How to Brief a Case

A. Decide on a Format and Stick to It

Structure is essential to a good brief. It enables you to arrange systematically the related parts that are scattered throughout most cases, thus making manageable and understandable what might otherwise seem to be an endless and unfathomable sea of information. There are, of course, an unlimited number of formats that can be utilized. However, it is best to find one that suits your needs and stick to it. Consistency breeds both efficiency and the security that when called upon you will know where to look in your brief for the information you are asked to give.

Any format, as long as it presents the essential elements of a case in an organized fashion, can be used. Experience, however, has led *Casenote® Legal Briefs* to develop and utilize the following format because of its logical flow and universal applicability.

NATURE OF CASE: This is a brief statement of the legal character and procedural status of the case (e.g., "Appeal of a burglary conviction").

There are many different alternatives open to a litigant dissatisfied with a court ruling. The key to determining which one has been used is to discover *who is asking this court for what.*

This first entry in the brief should be kept as *short as possible.* Use the court's terminology if you understand it. But since jurisdictions vary as to the titles of pleadings, the best entry is the one that addresses who wants what in this proceeding, not the one that sounds most like the court's language.

RULE OF LAW: A statement of the general principle of law that the case illustrates (e.g., "An acceptance that varies any term of the offer is considered a rejection and counteroffer").

Determining the rule of law of a case is a procedure similar to determining the issue of the case. Avoid being fooled by red herrings; there may be a few rules of law mentioned in the case excerpt, but usually only one is *the* rule with which the casebook editor is concerned. The techniques used to locate the issue, described below, may also be utilized to find the rule of law. Generally, your best guide is simply the chapter heading. It is a clue to the point the casebook editor seeks to make and should be kept in mind when reading every case in the respective section.

FACTS: A synopsis of only the essential facts of the case, i.e., those bearing upon or leading up to the issue.

The facts entry should be a short statement of the events and transactions that led one party to initiate legal proceedings against another in the first place. While some cases conveniently state the salient facts at the beginning of the decision, in other instances they will have to be culled from hiding places throughout the text, even from concurring and dissenting opinions. Some of the "facts" will often be in dispute and should be so noted. Conflicting evidence may be briefly pointed up. "Hard" facts must be included. Both must be *relevant* in order to be listed in the facts entry. It is impossible to tell what is relevant until the entire case is read, as the ultimate determination of the rights and liabilities of the parties may turn on something buried deep in the opinion.

Generally, the facts entry should not be longer than three to five *short* sentences.

It is often helpful to identify the role played by a party in a given context. For example, in a construction contract case the identification of a party as the "contractor" or "builder" alleviates the need to tell that that party was the one who was supposed to have built the house.

It is always helpful, and a good general practice, to identify the "plaintiff" and the "defendant." This may seem elementary and uncomplicated, but, especially in view of the creative editing practiced by some casebook editors, it is sometimes a difficult or even impossible task. Bear in mind that the *party presently* seeking something from this court may not be the plaintiff, and that sometimes only the cross-claim of a defendant is treated in the excerpt. Confusing or misaligning the parties can ruin your analysis and understanding of the case.

ISSUE: A statement of the general legal question answered by or illustrated in the case. For clarity, the issue is best put in the form of a question capable of a "yes" or "no" answer. In reality, the issue is simply the Rule of Law put in the form of a question (e.g., "May an offer be accepted by performance?").

The major problem presented in discerning what is *the* issue in the case is that an opinion usually purports to raise and answer several questions. However, except for rare cases, only one such question is really the issue in the case. Collateral issues not necessary to the resolution of the matter in controversy are handled by the court by language known as *"obiter dictum"* or merely *"dictum."* While dicta may be included later in the brief, they have no place under the issue heading.

To find the issue, ask *who wants what* and then go on to ask *why did that party succeed or fail in getting it.* Once this is determined, the "why" should be turned into a question.

The complexity of the issues in the cases will vary, but in all cases a single-sentence question should sum up the issue. *In a few cases,* there will be two, or even more rarely, three issues of equal importance to the resolution of the case. Each should be expressed in a single-sentence question.

Since many issues are resolved by a court in coming to a final disposition of a case, the casebook editor will reproduce the portion of the opinion containing the issue or issues most relevant to the area of law under scrutiny. A noted law professor gave this advice: "Close the book; look at the title on the cover." Chances are, if it is Property, you need not concern yourself with whether, for example, the federal government's treatment of the plaintiff's land really raises a federal question sufficient to support jurisdiction on this ground in federal court.

The same rule applies to chapter headings designating sub-areas within the subjects. They tip you off as to what the text is designed to teach. The cases are arranged in a casebook to show a progression or development of the law, so that the preceding cases may also help.

It is also most important to remember to *read the notes and questions* at the end of a case to determine what the editors wanted you to have gleaned from it.

HOLDING AND DECISION: This section should succinctly explain the rationale of the court in arriving at its decision. In capsulizing the "reasoning" of the court, it should always include an application of the general rule or rules of law to the specific facts of the case. Hidden justifications come to light in this entry: the reasons for the state of the law, the public policies, the biases and prejudices, those considerations that influence the justices' thinking and, ultimately, the outcome of the case. At the end, there should be a short indication of thedisposition or procedural resolution of the case (e.g., "Decision of the trial court for Mr. Smith (P) reversed").

The foregoing format is designed to help you "digest" the reams of case material with which you will be faced in your law school career. Once mastered by practice, it will place at your fingertips the information the authors of your casebooks have sought to impart to you in case-by-case illustration and analysis.

B. Be as Economical as Possible in Briefing Cases

Once armed with a format that encourages succinctness, it is as important to be economical with regard to the time spent on the actual reading of the case as it is to be economical in the writing of the brief itself. This does not mean "skimming" a case. Rather, it means reading the case with an "eye" trained to recognize into which "section" of your brief a particular passage or line fits and having a system for quickly and precisely marking the case so that the passages fitting any one particular part of the brief can be easily identified and brought together in a concise and accurate manner when the brief is actually written.

It is of no use to simply repeat everything in the opinion of the court; record only enough information to trigger your recollection of what the court said. Nevertheless, an accurate statement of the "law of the case," i.e., the legal principle applied to the facts, is absolutely essential to class preparation and to learning the law under the case method.

To that end, it is important to develop a "shorthand" that you can use to make marginal notations. These notations will tell you at a glance in which section of the brief you will be placing that particular passage or portion of the opinion.

Some students prefer to underline all the salient portions of the opinion (with a pencil or colored underliner marker), making marginal notations as they go along. Others prefer the color-coded method of underlining, utilizing different colors of markers to underline the salient portions of the case, each separate color being used to represent a different section of the brief. For example, blue underlining could be used for passages relating to the rule of law, yellow for those relating to the issue, and green for those relating to the holding and decision, etc. While it has its advocates, thecolor-coded method can be confusing and time-consuming (all that time spent on changing colored markers). Furthermore, it can interfere with the continuity and concentration many students deem essential to the reading of a case for maximum comprehension. In the end, however, it is a matter of personal preference and style. Just remember, whatever method you use, underlining must be used sparingly or its value is lost.

If you take the marginal notation route, an efficient and easy method is to go along underlining the key portions of the case and placing in the margin alongside them the following "markers" to indicate where a particular passage or line "belongs" in the brief you will write:

N	(NATURE OF CASE)
RL	(RULE OF LAW)
I	(ISSUE)
HL	(HOLDING AND DECISION, relates to the RULE OF LAW behind the decision)
HR	(HOLDING AND DECISION, gives the RATIONALE or reasoning behind the decision)
HA	(HOLDING AND DECISION, applies the general principle(s) of law to the facts of the case to arrive at the decision)

Remember that a particular passage may well contain information necessary to more than one part of your brief, in which case you simply note that in the margin. If you are using the color-coded underlining method instead of marginal notation, simply make asterisks or checks in the margin next to the passage in question in the colors that indicate the additional sections of the brief where it might be utilized.

The economy of utilizing "shorthand" in marking cases for briefing can be maintained in the actual brief writing process itself by utilizing "law student shorthand" within the brief. There are many commonly used words and phrases for which abbreviations can be substituted in your briefs (and in your class notes also). You can develop abbreviations that are personal to you and which will save you a lot of time. A reference list of briefing abbreviations can be found on page x of this book.

C. Use Both the Briefing Process and the Brief as a Learning Tool

Now that you have a format and the tools for briefing cases efficiently, the most important thing is to make the time spent in briefing profitable to you and to make the most advantageous use of the briefs you create. Of course, the briefs are invaluable for classroom reference when you are called upon to explain or analyze a particular case. However, they are also useful in reviewing for exams. A quick glance at the fact summary should bring the case to mind, and a rereading of the rule of law should enable you to go over the underlying legal concept in your mind, how it was applied in that particular case, and how it might apply in other factual settings.

As to the value to be derived from engaging in the briefing process itself, there is an immediate benefit that arises from being forced to sift through the essential facts and reasoning from the court's opinion and to succinctly express them in your own words in your brief. The process ensures that you understand the case and the point that it illustrates, and that means you will be ready to absorb further analysis and information brought forth in class. It also ensures you will have something to say when called upon in class. The briefing process helps develop a mental agility for getting to the *gist* of a case and for identifying, expounding on, and applying the legal concepts and issues found there. The briefing process is the mental process on which you must rely in taking law school examinations; it is also the mental process upon which lawyers rely in serving their clients and in making a living.

Abbreviations for Briefs

acceptance	acp
affirmed	aff
answer	ans
assumption of risk	a/r
attorney	atty
beyond a reasonable doubt	b/r/d
bona fide purchaser	BFP
breach of contract	br/k
cause of action	c/a
common law	c/l
Constitution	Con
constitutional	con
contract	K
contributory negligence	c/n
cross	x
cross-complaint	x/c
cross-examination	x/ex
cruel and unusual punishment	c/u/p
defendant	D
dismissed	dis
double jeopardy	d/j
due process	d/p
equal protection	e/p
equity	eq
evidence	ev
exclude	exc
exclusionary rule	exc/r
felony	f/n
freedom of speech	f/s
good faith	g/f
habeas corpus	h/c
hearsay	hr
husband	H
injunction	inj
in loco parentis	ILP
inter vivos	I/v
joint tenancy	j/t
judgment	judgt
jurisdiction	jur
last clear chance	LCC
long-arm statute	LAS
majority view	maj
meeting of minds	MOM
minority view	min
Miranda rule	Mir/r
Miranda warnings	Mir/w
negligence	neg
notice	ntc
nuisance	nus
obligation	ob
obscene	obs
offer	O
offeree	OE
offeror	OR
ordinance	ord
pain and suffering	p/s
parol evidence	p/e
plaintiff	P
prima facie	p/f
probable cause	p/c
proximate cause	px/c
real property	r/p
reasonable doubt	r/d
reasonable man	r/m
rebuttable presumption	rb/p
remanded	rem
res ipsa loquitur	RIL
respondeat superior	r/s
Restatement	RS
reversed	rev
Rule Against Perpetuities	RAP
search and seizure	s/s
search warrant	s/w
self-defense	s/d
specific performance	s/p
statute	S
statute of frauds	S/F
statute of limitations	S/L
summary judgment	s/j
tenancy at will	t/w
tenancy in common	t/c
tenant	t
third party	TP
third party beneficiary	TPB
transferred intent	TI
unconscionable	uncon
unconstitutional	unconst
undue influence	u/e
Uniform Commercial Code	UCC
unilateral	uni
vendee	VE
vendor	VR
versus	v
void for vagueness	VFV
weight of authority	w/a
weight of the evidence	w/e
wife	W
with	w/
within	w/i
without	w/o
without prejudice	w/o/p
wrongful death	wr/d

Table of Cases

CHAPTER 1

An Overview of Procedure

Quick Reference Rules of Law

Hawkins v. Masters Farms, Inc.

Representative of estate (P) v. Tractor driver (D)

2003 WL 21555767 (D. Kan. 2003)

NATURE OF CASE: Motion to dismiss for lack of subject matter jurisdiction.

FACT SUMMARY: James Creal was killed when his automobile was struck by a tractor owned by Masters Farms, Inc. (D). Creal's estate (P) brought suit against Masters Farms, Inc. (D) in federal court alleging diversity subject matter jurisdiction. Masters Farms, Inc. (D) moved to dismiss on grounds of incomplete diversity among the parties.

RULE OF LAW

For purposes of determining diversity jurisdiction, a person is a "citizen" of the state in which he or she is "domiciled," which for adults is established by physical presence in a place in connection with the intent to remain there.

FACTS: On December 8, 2000, James Creal was killed in an automobile accident just south of Troy, Kansas, when his car was struck by a tractor driven by Masters (D), a citizen of Kansas. At the time of his death, James Creal was living in Kansas with his wife and her children. James Creal had lived in Missouri most of his life, while Mrs. Creal had resided in Kansas the majority of her life. When Mrs. Creal moved into an apartment in Troy, Kansas, in March 2000, James Creal brought his clothes, furniture, and many other items and moved to the new apartment. The Creals were married in July 2000. In November, the Creals moved into a house in Troy, Kansas. His death certificate listed Kansas as his residence. The representatives of James Creal (P) brought suit against Masters (D) in the federal district court for Kansas, alleging the existence of diversity jurisdiction under 28 U.S.C. § 1332. Masters (D) moved to dismiss, disputing that there was complete diversity among the parties.

ISSUE: For purposes of determining diversity jurisdiction, is a person a "citizen" of the state in which he or she is "domiciled," which for adults is established by physical presence in a place in connection with the intent to remain there?

HOLDING AND DECISION: (Van Bebber, J.) Yes. For purposes of determining diversity jurisdiction, a person is a "citizen" of the state in which he or she is "domiciled," which for adults is established by physical presence in a place in connection with the intent to remain there. Here, at the time of his death, Creal had not only established a physical presence in the State of Kansas, but also displayed intent to remain there. Although he lived the majority of his life in Missouri, he had been living in Kansas with his wife of five months for nearly one year at the time he died. Among other things, he had moved household items into the Kansas home; he contributed to household costs; and he purchased a new bedroom set with his wife. Any non-specific so-called "floating intention" of Creal to return to his former Missouri domicile would be insufficient to overcome the evidence that he was domiciled in Kansas at the time of his death. Masters's (D) motion to dismiss is granted.

ANALYSIS

In *Hawkins*, the court noted that the party seeking to invoke federal jurisdiction bears the burden of proving that jurisdiction is proper. Because federal courts are courts of limited jurisdiction, the presumption is against federal jurisdiction.

Quicknotes

DIVERSITY OF CITIZENSHIP Parties are citizens of different states, or one party is an alien; a factor, along with a statutorily set dollar value of the matter in controversy, that allows a federal district court to exercise its authority to hear a lawsuit based on diversity jurisdiction.

DIVERSITY JURISDICTION The authority of a federal court to hear and determine cases involving parties who are of different states and an amount in controversy greater than a statutorily set amount.

FEDERAL JURISDICTION The authority of federal courts to hear and determine cases of a particular nature derived from the United States Constitution and rules promulgated by Congress pursuant thereto.

Bridges v. Diesel Service, Inc.

Disabled employee (P) v. Employer (D)

1994 U.S. Dist. LEXIS 9429 (E.D. Pa. 1994)

NATURE OF CASE: Motion for sanctions pursuant to Fed. R. Civ. P. 11.

FACT SUMMARY: Bridges (P) commenced this action against Diesel Service, Inc. (D) under the Americans with Disabilities Act (ADA) alleging that his employer dismissed him from his job as a result of a disability.

RULE OF LAW

Fed. R. Civ. P. 11 imposes an obligation on counsel and client to stop, think, investigate, and research before filing papers either to initiate the suit or to conduct the litigation.

FACTS: Bridges (P) commenced this action against Diesel Service, Inc. (D) under the Americans with Disabilities Act (ADA) alleging that his employer dismissed him from his job as a result of a disability. By an order dated June 29, 1994, the court dismissed Bridges's (P) complaint without prejudice for failure to exhaust administrative remedies. In particular, Bridges (P) did not file a charge with the Equal Employment Opportunity Commission (EEOC) until after commencement of this action. Diesel Service, Inc. (D) then moved for sanctions pursuant to Fed. R. Civ. P. 11.

ISSUE: Does Fed. R. Civ. P. 11 impose an obligation on counsel and client to stop, think, investigate, and research before filing papers either to initiate the suit or to conduct the litigation?

HOLDING AND DECISION: (Huyett, J.) Yes. Fed. R. Civ. P. 11 imposes an obligation on counsel and client to stop, think, investigate, and research before filing papers either to initiate the suit or to conduct the litigation. The court is not convinced that Plaintiff's lawyer displayed a competent level of legal research. A brief review of case law would have revealed the EEOC filing requirement. Further, an award of sanctions for failure to exhaust administrative remedies is not unprecedented. However, the court will not grant sanctions. The prime goal of Rule 11 sanctions is deterrence of improper conduct. In this case, monetary sanctions are not necessary to deter future misconduct since plaintiff's counsel immediately acknowledged his error and attempted to rectify the situation. Motion is denied.

ANALYSIS

It is possible that the court treated plaintiff's counsel with lenience in this case, since the action was brought under the Americans with Disabilities Act. As the court states in its decision, "The Court is aware of the need to avoid 'chilling' Title VII litigation." Generally, Fed. R. Civ. P. 11 sanctions are awarded where the complaint filed asserts patently unmeritorious or frivolous allegations.

Quicknotes

ADMINISTRATIVE REMEDIES Relief sought before an administrative body as opposed to a court.

FED. R. CIV. P. 11 Sets forth (a) the requirement that every pleading or written paper be signed by at least one attorney of record; (b) that the attorney make certain representations to the court upon the signing of such document; and (c) the sanctions for violation of the provision.

Bell v. Novick Transfer Co.

Automobile passenger (P) v. Trucking company (D)

17 F.R.D. 279 (D. Md. 1955)

NATURE OF CASE: Motion to dismiss for failure to state a claim.

FACT SUMMARY: Bell (P) filed a tort complaint in federal court after removal that stated only that Novick Transfer Co.'s (D) agent drove a truck that negligently collided with the car in which Bell (P) was riding, causing injury to Bell (P).

RULE OF LAW

A complaint that alleges only that a defendant negligently drove a motor vehicle and thereby injured the plaintiff is sufficient under Fed. R. Civ. P. 8.

FACTS: After Bell's (P) tort action arising out of an automobile-truck accident was removed to federal court, Bell (P) filed a complaint there that alleged only that an agent of Novick Transfer Co. (Novick) (D) drove a truck negligently so as to collide with a car in which Bell (P) was riding, causing injury to Bell (P). Novick (D) moved to dismiss the complaint for failure to state a cause of action.

ISSUE: Is a complaint that alleges only that defendant negligently drove a motor vehicle and thereby injured the plaintiff sufficient under Fed. R. Civ. P. 8?

HOLDING AND DECISION: (Thompsen, J.) Yes. This tort action was originally filed in Court of Common Pleas of Baltimore City but was removed to federal court. After such a removal, the Federal Rules of Civil Procedure apply rather than the laws of the State of Maryland. Thus, while Maryland law might regard the complaint here as insufficient for failure to state a cause of action, the inquiry here is to be made in light of the Federal Rules of Civil Procedure. Rule 8 controls the sufficiency of complaints and requires only "a short and plain statement of the claim showing the pleader is entitled to relief." The complaint in this case contains such a statement and sufficiently states a cause of action under Rule 8. A complaint that alleges only that a defendant negligently drove a motor vehicle and thereby injured the plaintiff is sufficient under Rule 8. Motion is overruled.

ANALYSIS

A complaint is designed to apprise the defendant of the claim against which he or she is to defend. The argument against sufficiency in this case is that the defendant is not told what negligent acts he has allegedly committed, other than the general allegation of "negligence," giving rise to liability. However, the policy of granting everyone access to the courts militates toward permitting generalized allegations and forcing the defendant to move for a more particularized statement under Fed. R. Civ. P. 12(e).

Quicknotes

FED. R. CIV. P. 8 Sets forth the general rules of pleading a claim for relief.

MOTION TO DISMISS Motion to terminate a trial based on the adequacy of the pleadings, improper service or venue, etc.

REMOVAL Petition by a defendant to move the case to another court.

Fisher v. Ciba Specialty Chemicals Corp.

Property owner (P) v. Chemicals manufacturing plant owner (D)

245 F.R.D. 539 (S.D. Ala. 2007)

NATURE OF CASE: Motion to sever, pursuant to Fed. R. Civ. P. 20 and 21, in action alleging diminution of property value as the result of environmental contamination.

FACT SUMMARY: Ciba Specialty Chemicals Corp. (Ciba) (D) moved to sever, pursuant to Fed. R. Civ. P. 20 and 21, claims brought by five property owners (P) alleging that Ciba's (D) chemicals manufacturing plant contaminated and reduced the value of their property. Ciba (D) asserted inefficiency and prejudice as the primary grounds for its motion, which the property owner (P) opposed.

RULE OF LAW

Under Fed. R. Civ. P. 20 and 21, a cause of action based on multiple individual claims will not be severed into separate trials where it is anticipated that, although there will be some individual-specific evidence, there will be substantial overlapping background evidence for all plaintiffs' claims; the same roster of experts will be called; and any potential prejudice to the defendant can be mitigated through limiting instructions.

FACTS: Five individual property owners (P) joined together and brought suit against Ciba Specialty Chemicals Corp. (Ciba) (D), alleging that Ciba's (D) chemicals manufacturing plant contaminated and reduced the value of their property with widespread environmental pollutants, including DDT. Ciba (D) moved, pursuant to Fed. R. Civ. P. 20 and 21, to sever the action into five separate trials. Ciba (D) argued that (1) the property owners' claims did not arise from the same transaction or occurrence; (2) they would rely on individualized evidence to prove their claims; (3) Ciba (D) would invoke individual-specific defenses; and (4) a common trial would be prejudicial to Ciba (D). The property owners (P) opposed the motion, arguing that severing their essentially identical claims would cause great inefficiency, and undue delay and undue expense, while also burdening the court with presiding over a largely similar trial five times in a row. The district court considered the motion.

ISSUE: Under Fed. R. Civ. P. 20 and 21, will a cause of action based on multiple individual claims be severed into separate trials where it is anticipated that, although there will be some individual-specific evidence, there will be substantial overlapping background evidence for all plaintiffs' claims; the same roster of experts will be called; and any potential prejudice to the defendant can be mitigated through limiting instructions?

HOLDING AND DECISION: (Steele, J.) No. Under Fed. R. Civ. P. 20 and 21, a cause of action based on multiple individual claims will not be severed into separate trials where it is anticipated that, although there will be some individual-specific evidence, there will be substantial overlapping background evidence for all plaintiffs' claims; the same roster of experts will be called; and any potential prejudice to the defendant can be mitigated through limiting instructions. Whether to grant the motion is within the court's discretion. Factors considered in determining whether to sever include whether the claims arise from the same transaction or occurrence, whether they present some common question of law or fact, whether severance would facilitate settlement or judicial economy, and the relative prejudice to each side if the motion is granted or denied. The commonality of law and fact issues need not be absolute; only some law or fact questions need to be common to all parties. Under the circumstances of the case, holding a single trial will present both efficiencies and inefficiencies. However, the efficiencies outweigh the inefficiencies. First, it is anticipated that there will be substantial overlapping background evidence for all plaintiffs' claims concerning the environmental history and activities of the Ciba (D) plant, and the interactions of Ciba (D) with the media, government regulators, and alleged co-conspirators. Second, it is probable that the same roster of nine expert witnesses, all of whom live out of state, will be called to testify with respect to each plaintiff's claims. To require these nine experts (as well as out-of-state counsel) to travel to the court five times in quick succession (or to sit and wait in a hotel for days on end) to testify in five different trials would be financially foolhardy and needlessly wasteful of the parties' economic resources, potentially even rendering these trials cost-prohibitive. Moreover, if these nine experts would be testifying to substantially similar, partially overlapping opinions in each of these five trials, the attendant drag on the efficient administration of justice would be considerable, as the court would be subjected to something akin to a judicial *Groundhog Day*. Additionally, Ciba's (D) claims of extreme prejudice must be rejected. Ciba (D) asserts that it will be prejudiced by the holding of a single trial because: (1) a multiplicity of plaintiff-specific facts will confuse the jury; (2) to the extent that one plaintiff's claims are stronger than the others', evidence as to that plaintiff may unfairly taint the jury as to the other plaintiffs' claims; and (3) consolidation for trial will allow plaintiffs to bolster their individually

Continued on next page.

weak cases by a suggestion that contamination is widespread. As to jury confusion, federal juries are routinely asked to parse facts that are relevant to particular claims or particular parties and are able to do so without difficulty so long as counsel presents the evidence in a cogent, orderly fashion that makes clear which evidence attaches to which particular claims or defenses. As to any "tainting," limiting instructions may be drafted to circumscribe the uses for which particular evidence may be considered, as well as pattern charges stressing that the claims and defenses of each party must be considered separately and independently from those of each other party. Finally, it is anticipated that the plaintiffs will each make the case that contamination from Ciba's (D) plant is widespread, so that this "suggestion" will be before the jury in plaintiffs' evidentiary submission at trial, irrespective of whether severance is granted. For all these reasons, Ciba's (D) motion to sever is denied.

ANALYSIS

Even if a court has found under Fed. R. Civ. P. 23 at the class certification stage that common issues do not predominate over individual-specific issues, such a finding, and a ruling against the plaintiffs based on it in no way suggests (much less mandates) a like outcome with respect to a motion under Fed. R. Civ. P. 20. That is because there is no predomination prerequisite for joinder of multiple plaintiffs' claims, and Fed. R. Civ. P. 20 contemplates a much lower threshold for allowing plaintiffs' claims to proceed to trial together than is required by Fed. R. Civ. P. 23 for class certification. As this case illustrates, the touchstone of the Fed. R. Civ. P. 20 joinder/severance analysis is whether the interests of efficiency and judicial economy would be advanced by allowing the claims to travel together, and whether any party would be prejudiced if they did.

Quicknotes

SEVERANCE Dividing or separating; setting aside one or more claims in a lawsuit to be tried separately.

Gordon v. T.G.R. Logistics, Inc.

Automobile accident victim (P) v. Corporation (D)

2017 WL 1947537 (D. Wyo. 2017)

NATURE OF CASE: Consideration of defendant's motion to compel production of plaintiff's Facebook account history for several years prior to the accident giving rise to the accident.

FACT SUMMARY: Gordon (P) suffered severe physical injuries when her vehicle was struck by a tractor-trailer unit owned by T.G.R. Logistics (D). Gordon (P) filed claims for both physical and emotional injuries.

RULE OF LAW

When determining the scope of permissible discovery pursuant to Fed. R. Civ. P. 26(b)(1), courts must determine if the information sought is privileged, relevant to a claim or defense, and proportional to the case.

FACTS: Gordon (P) suffered severe physical injuries when her vehicle was struck by a tractor-trailer unit owned by T.G.R. Logistics (D). Gordon's (P) claimed injuries included physical injuries, a traumatic brain injury, posttraumatic stress disorder, and depression. During discovery, T.G.R. Logistics (D) served a discovery request upon Gordon (P) for her entire Facebook account history, including the years prior to the accident. After Gordon (P) objected to the request, T.G.R. Logistics (D) filed a motion to compel the discovery.

ISSUE: When determining the scope of permissible discovery pursuant to Fed. R. Civ. P. 26(b)(1), must courts determine if the information sought is privileged, relevant to a claim or defense, and proportional to the case?

HOLDING AND DECISION: (Carman, J.) Yes. When determining the scope of permissible discovery pursuant to Fed. R. Civ. P. 26(b)(1), courts must determine if the information sought is privileged, relevant to a claim or defense, and proportional to the case. In this case, only the latter two prongs of the analysis are at issue. Social media presents significant issues regarding relevance and proportionality. Individuals now place vast troves of personal information online and that information may be relevant to the litigation. Production of such information may also not be expensive. However, simply because the production of the information may be easy or uncomplicated does not mean that the production is not burdensome. Here, T.G.R. Logistics (D) is correct that the production of the account history would not be expensive. The information sought could also lead to Gordon (P) having to explain every post where she expressed angst or emotional distress, including such instances that are personal or embarrassing. T.G.R. Logistics (D) counters by now offering to reduce its request to only three years prior to the accident, as well as all post-accident history. This is too broad a request. Granting access to the account prior to the accident would likely produce only minimal relevant information while exposing Gordon's (P) private posts unnecessarily. This would exceed the limits of proportionality. Gordon (P) must, however, produce all post-accident history as it relates to her emotional turmoil, mental disability, or other events that relate to emotional distress or her physical injuries. She should also produce any history or photos that show her level of activity since the date of the accident. Defendant's motion to compel is thus denied in part and granted in part.

ANALYSIS

In any personal injury claim, defendants will scour a plaintiff's social media accounts for both evidence of injuries and emotional distress prior to the accident date, as well as any evidence that the plaintiff's claimed damages are not as bad as claimed. Courts rely on the two elements discussed in this case–relevance and proportionality–to fashion the appropriate scope of discovery. Depending on the severity of the claimed injuries, these disputes over the scope of discovery become paramount during the early stages of the litigation.

Quicknotes

DISCOVERY Pretrial procedure during which one party makes certain information available to the other.

RELEVANCE The admissibility of evidence based on whether it has any tendency to prove or disprove a matter at issue in the case.

Houchens v. American Home Assurance Co.

Spouse of decedent (P) v. Life insurance company (D)

927 F.2d 163 (4th Cir. 1991)

NATURE OF CASE: Appeal of dismissal of action for damages for breach of contract.

FACT SUMMARY: On American Home Assurance Co.'s (D) summary judgment motion, the court dismissed Houchens's (P) suit for payment on two accidental death policies because of insufficient evidence that Houchens's (P) husband died accidentally.

RULE OF LAW

Under Fed. R. Civ. P. 56, a federal court must enter summary judgment if after complete discovery a party fails to show that the evidence, viewed in the light most favorable to that party, is sufficient to establish the existence of an essential element on which that party has the burden of proof.

FACTS: Houchens's (P) husband disappeared in Thailand in August 1980, and was not heard from since. Under Virginia law, a person who is missing for seven years is presumed dead. In 1988, Houchens (P) had her husband declared legally dead. Houchens (P) attempted to collect on two life insurance policies issued by American Home Assurance Co. (American) (D), under which the proceeds would be paid only upon proof that the insured's death was accidental. American (D) refused to pay, and Houchens (P) sued in federal court for breach of contract. American (D) moved for summary judgment, arguing there was no evidence that the insured had died or that he had died accidentally. The district court granted the motion and dismissed the case, and Houchens (P) appealed.

ISSUE: Under Fed. R. Civ. P. 56, must a federal court enter summary judgment if a party fails to show that the evidence, viewed in the light most favorable to that party, is sufficient to establish the existence of an essential element on which that party has the burden of proof?

HOLDING AND DECISION: (Ervin, J.) Yes. Under Fed. R. Civ. P. 56, a federal court must enter summary judgment if a party fails to show that the evidence, viewed in the light most favorable to that party, is sufficient to establish the existence of an essential element on which that party has the burden of proof. Under Rule 56(c), a summary judgment motion must be granted where there is "no genuine issue as to any material fact." Here, Houchens (P) is entitled to the Virginia presumption that her husband is dead. However, for recovery on the policy it still must be shown that her husband's death was accidental. The meager circumstances surrounding his disappearance do not provide sufficient evidence to allow a reasonable jury to conclude that he died accidentally. Under Virginia law, Houchens (D) had the burden of proof as to accident, a necessary element of her case. She had insufficient evidence to meet this burden. Thus, as there was no genuine issue as to a material fact, the summary judgment motion was properly granted. Affirmed.

ANALYSIS

Houchens (P) cited two cases where the issue was the same and a summary judgment motion by the insurance company defendant was denied. In *Valley National Bank of Arizona v. J.C. Penney Ins. Co.*, Ariz. Ct. App., 129 Ariz. 108, 628 P.2d 991 (1981), the insured disappeared, and his skeletal remains were later found with bullet casings nearby. In *Martin v. Insurance Co. of America*, 1 Wash. App. 218, 460 P.2d 682 (1969), the insured disappeared in fog and snow on a steep and wooded mountainside after having last been seen, asking for directions, without a compass at the 3,000-foot level. In each of these cases, the court found that there was a genuine issue of material fact because there was sufficient evidence, unlike in the *Houchens* case, for a jury to find that the insured died accidentally.

Quicknotes

BURDEN OF PROOF The duty of a party to introduce evidence to support a fact that is in dispute in an action.

FED. R. CIV. P. 56 Governs the standard for summary judgment.

SUMMARY JUDGMENT Judgment rendered by a court in response to a motion by one of the parties, claiming that the lack of a question of material fact in respect to an issue warrants disposition of the issue without consideration by the jury.

Norton v. Snapper Power Equipment

Gardener (P) v. Lawn mower manufacturer (D)

806 F.2d 1545 (11th Cir. 1987)

NATURE OF CASE: Appeal from judgment notwithstanding the verdict denying damages for personal injuries.

FACT SUMMARY: In Norton's (P) suit for damages against Snapper Power Equipment (Snapper) (D), Snapper (D) moved for and was granted a judgment notwithstanding the verdict, contending that since a reconstruction of Norton's (P) accident with a Snapper (D) riding mower was impossible, the jury could not determine whether a blade-stopping device would have eliminated or lessened Norton's (P) injury.

RULE OF LAW

A judgment notwithstanding the verdict should be granted only where the evidence so strongly points in favor of a moving party that reasonable people could not arrive at a contrary verdict.

FACTS: Norton (P), a commercial gardener, was injured while riding a lawn mower manufactured by Snapper Power Equipment (Snapper) (D). Norton (P) sued Snapper (D) for damages based on strict liability. At the close of Norton's (P) case, and against the close of all evidence, Snapper (D) moved for a directed verdict. The court left the strict liability claim for the jury, and the jury returned a verdict for Norton (P), holding Snapper (D) liable for 80 percent of the injuries. After dismissing the jury, the court indicated that it would enter a judgment notwithstanding the verdict based on Snapper's (D) contention that since a reconstruction of Norton's (P) accident with the mower was impossible, the jury could not determine whether a blade-stopping device would have eliminated or lessened Norton's (P) injury. Norton (P) appealed.

ISSUE: Should a judgment notwithstanding the verdict be granted only where the evidence so strongly points in favor of a moving party that reasonable people could not arrive at a contrary verdict?

HOLDING AND DECISION: (Clark, J.) Yes. A judgment notwithstanding the verdict should be granted only where the evidence so strongly points in favor of a moving party that reasonable people could not arrive at a contrary verdict. The issues here were whether the failure to install "dead man" devices rendered the mower defective, and if the mower was defective, whether the lack of a "dead man" control caused the injury. Snapper (D) claims that there was little or no evidence to support the jury's verdict. The jury is, however, permitted to reconstruct the series of events by drawing an inference upon an inference. The causation evidence here, although circumstantial, was far more impressive than Snapper (D) contends, and Snapper (D) was given every opportunity to point out the weaknesses in Norton's (P) proof but was unpersuasive to the jury. Reversed and remanded.

ANALYSIS

Within ten days of an adverse verdict, the loser may move for a judgment notwithstanding the verdict. This motion asserts that even if all the winner's evidence is true, the loser is entitled to a verdict as a matter of law. A motion for a new trial may be based either on an error of law or on an erroneous charge.

Quicknotes

DIRECTED VERDICT A verdict ordered by the court in a jury trial.

JUDGMENT NOTWITHSTANDING THE VERDICT (JUDGMENT N.O.V.) A judgment entered by the trial judge reversing a jury verdict if the jury's determination has no basis in law or fact.

STRICT LIABILITY Liability for all injuries proximately caused by a party's conducting of certain inherently dangerous activities without regard to negligence or fault.

Ison v. Thomas

Accident victim (P) v. Car driver (D)

Ky. Ct. App., 2007 WL 1194374 (2007)

NATURE OF CASE: Appeal from dismissal on summary judgment of a claim for personal injuries.

FACT SUMMARY: Ison's (P) claim against Thomas (D) for personal injuries was dismissed on the grounds that he had previously prevailed against Thomas (D) on a claim for property damages and was precluded from raising the personal injury claim under the rule against splitting one's cause of action.

RULE OF LAW

Where a plaintiff brings one action after another, and the claims in the subsequent action could have been brought in the prior action, the rule against splitting one's cause of action is not inapplicable if the plaintiff prevails in the prior action.

FACTS: Thomas (D) was found liable to Ison (P) for property damages arising from a car accident, and a jury awarded Ison (P) $5,000. Subsequently, Ison (P) brought suit against Thomas (D) for personal injuries arising from the same accident. Ison's (P) claim was dismissed on summary judgment under the rule against splitting one's cause of action. The trial court held that Ison's (P) personal injury claim was part of the same cause of action as his property damage claim and so had merged with the prior judgment. Ison (P) appealed, claiming that the trial court had misapplied the rule against splitting one's cause of action. The state's intermediate appellate court granted review.

ISSUE: Where a plaintiff brings one action after another, and the claims in the subsequent action could have been brought in the prior action, is the rule against splitting one's cause of action inapplicable if the plaintiff prevails in the prior action?

HOLDING AND DECISION: (Abramson, J.) No. Where a plaintiff brings one action after another, and the claims in the subsequent action could have been brought in the prior action, the rule against splitting one's cause of action is not inapplicable if the plaintiff prevails in the prior action. The rule against splitting one's cause of action is an aspect of the doctrine of res judicata. When a matter is in litigation, (1) parties are required to bring forward their whole case, and (2) the plea of res judicata applies not only to the points upon which the court was required by the parties to form an opinion and pronounce judgment, but to every point that properly belonged to the subject of litigation, and that the parties, exercising reasonable diligence, might have brought forward at the time. If the plaintiff prevails on his or her initial claim, other claims arising from the same transaction are said to merge with his judgment, and if the plaintiff loses initially, that judgment is said to bar any such subsequent claim. Although Thomas (D) did not raise res judicata as an affirmative defense in his answer, but raised it in his motion for summary judgment, that does not automatically waive this defense, provided Ison (P) was not prejudiced. Because the defense was raised before either party had expended much on discovery, Ison (P) was not prejudiced thereby. In sum, all claims against a single defendant arising from a single negligent incident must be brought in a single action. Ison (P) improperly split his claim for property damages from his claim for personal injury damages, where both claims arose against a single defendant as a result of a single accident. The damages claims should have been brought together, and because they were not, the trial court correctly ruled that the subsequent action is barred. Affirmed.

ANALYSIS

The decision in this case echoes the Restatement (Second) Judgments, § 24, which provides that "[w]hen a valid and final judgment rendered in an action extinguishes the plaintiff's claim pursuant to the rules of merger or bar . . . the claim extinguished includes all rights of the plaintiff to remedies against the defendant with respect to all or any part of the transaction, or series of connected transactions, out of which the action arose." The example used by the Restatement to illustrate this point is on all fours with the case at bar: "A and B, driving their respective cars, have a collision injuring A and damaging his car. The occurrence is single, and so is A's claim. If A obtains a judgment against B on the ground of negligence for the damage to the car, he is prevented by the doctrine of merger from subsequently maintaining an action for the harm to his person."

Quicknotes

CAUSE OF ACTION A fact or set of facts the occurrence of which entitles a party to seek judicial relief.

ON ALL FOURS Two cases are "on all fours" when they are similar in terms of the facts and the questions of law involved.

RES JUDICATA The rule of law that a final judgment by a court precludes subsequent litigation between the parties regarding the same cause of action.

Reise v. Board of Regents of the University of Wisconsin

Law school faculty applicant (P) v. State university (D)

957 F.2d 293 (7th Cir. 1992)

NATURE OF CASE: Appeal from order to submit to a mental examination.

FACT SUMMARY: E. H. Reise (P), who claimed he was discriminated against in his application to become a law school faculty member at the Law School of the University of Wisconsin at Madison (D), and that he suffered $4 million in damages from the resulting mental anguish, emotional distress, and illness, contended that it was erroneous to order him to submit to a mental examination.

RULE OF LAW

An interlocutory discovery order requiring a mental examination is not appealable prior to a final decision.

FACTS: E. H. Reise (P), a white male who graduated in the top of his class at the Law School of the University of Wisconsin at Madison (Law School) (D), applied for a faculty position at the Law School (D). When his application was denied, he brought suit, claiming that the denial was discriminatory, as in recent years the Law School (D) had been unwilling to consider anyone, no matter how skilled, who was not Black, female, or otherwise eligible for preferential treatment. According to Reise (P), only one of the last 13 appointments to the faculty has been a white male. The Law School (D) countered that all the persons it hired were better lawyers and scholars than Reise (P). Reise (P) sought $4 million in damages from mental anguish, emotional distress, and illness that allegedly resulted from the Law School's (D) decision not to hire him. The trial court ordered that he submit to a mental examination under Fed. R. Civ. P. 35. Reise (P) objected on the grounds that an examination would reveal nothing of value, since he was over his distress and was not seeking damages on account of his current mental condition. Reise (P) appealed the order, and the U.S. Court of Appeals for the Seventh Circuit granted review.

ISSUE: Is an interlocutory discovery order requiring a mental examination appealable prior to a final decision?

HOLDING AND DECISION: (Easterbrook, J.) No. An interlocutory discovery order requiring a mental examination is not appealable prior to a final decision. Discovery orders, including orders to submit to an examination, are readily reviewable after final decision. A party aggrieved by the order assures eventual review by refusing to comply. The district judge then imposes sanctions under Fed. R. Civ. P. 37(b)(2). If Reise (P) were not to comply with the trial court's order, it is most likely that the court would impose a sanction striking Reise's (P) claim for damages on account of mental and physical distress. If Reise (P) then prevailed on the merits but did not obtain damages because of the order striking his claim, he could obtain full review on appeal: if the district judge abused his discretion in requiring Reise (P) to submit to an examination, the case would be remanded for further proceedings. Because almost all interlocutory appeals from discovery orders would end in affirmance (the district court possesses discretion, and review is deferential), the costs of delay via appeal, and the costs to the judicial system of entertaining these appeals, exceed in the aggregate the costs of the few erroneous discovery orders that might be corrected were appeals available. Further, requiring the complaining party to take some risk winnows weak claims, since only persons who have substantial objections to the examination and believe their legal positions strong will follow a path that could end in defeat. Among those who take the risk by balking at the order, some will lose on the merits, and their discovery disputes will become moot. Most of the remaining cases will end in affirmance, given deferential review. The number of retrials entailed by the procedure is small, the number of appeals avoided large. For all these reasons, the order is not appealable, and it is dismissed for lack of jurisdiction.

ANALYSIS

A "final" decision usually means the order ending the litigation, and, thus, an examination ordered under Fed. R. Civ. P. 35 does not meet that definition. Although the travail and expense of discovery and trial cannot be reversed at the end of the case, this alone has never been thought sufficient to allow pre-trial appeals. Indeed, even orders to produce information over strong objections based on privilege are not appealable, despite the claim that once the information is revealed the privilege is gone.

Quicknotes

DISCOVERY Pretrial procedure during which one party makes certain information available to the other.

INTERLOCUTORY APPEAL The appeal of an issue that does not resolve the disposition of the case but is essential to a determination of the parties' legal rights.

CHAPTER 2

Personal Jurisdiction and Notice

Quick Reference Rules of Law

Pennoyer v. Neff

Purchaser of property (D) v. Real property owner (P)

95 U.S. 714 (1877)

NATURE OF CASE: Action to recover possession of land.

FACT SUMMARY: Neff (P) attacked the validity of a sheriff's sale of his property to satisfy a personal judgment obtained against him where service was by publication.

RULE OF LAW

Where the object of an action is to determine the personal rights and obligations of the parties, service by publication against a nonresident is ineffective to confer jurisdiction upon the court.

FACTS: Neff (P) owned real property in Oregon. Mitchell brought suit in Oregon to recover legal fees allegedly owed him by Neff (P). Neff (P), a nonresident, was served by publication and Mitchell obtained a default judgment. The court ordered Neff's (P) land sold at a sheriff's sale to satisfy the judgment. Pennoyer (D) purchased the property. Neff (P) subsequently learned of the sale and brought suit in Oregon to recover possession of the property. Neff (P) alleged that the court ordering the sale had never acquired in personam jurisdiction over him. Therefore, the court could not adjudicate the personal rights between Neff (P) and Mitchell, and the default judgment had been improperly entered.

ISSUE: Where the object of an action is to determine the personal rights and obligations of the parties, is service by publication against a nonresident ineffective to confer jurisdiction upon the court?

HOLDING AND DECISION: (Field, J.) No. Where the object of an action is to determine the personal rights and obligations of the parties, service by publication against a nonresident is ineffective to confer jurisdiction upon the court. Substituted service of process in actions against nonresidents of a state is effective only in proceedings in rem. No state can exercise direct jurisdiction and authority over persons or property outside of its boundaries. The validity of every judgment depends upon the jurisdiction of the court rendering judgment. Thus, Mitchell could not obtain a personal judgment against Neff (P) without first obtaining in personam jurisdiction. Substituted service by publication is ineffective to confer personal jurisdiction over a nonresident. The sale was therefore void. A different result could have been reached if Mitchell had first obtained in rem jurisdiction by seizing the property at the time suit was commenced. Affirmed.

ANALYSIS

Although no state can exercise direct jurisdiction and authority over people or property outside the state, the state may exercise jurisdiction over persons and property inside the state in ways that will affect persons and property outside the state. *Pennoyer v. Neff* established that every state had the power to regulate the way in which property within the state is acquired, enjoyed, and transferred. But a state cannot bring a person or property outside the state into its jurisdiction simply by using substituted service.

Quicknotes

IN PERSONAM JURISDICTION The power of a court over a person, as opposed to a court's power over a person's interest in property.

IN REM JURISDICTION A court's authority over an object so that its judgment is binding in respect to the rights and interests of all parties in that object.

SERVICE OF PROCESS The communication of reasonable notice of a court proceeding to a defendant in order to provide him or her with an opportunity to be heard.

International Shoe Co. v. Washington

Delaware corporation (D) v. State (P)

326 U.S. 310 (1945)

NATURE OF CASE: Proceedings to recover unemployment contributions.

FACT SUMMARY: A state statute authorized the mailing of notice of assessment of delinquent contributions for unemployment compensation to nonresident employers. International Shoe Co. (International) (D) was a nonresident corporation. Notice of assessment was served on one of its salespersons within the state and was mailed to International's (D) office.

RULE OF LAW

For a state to subject a nonresident defendant to in personam jurisdiction, due process requires that the nonresident defendant have certain minimum contacts with the state such that the maintenance of the suit does not offend traditional notions of fair play and substantial justice.

FACTS: A Washington statute set up a scheme of unemployment compensation that required contributions by employers. The statute authorized the commissioner, Washington (P), to issue an order and notice of assessment of delinquent contributions by mailing the notice to nonresident employers. International Shoe Co. (International) (D) was a Delaware corporation having its principal place of business in Missouri. International (D) employed 11 to 13 salespersons under the supervision of managers in Missouri. These salespeople resided in Washington, did most of their work there, and had no authority to enter into contracts or make collections. International (D) did not have an office in Washington and made no contracts there. Notice of assessment was served upon one of International's (D) Washington salespersons and a copy of the notice was sent by registered mail to International's (D) Missouri address. The lower courts ruled that Washington (P) was entitled to recover the unpaid contributions.

ISSUE: For a state to subject a nonresident defendant to in personam jurisdiction, does due process require that the nonresident have certain minimum contacts with the state such that the maintenance of the suit does not offend notions of fair play and substantial justice?

HOLDING AND DECISION: (Stone, C.J.) Yes. For a state to subject a nonresident defendant to in personam jurisdiction, due process requires that the nonresident defendant have certain minimum contacts with the state such that the maintenance of the suit does not offend traditional notions of fair play and substantial justice. Historically the jurisdiction of courts to render judgment in personam is grounded on their power over the defendant's person, and the defendant's presence within the territorial jurisdiction of a court was necessary to a valid judgment. But now, due process requires only that in order to subject a defendant to a judgment in personam, if he or she is not present within the territorial jurisdiction, the person has certain minimum contacts with the territory such that the maintenance of the suit does not offend traditional notions of fair play and substantial justice. The contacts must be such as to make it reasonable, in the context of our federal system, to require a defendant corporation to defend the suit brought there. An estimate of the inconveniences that would result to the corporation from a trial away from its "home" is relevant. To require a corporation to defend a suit away from home where its contact has been casual or its activities isolated has been thought to lay too unreasonable a burden on the corporation. However, even single or occasional acts may, because of their nature, quality, and circumstances, be deemed sufficient to render a corporation liable to suit. Hence, the criteria to determine whether jurisdiction is justified are not simply mechanical or quantitative. Satisfaction of due process depends on the quality and nature of the activity in relation to the fair and orderly administration of the laws. In this case International Shoe Co.'s (International) (D) activities were neither irregular nor casual. Rather, they were systematic and continuous. The obligation sued upon here arose out of these activities. They were sufficient to establish sufficient contacts or ties to make it reasonable to permit Washington (P) to enforce the obligations International (D) incurred there. Affirmed.

DISSENT: (Black, J.) The United States Constitution leaves to each state the power to tax and to open the doors of its courts for its citizens to sue corporations who do business in the state. It is a judicial deprivation to condition the exercise of this power on this court's notion of "fair play."

ANALYSIS

Before this decision three theories had evolved to provide for suits by and against foreign corporations. The first was the consent theory. It rested on the proposition that since a foreign corporation could not carry on its business within a state without the permission of that state, the state could require a corporation to appoint

Continued on next page.

an agent to receive service of process within the state. However, it soon became established law that a foreign corporation could not be prevented by a state from carrying on interstate commerce within its borders. The presence doctrine required that the corporation was "doing business" and "present" in the state. The third theory used either the present or consent doctrine, and it was necessary to determine whether the corporation was doing business within the state either to decide whether its consent could properly be implied or to discover whether the corporation was present.

Quicknotes

CONSENT JURISDICTION The forum having jurisdiction over a lawsuit as agreed upon by the parties prior to litigation.

IN PERSONAM JURISDICTION The power of a court over a person, as opposed to a court's power over a person's interest in property.

MINIMUM CONTACTS The minimum degree of contact necessary in order to sustain a cause of action within a particular forum, consistent with the requirements of due process.

McGee v. International Life Insurance Co.

Beneficiary (P) v. Insurance company (D)

355 U.S. 220 (1957)

NATURE OF CASE: Suit to enforce payment of life insurance proceeds.

FACT SUMMARY: McGee (P) was the beneficiary of a life insurance policy on a California resident who had purchased the policy from an insurer who was subsequently bought by International Life Insurance Co. (D). McGee obtained a judgment for the proceeds in California and attempted to enforce the judgment in Texas.

RULE OF LAW

Due process requires only that in order to subject a nonresident defendant to the personal jurisdiction of the forum, the suit be based on a contract that has substantial connection with the forum.

FACTS: Lowell Franklin, a resident of California, purchased a life insurance policy from an insurer. The reinsurer, International Life Insurance Co. (D), mailed a reinsurance certificate to the California resident offering to insure him. Franklin accepted this offer and paid all premiums by mail from his California home to the reinsurer's Texas office. The insured died, and the beneficiary, McGee (P), notified the insurer (D) of the death. The insurer (D) refused to make payment, and McGee (P) sued the insurer in California, obtaining a judgment.

ISSUE: Does due process require only that in order to subject a nonresident defendant to the personal jurisdiction of the forum, the suit be based on a contract that has substantial connection with the forum?

HOLDING AND DECISION: (Black, J.) Yes. Due process requires only that in order to subject a nonresident defendant to the personal jurisdiction of the forum, the suit be based on a contract that has substantial connection with the forum. Here, the insurance contract was delivered to California, and the premiums were payable there. The beneficiary and policyholders are California residents. It cannot be denied that California has a manifest interest in providing effective means of redress for its residents when their insurers refuse to pay claims. These residents would be at a severe disadvantage if forced to follow the insurance company to a distant state in order to hold it legally accountable.

ANALYSIS

The fact of solicitation of the policy in California was a key element of this decision. That solicitation, albeit a single incident, could reasonably be thought to have put International Life Insurance Co. (D) on notice that it might be sued in California. If, on the other hand, the insured had taken out the policy in Texas and then moved to California, where he was the sole policyholder, this foreseeability argument would be greatly diluted. However, if the insured was one of a number of California policyholders, the exercise of personal jurisdiction there could be expected.

Quicknotes

FULL FAITH AND CREDIT Doctrine that a judgment by a court of one state shall be given the same effect in another state.

MINIMUM CONTACTS The minimum degree of contact necessary in order to sustain a cause of action within a particular forum, consistent with the requirements of due process.

Hanson v. Denckla

Will legatees (P) v. Trust beneficiaries (D)

357 U.S. 235 (1958)

NATURE OF CASE: Appeal from disposition of property in a trust.

FACT SUMMARY: Mrs. Donner, mother of three daughters, established a trust in Delaware and later moved to Florida where she died.

RULE OF LAW

For there to be "minimal contacts" sufficient to support in personam jurisdiction, it is essential that there be some act by which the defendant purposefully avails itself of the privilege of conducting activities within the forum state, thus invoking the benefits and protections of its laws.

FACTS: Mrs. Donner established a trust in Delaware and later moved to Florida, where she died. A will contest ensued among her three daughters: if Florida could acquire jurisdiction over the Delaware trust, two daughters would get the entire estate; if the Delaware courts had jurisdiction, all three daughters would share equally.

ISSUE: For there to be "minimal contacts" sufficient to support in personam jurisdiction, is it essential that there be some act by which the defendant purposefully avails itself of the privilege of conducting activities within the forum state, thus invoking the benefits and protections of its laws?

HOLDING AND DECISION: (Warren, C.J.) Yes. For there to be "minimal contacts" sufficient to support in personam jurisdiction, it is essential that there be some act by which the defendant purposefully avails itself of the privilege of conducting activities with the forum state, thus invoking the benefits and protections of its laws. In this case, no such contacts could be found. The Delaware trustee had no office in Florida and conducted no business there. No trust assets were ever held in Florida or administered there, and there was no solicitation of business in that state either in person or by mail. Consequently, this suit was not one to enforce an obligation that arose from a privilege exercised in Florida. However minimal the burden of defending in a foreign tribunal, a defendant may not be called upon to do so unless he or she has had the minimum contacts with that state that are a prerequisite to its exercise of power over him or her. Florida lacked jurisdiction.

ANALYSIS

The case really revolves around the validity of the inter vivos trust. The trust was created in Delaware, and the corpus remains there. The fact that some Florida residents are beneficiaries thereunder, or that they wish to defeat the trust, is not a compelling state interest. It certainly is not a more substantial interest than is Delaware's right to construe the validity of a trust created under its laws and the corpus of which is within its jurisdiction. The fact that the settlor was a Florida resident is immaterial. She was not a resident when the trust was created, nor was she attempting to have the trust set aside.

Quicknotes

IN PERSONAM JURISDICTION The power of a court over a person as opposed to a court's power over a person's interest in property.

INTER VIVOS TRUST Property that is held by one person for the benefit of another and which is created by an instrument that takes effect during the life of the grantor.

MINIMUM CONTACTS The minimum degree of contact necessary in order to sustain a cause of action within a particular forum, consistent with the requirements of due process.

RESIDUARY CLAUSE (OF WILL) A clause contained in a will disposing of the assets remaining following distribution of the estate.

World-Wide Volkswagen Corp. v. Woodson

Automobile distributor (P) v. Court (D)

444 U.S. 286 (1980)

NATURE OF CASE: Petition for a writ prohibiting the exercise of in personam jurisdiction.

FACT SUMMARY: World-Wide Volkswagen Corp. (P) sought a writ of prohibition to keep district court Judge Woodson (D) from exercising in personam jurisdiction over it, alleging it did not have sufficient "contacts" with the forum state of Oklahoma to render it subject to such jurisdiction.

RULE OF LAW

A state court may exercise personal jurisdiction over a nonresident defendant only so long as there exist sufficient "minimum contacts" between him or her and the forum state such that maintenance of the suit does not offend "traditional notions of fair play and substantial justice."

FACTS: World-Wide Volkswagen Corp. (World-Wide) (P) was the regional distributor of Audi automobiles for the tri-state area of New York, New Jersey, and Connecticut. It was the distributor of the particular Audi that the Robinsons purchased from a New York dealer and drove to Oklahoma, where three family members were severely burned when another car struck their Audi in the rear. The Robinsons brought a products-liability action in an Oklahoma district court, suing the New York dealership and World-Wide (a New York corporation) (P). Claiming that no evidence showed it had any connection with Oklahoma whatsoever, World-Wide (P) sought a writ of prohibition to keep district court Judge Woodson (D) from exercising in personam jurisdiction. World-Wide (P) argued that a lack of sufficient contacts with the forum state made assertion of such jurisdiction improper under the Due Process Clause. The Oklahoma Supreme Court denied the writ, noting that World-Wide (P) could foresee that the automobiles it sold would be taken into other states, including Oklahoma. The United States Supreme Court granted certiorari.

ISSUE: May a state court exercise personal jurisdiction over a nonresident defendant only so long as there exist sufficient "minimum contacts" between him or her and the forum state such that maintenance of the suit does not offend "traditional notions of fair play and substantial justice?"

HOLDING AND DECISION: (White, J.) Yes. A state court may exercise personal jurisdiction over a nonresident defendant only so long as there exist sufficient "minimum contacts" with the forum state such that maintenance of the suit does not offend "traditional notions of fair play and substantial justice." Here, World-Wide (P) had no "contacts, ties, or relations" with Oklahoma, so personal jurisdiction could not be exercised. As for the notion that it was foreseeable that cars sold in New York would wind up in Oklahoma, the foreseeability that is critical to due process analysis is not the mere likelihood that a product will find its way into the forum state. Rather, it is that the defendant's conduct and connection with the forum state are such that he or she should reasonably anticipate being taken to court there. Such conduct and connection are simply missing in this case. Reversed.

DISSENT: (Brennan, J.) The automobile is designed specifically to facilitate travel from place to place, and the sale of one purposefully injects it into the stream of interstate commerce. Thus, this case is not unlike those where in personam jurisdiction is properly exercised over one who purposefully places his or her product into the stream of interstate commerce with the expectation it will be purchased by consumers in other states. Furthermore, a large part of the value of automobiles is the extensive, nationwide network of highways. State maintenance of such roads contributes to the value of World-Wide's (P) business. World-Wide (P) also participates in a network of related dealerships with nationwide service facilities. Having such facilities in Oklahoma also adds to the value of World-Wide's (P) business. Thus, it has the required minimum contacts with Oklahoma to render this exercise of personal jurisdiction constitutional.

ANALYSIS

Over the years, modern transportation and communication have made foreign-state suits much less of a burden to defendants. This resulted in a relaxing of the due process limits placed on state jurisdiction down to the "minimum contacts" concept. However, even if there were no inconvenience to the defendant, a state could not exercise personal jurisdiction over him or her if the defendant had no "contacts, ties, or relations." This is true even if that state had a strong interest in applying its law to the controversy, and it was the most convenient location for litigation, etc. The reason is that the Due Process Clause serves two distinct functions: the first is as a guarantor against inconvenient litigation but the second is as a guardian of interstate federalism. It is in this second capacity that the Due Process Clause would prevent assumption of jurisdiction in the

Continued on next page.

aforementioned instance by recognizing the "territorial limitations on the power of the respective states."

Quicknotes

DUE PROCESS CLAUSE Language in the Fifth and Fourteenth Amendments to the United States Constitution providing that no person shall be deprived of "life, liberty, or property without due process of law."

IN PERSONAM JURISDICTION The jurisdiction of a court over a person, as opposed to a court's power over a person's interest in property.

MINIMUM CONTACTS The minimum degree of contact necessary in order to sustain a cause of action within a particular forum, consistent with the requirements of due process.

J. McIntyre Machinery, Ltd. v. Nicastro

Product manufacturer (D) v. Injured worker (P)

564 U.S. 873 (2011)

NATURE OF CASE: Appeal of judgment by state supreme court.

FACT SUMMARY: A person who was injured when he used a piece of heavy machinery sued the foreign manufacturer in New Jersey state court. The company disputed the state's jurisdiction.

RULE OF LAW

In products liability cases, the "stream-of-commerce" doctrine cannot displace the general rule that the exercise of judicial power is not lawful unless the defendant purposefully avails itself of the privilege of conducting activities within the forum state, thus invoking the benefits and protections of its laws.

FACTS: Robert Nicastro (P) injured his hand while using a metal-shearing machine that was manufactured by J. McIntyre Machinery, Ltd. (J. McIntyre) (D). The machine was manufactured in England, where J. McIntyre (D) is incorporated and operates, and the injury occurred in New Jersey. Nicastro (P) filed suit in New Jersey. The New Jersey Supreme Court found that it had jurisdiction over J. McIntyre (D) because J. McIntyre (D) machines were sold in the United States, the company attended annual conventions for the scrap recycling industry to advertise, four machines were identified in New Jersey, and J. McIntyre (D) guided advertising and sales efforts for the U.S. distributor. J. McIntyre (D) appealed.

ISSUE: In products liability cases, can the "stream-of-commerce" doctrine displace the general rule that the exercise of judicial power is not lawful unless the defendant purposefully avails itself of the privilege of conducting activities within the forum state, thus invoking the benefits and protections of its laws?

HOLDING AND DECISION: (Kennedy, J.) No. In products liability cases, the "stream-of-commerce" doctrine cannot displace the general rule that the exercise of judicial power is not lawful unless the defendant purposefully avails itself of the privilege of conducting activities within the forum state, thus invoking the benefits and protections of its laws. The Supreme Court of New Jersey held that New Jersey's courts can exercise jurisdiction over a foreign manufacturer of a product as long as the manufacturer knows or reasonably should know that its products are distributed through a nationwide distribution system that might lead to those products being sold in any of the 50 states. That rule is from *Asahi Metal Industry Co. v. Superior Court of Cal., Solano County*, 480 U.S. 102 (1987). Based on that test, the court concluded that the British manufacturer of scrap metal machines was subject to New Jersey jurisdiction, even though the company had at no time advertised in, sent goods to, or in any way targeted the state. Those who live or operate primarily outside a state have a due process right not to be subjected to judgment in its courts, as a general rule. Where the individual or corporation explicitly consents to jurisdiction, is present in a state at the time a suit starts, is a citizen or has a domicile within the state, or is incorporated in the state, jurisdiction is proper, because all of those situations indicate an intent to submit to the laws of the state. The stream-of-commerce exception to the general rule refers to the movement of goods from manufacturers through distributors to consumers, and advocates of the exception argue that the placement of goods into the stream of commerce with the expectation that they will be purchased by consumers indicates purposeful availment. But the exception holds only where the activities manifest an intention to submit to the power of the sovereign. In this case, J. McIntyre (D) directed marketing and sales efforts at the United States, but not directly to New Jersey, and because of that, a federal court might have jurisdiction, but a New Jersey state court does not. It is J. McIntyre's (D) purposeful contacts with New Jersey, not with the United States, that are relevant. Because J. McIntyre has not engaged in conduct purposefully directed at New Jersey, New Jersey state courts did not have jurisdiction to hear the case. Reversed.

CONCURRENCE: (Breyer, J.) The judgment is correct, but it is determined by precedent. There is no reason to construct new general rules that limit jurisdiction, since on the basis of existing precedent, the case can be decided. No precedent finds that a single isolated sale, even if accompanied by the sales here, is sufficient. Nicastro (P) failed to meet his burden of showing that it was constitutionally proper to exercise jurisdiction over petitioner J. McIntyre (D).

DISSENT: (Ginsburg, J.) J. McIntyre (D) wanted to establish a market for its product in the United States and took steps to do so. Where in the United States buyers of the product live or operate is irrelevant to the manufacturer. The company simply wants to sell its product in the United States. Under *International Shoe Co. v. Washington*, 326 U.S. 310 (1945), personal jurisdiction is established.

Continued on next page.

ANALYSIS

The absence of a majority opinion makes it difficult to identify a reliable rule. Three justices voted to reverse on the basis of a new rule that limits jurisdiction more severely than precedent; three others voted to reverse on the basis of precedent, with making a new rule; and three others voted to affirm on the basis of precedent.

Quicknotes

FORUM STATE The state in which a court, or other location in which a legal remedy may be sought, is located.

PURPOSEFUL AVAILMENT An element in determining whether a defendant had the required minimum contacts in a forum necessary in order for a court to exercise jurisdiction over the party, whereby the court determines whether the defendant intentionally conducted activities in the forum and thus knows, or could reasonably expect, that such conduct could give rise to litigation in that forum.

Goodyear Dunlop Tires Operations, S.A. v. Brown

Foreign subsidiaries of U.S. corporation (D) v. Decedents' parents (P)

564 U.S. 915 (2011)

NATURE OF CASE: Appeal of state court's assertion of jurisdiction.

FACTS SUMMARY: The parents of two American boys killed in a bus accident in France brought suit in North Carolina, where the boys lived, against the tire company.

RULE OF LAW

A state may not exercise general personal jurisdiction over a foreign subsidiary of a U.S. corporation where the subsidiary lacks continuous and systematic business contacts with the state.

FACTS: The parents (P) of two American boys who were killed in a bus accident in France brought suit in North Carolina state court against Goodyear Tire and Rubber Company (D) and three Goodyear subsidiaries (D) operating in Turkey, France, and Luxembourg. The parents (P) claimed that the accident resulted from a defective tire manufactured at the Turkish subsidiary's plant. Although Goodyear USA (D) operates in North Carolina, the three foreign subsidiaries (D) have no place of business, employees, or bank accounts in the state and neither solicit nor do business in the state. A small percentage of the subsidiaries' (D) tires were distributed in North Carolina by other Goodyear USA (D) affiliates, however. The subsidiaries (D) moved to dismiss the claims against them for lack of personal jurisdiction. The trial court denied the motion, and the North Carolina Court of Appeals affirmed, holding that the court had general jurisdiction over the subsidiaries (D) because their tires had reached the state through "the stream of commerce."

ISSUE: May a state exercise general personal jurisdiction over a foreign subsidiary of a U.S. corporation where the subsidiary lacks continuous and systematic business contacts with the state?

HOLDING AND DECISION: (Ginsburg, J.) No. A state may not exercise general personal jurisdiction over a foreign subsidiary of a U.S. corporation where the subsidiary lacks continuous and systematic business contacts with the state. As stated in *International Shoe Co. v. Washington*, 326 U. S. 310, 316 (1945), and its progeny, a distinction exists between general and specific personal jurisdiction. General personal jurisdiction arises from a defendant's "continuous and systematic" affiliation with a state and permits a state to exercise personal jurisdiction over the defendant for any claim, regardless of whether the claim itself has any connection to the defendant's activities in the state. Specific personal jurisdiction arises from a connection between the state and the underlying claim and permits a state to exercise jurisdiction only with respect to that claim. In this case, the North Carolina courts conflated the two types of jurisdiction, improperly using the isolated presence of the subsidiaries' products in the state as a result of others' actions to justify jurisdiction over the subsidiaries for claims having nothing to do with those products. Reversed.

ANALYSIS

Key to this case is the distinction between two types of personal jurisdiction: general and specific. General jurisdiction is all-purpose, in the sense that it allows any claim to be brought against a defendant as long as the defendant has "systematic and continuous" contacts with that forum. Specific jurisdiction exists where there is a connection between a forum and a particular controversy, and it is limited to that controversy. In this case, only general jurisdiction was in issue: The site of the accident and the factory where the tires were made were both outside of North Carolina, so there was no connection between the state and the controversy, and specific jurisdiction was therefore not properly at issue. As to whether general jurisdiction existed, the Court focused on the "stream of commerce" and reached the conclusion that jurisdiction did not exist.

Quicknotes

GENERAL JURISDICTION The court's authority to hear and determine all cases of a particular type.

PERSONAL JURISDICTION The court's authority over a person or parties to a lawsuit.

Daimler AG v. Bauman

Foreign corporation (D) v. Foreign residents (P)

571 U.S. 117 (2014)

NATURE OF CASE: Appeal from reversal of dismissal, for lack of personal jurisdiction, of action asserting claims under the Alien Tort Statute and the Torture Victim Protection Act of 1991, as well as under state and foreign law.

FACT SUMMARY: Argentinian residents (P) brought suit against Daimler AG (Daimler) (D) in U.S. federal district court asserting various claims under the Alien Tort Statute and the Torture Victim Protection Act of 1991, as well as under state and foreign law, claiming that MB Argentina, an Argentinian subsidiary of Daimler (D), collaborated with state security forces during Argentina's 1976–1983 "Dirty War" to kidnap, detain, torture, and kill certain MB Argentina workers, among them, plaintiffs or persons closely related to the plaintiffs. Daimler (D) moved to dismiss for lack of personal jurisdiction, as none of MB Argentina's alleged actions occurred in the United States, because Daimler (D) had insufficient presence in the United States, and because jurisdiction could not be predicated on the presence in the United States of its indirect subsidiary, MBUSA.

RULE OF LAW

Notwithstanding significant contacts that may be imputed to a foreign corporation, the corporation is not subject to general jurisdiction in a state where the corporation is not at "home," i.e., where it is incorporated or has its principal place of business.

FACTS: Residents of Argentina (P) filed suit against Daimler AG (Daimler) (D) in California federal district court, alleging that MB Argentina, an Argentinian subsidiary of Daimler, collaborated with state security forces during Argentina's 1976–1983 "Dirty War" to kidnap, detain, torture, and kill certain MB Argentina workers, among them, plaintiffs or persons closely related to plaintiffs. Based on those allegations, plaintiffs asserted claims under the Alien Tort Statute and the Torture Victim Protection Act of 1991, as well as under California and Argentina law. Personal jurisdiction over Daimler (D) was predicated on the California contacts of MBUSA, an indirect Daimler (D) subsidiary, one incorporated in Delaware with its principal place of business in New Jersey. MBUSA, as an independent contractor, distributes vehicles manufactured by Daimler (D) to independent dealerships throughout the United States, including California. Daimler (D) moved to dismiss the action for want of personal jurisdiction. Opposing that motion, plaintiffs argued that jurisdiction over Daimler (D) could be founded on the California contacts of MBUSA. The district court granted Daimler's (D) motion to dismiss, finding that Daimler (D) itself has insufficient contacts with California to support jurisdiction, and that MBUSA did not act as Daimler's (D) agent. Reversing, the court of appeals held that MBUSA, which it assumed to fall within the California courts' all-purpose jurisdiction, was Daimler's (D) "agent" for jurisdictional purposes, so that Daimler (D), too, should generally be answerable to suit in California. The United States Supreme Court granted certiorari.

ISSUE: Notwithstanding significant contacts that may be imputed to a foreign corporation, is the corporation subject to general jurisdiction in a state where the corporation is not at "home," i.e., where it is incorporated or has its principal place of business?

HOLDING AND DECISION: (Ginsburg, J.) No. Notwithstanding significant contacts that may be imputed to a foreign corporation, the corporation is not subject to general jurisdiction in a state where the corporation is not at "home," i.e., where it is incorporated or has its principal place of business. Since *International Shoe* [*v. Washington*, 326 U.S. 310 (1945)], specific jurisdiction has become the centerpiece of modern jurisdiction theory. This Court's general jurisdiction opinions, in contrast, have been few. As is evident from these post-*International Shoe* decisions, while specific jurisdiction has been cut loose from *Pennoyer's* sway (*Pennoyer* [*v. Neff*, 95 U.S. 714 (1877)], which held that a tribunal's jurisdiction over persons reaches no farther than the geographic bounds of the forum), general jurisdiction has not been stretched beyond limits traditionally recognized. As the Court has increasingly focused on the relationship among the defendant, the forum, and the litigation, i.e., the attributes of specific jurisdiction, general jurisdiction has come to occupy a less dominant place in the contemporary scheme. Taking these trends into account, even assuming, arguendo, that MBUSA qualifies as at home in California, Daimler's (D) affiliations with California are not sufficient to subject it to the general jurisdiction of California courts. Assuming MBUSA is at home in California and that MBUSA's contacts are imputable to Daimler (D), nevertheless there would still be no basis to subject Daimler (D) to general jurisdiction in California. The paradigm all-purpose forums for general jurisdiction are a corporation's place of incorporation and principal place of business. Plaintiffs' reasoning, however, would reach well beyond these exemplar bases

Continued on next page.

to approve the exercise of general jurisdiction in every state in which a corporation "engages in a substantial, continuous, and systematic course of business." Instead, the proper inquiry is whether a foreign corporation's affiliations with the state are so continuous and systematic as to render it essentially at home in the forum state. Neither Daimler (D) nor MBUSA is incorporated in California, nor does either entity have its principal place of business there. If Daimler's (D) California activities sufficed to allow adjudication of this Argentina-rooted case in California, the same global reach would presumably be available in every other state in which MBUSA's sales are sizable. The Court has never before sanctioned a view of general jurisdiction so grasping. The court of appeals, therefore, had no warrant to conclude that Daimler (D), even with MBUSA's contacts attributed to it, was at home in California, and hence subject to suit there on claims by foreign plaintiffs having nothing to do with anything that occurred or had its principal impact in California. Finally, the transnational context of this dispute bears attention. It is significant that the court of appeals paid little heed to the risks to international comity posed by its expansive view of general jurisdiction, which are not embraced by other nations. For these reasons, the exercise of personal jurisdiction over Daimler (D) would be inappropriate. Reversed.

CONCURRENCE: (Sotomayor, J.) The result of the Court's decision is correct, but not its approach. Here, Daimler (D) has conceded that California courts may exercise general jurisdiction over MBUSA on the basis of its contacts with California, and the Court assumes that MBUSA's contacts may be attributed to Daimler (D) for the purpose of deciding whether Daimler (D) is also subject to general jurisdiction. However, the Court errs in holding that these contacts are insufficient to permit the exercise of general jurisdiction over Daimler (D)—not because the contacts are too few, but because Daimler's (D) contacts with other forums are too many. In other words, the Court does not dispute that the presence of multiple offices, the direct distribution of thousands of products accounting for billions of dollars in sales, and continuous interaction with customers throughout a state would be enough to support the exercise of general jurisdiction over some businesses. Daimler (D) is just not one of those businesses, the Court concludes, because its California contacts must be viewed in the context of its extensive "nationwide and worldwide" operations. Such an approach is wrong, as it ignores the lodestar of our personal jurisdiction jurisprudence: A state may subject a defendant to the burden of suit if the defendant has sufficiently taken advantage of the state's laws and protections through its contacts in the state; whether the defendant has contacts elsewhere is immaterial. The Court instead should have reached the conclusion that exercising jurisdiction over Daimler (D) in this case was inappropriate because, no matter how extensive Daimler's (D) contacts with California, that state's exercise of jurisdiction would be unreasonable given the case involves foreign plaintiffs suing a foreign defendant based on foreign conduct and given a more appropriate forum is available.

ANALYSIS

Arguably, the majority's approach will result in several injustices. For example, it could result in small businesses being treated unfairly in comparison to national and multinational conglomerates: whereas a larger company will often be immunized from general jurisdiction in a state on account of its extensive contacts outside the forum, a small business will not be. The approach could also ostensibly create the incongruous result that an individual defendant whose only contact with a forum state is a one-time visit will be subject to general jurisdiction if served with process during that visit, but a large corporation that owns property, employs workers, and does billions of dollars' worth of business in the state will not be, simply because the corporation has similar contacts elsewhere (though the visiting individual surely does as well). Finally, the majority's approach could significantly shift the risk of loss from multinational corporations to the individuals harmed by their actions, since such corporations would be immunized from suit in any state, even if—and possibly because—the corporation has a massive presence in multiple states.

Quicknotes

GENERAL JURISDICTION The court's authority to hear and determine all cases of a particular type.

PERSONAL JURISDICTION The court's authority over a person or parties to a lawsuit.

Bristol-Myers Squibb Co. v. Superior Court

Corporation (D) v. Class of individuals (P)

582 U.S. ___, 137 S. Ct. 1773 (2017)

NATURE OF CASE: Appeal from the California Supreme Court's decision in favor of the plaintiffs.

FACT SUMMARY: More than 600 plaintiffs alleged they suffered physical injuries caused by a drug, Plavix, manufactured by Bristol-Myers Squibb (BMS) (D), including 592 residents of other states.

RULE OF LAW

For a state court to exercise specific jurisdiction over a claim, the lawsuit must arise out of or relate to the defendant's contacts with the state.

FACTS: More than 600 plaintiffs alleged they suffered physical injuries caused by a drug, Plavix, a blood thinning pharmaceutical, manufactured by Bristol-Myers Squibb (BMS) (D). The cases were all filed in California Superior Court. The plaintiffs included 86 residents of California and 592 residents of thirty-three other states. BMS (D) is incorporated in Delaware and headquartered in New York. BMS (D) has 400 employees working in California, including 250 sales representatives. Between 2007 and 2012, BMS (D) took in over $900 million in sales from Plavix. Significantly, the 592 residents of the other states did not allege they obtained Plavix in California or from a source in California. They did not claim they were injured in California nor did they receive any medical treatment in the state. After initial proceedings at the lower court levels, the California Supreme Court eventually decided that the California courts had specific jurisdiction over the claims filed by the nonresidents. BMS (D) appealed to the United States Supreme Court.

ISSUE: For a state court to exercise specific jurisdiction over a claim, must the lawsuit arise out of or relate to the defendant's contacts with the state?

HOLDING AND DECISION: (Alito, J.) Yes. For a state court to exercise specific jurisdiction over a claim, the lawsuit must arise out of or relate to the defendant's contacts with the state. A state court with general jurisdiction may adjudicate any claim made against a defendant, even if all the claims arise in a different state. General jurisdiction typically applies when a corporation has its headquarters in a particular state. Conversely, specific jurisdiction over a claim only arises when there is a connection between the state and the underlying case, usually via an activity or occurrence that takes place within the state. When assessing personal jurisdiction, courts must consider several factors. These include the interests of the forum state and of the plaintiff in proceeding with the cause in the plaintiff's forum of choice, but the main concern is the burden upon the defendant. Personal jurisdiction is limited by the territorial limitations of the state. Here, the California Supreme Court improperly concluded that its courts had jurisdiction over the claims of the nonresidents simply because their claims were similar to those of the state residents. This appears to be a form of general jurisdiction that is not supported by any prior decisions of this Court. Here, there are no connections between California and the claims of the nonresidents. Those plaintiffs did not purchase the drug in California, did not take the drug there, and were not treated for any injuries in the state. Accordingly, there are no facts present to establish specific jurisdiction over the claims of the nonresidents. Reversed and remanded.

DISSENT: (Sotomayor, J.) The majority's decision will make it difficult for class actions to proceed in one particular state court. Defendant corporations will now be forced to litigate separate claims in multiple jurisdictions. Clearly Bristol-Myers Squibb (BMS) (D) availed itself of the protections of the state of California by employing 400 people in the state and selling over $900 million dollars of the product in the state. The claims of the nonresidents also relate to BMS's (D) in-state activities. The nonresidents' claims are materially identical to the actions of BMS (D) in California.

ANALYSIS

It is not yet apparent whether this decision has had a significant impact on the filing of class action lawsuits across the country. The decision clearly limits, if not bars, the ability of nonresident plaintiffs to file claims in a jurisdiction where specific jurisdiction will not be present over their claims.

Quicknotes

CLASS ACTION A suit commenced by a representative on behalf of an ascertainable group that is too large to appear in court, shares a commonality of interests, and will benefit from a successful result.

PERSONAL JURISDICTION The court's authority over a person or parties to a lawsuit.

Ford Motor Co. v. Montana Eighth Judicial Dist. Court

Motor vehicle manufacturer (D) v. Individuals injured or killed by defective motor vehicle (P)

529 U.S. ___, 141 S. Ct. 1017 (2021)

NATURE OF CASE: Appeals from judgments of two separate state supreme courts in products liability actions holding that a motor vehicle manufacturer's contacts with the respective states was sufficient to support specific jurisdiction over the manufacturer in actions brought by residents of the states alleging that defects in the manufacturer's vehicles caused in-state injury to the residents.

FACT SUMMARY: Ford Motor Company (Ford) (D), a global auto company, asserted that it had insufficient contacts with states to support specific jurisdiction over it in products liability actions involving state residents who were injured or killed by allegedly defective Ford (D) motor vehicles where, notwithstanding that Ford (D) did substantial business in the states, the particular vehicles involved had not been designed, manufactured, or first sold in the states.

RULE OF LAW

In a products liability action, there is specific jurisdiction over a company whose product is claimed to be defective and to have caused in-state injury where, although the company did not design, manufacture, or first sell the product in the state where the injury occurred, the company did substantial business in the state, including advertising, selling, and servicing the type of product at issue.

FACTS: Ford Motor Company (Ford) (D), a global auto company, is incorporated in Delaware and headquartered in Michigan. Ford (D) markets, sells, and services its products across the United States and overseas. It has 3,200 licensed dealerships and conducts wide-ranging promotional activities across the United States. Ford (D) also encourages a resale market for its vehicles. In each of two cases, a state court exercised jurisdiction over Ford (D) in a products liability suit stemming from a car accident that injured a resident in the state. The first suit alleged that a 1996 Ford Explorer had malfunctioned, killing Markkaya Gullett (Gullett) near her home in Montana. The representative (P) of Gullett's estate sued Ford (D) in Montana state court. In the second suit, Adam Bandemer (Bandemer) (P) claimed that he was injured in a collision on a Minnesota road involving a defective 1994 (Ford (D)) Crown Victoria. Ford (D) moved to dismiss both suits for lack of personal jurisdiction. It argued that each state court had jurisdiction only if Ford's (D) conduct in the state had given rise to the plaintiff's claims. According to Ford (D), that causal link existed only if the company had designed, manufactured, or first sold in the state the particular vehicle involved in the accident. In neither suit could the plaintiff make that showing. The vehicles were designed and manufactured in other jurisdictions (designed in Michigan, manufactured, respectively, in Kentucky and Canada), and Ford (D) had originally sold the cars at issue outside the forum states (respectively, Washington and North Dakota). Only later resales and relocations by consumers had brought the vehicles to Montana and Minnesota. Although Ford (D) had not designed, manufactured, or first sold the particular vehicles at issue in the forum states, Ford (D) did substantial business in the states, including advertising, selling, and servicing the model of vehicle the respective suits claimed was defective. Both the Minnesota Supreme Court and the Montana Supreme Court rejected Ford's (D) argument. Affirming lower courts in its state, each state supreme court held that Ford's (D) activities in the state had the needed connection to the plaintiff's allegations that a defective Ford (D) caused in-state injury to support specific jurisdiction over Ford (D). Ford (D) appealed in each case, and the United States Supreme Court granted certiorari in each.

ISSUE: In a products liability action, is there specific jurisdiction over a company whose product is claimed to be defective and to have caused in-state injury where, although the company did not design, manufacture, or first sell the product in the state where the injury occurred, the company did substantial business in the state, including advertising, selling, and servicing the type of product at issue?

HOLDING AND DECISION: (Kagan, J.) Yes. In a products liability action, there is specific jurisdiction over a company whose product is claimed to be defective and to have caused in-state injury where, although the company did not design, manufacture, or first sell the product in the state where the injury occurred, the company did substantial business in the state, including advertising, selling, and servicing the type of product at issue. The Fourteenth Amendment's Due Process Clause limits a state court's power to exercise jurisdiction over a defendant. The canonical decision in this area remains *International Shoe Co. v. Washington*, 326 U.S. 310 (1945). There, the Court held that a tribunal's authority depends on the defendant's having such "contacts" with the forum state that "the maintenance of the suit" is "reasonable" and "does not offend traditional notions of fair play and substantial justice." In applying that formulation, the

Continued on next page.

Court has long focused on the nature and extent of the defendant's relationship to the forum state. That focus has led to the recognition of two types of personal jurisdiction: general and specific jurisdiction. A state court may exercise general jurisdiction only when a defendant is essentially at home in the state. Specific jurisdiction covers defendants less intimately connected with a state, but only as to a narrower class of claims. To be subject to specific jurisdiction, the defendant must take some act by which it purposefully avails itself of the privilege of conducting activities within the forum state. Additionally, as held in *Bristol-Myers Squibb Co.* v. *Superior Court of Cal., San Francisco Cty.*, 582 U.S. ___, 137 S. Ct. 1773 (2017), the plaintiff's claims must arise out of or relate to the defendant's contacts with the forum. Here, Ford (D) admits that it has purposefully availed itself of the privilege of conducting activities in both Minnesota and Montana. However, Ford (D) contends instead that those activities are insufficiently connected to the suits. In Ford's (D) view, due process requires a causal link locating jurisdiction only in the state where Ford (D) sold the car in question, or the states where Ford (D) designed and manufactured the vehicle. Therefore, according to Ford (D), because none of these things occurred in Montana or Minnesota, those states' courts have no power over these cases. Ford's (D) causation-only approach is unavailing, however, because it finds no support in the Court's requirement of a "connection" between a plaintiff's suit and a defendant's activities. The most common formulation of that rule, expressed in *Bristol-Meyer*, demands that the suit arise out of or relate to the defendant's contacts with the forum. The second half of that formulation, following the word "or," extends beyond causality. So the inquiry is not whether a causal test would put jurisdiction elsewhere, given that another state's courts could also have jurisdiction, because of a non-causal affiliation between the forum and the underlying controversy, principally, an activity or an occurrence involving the defendant that takes place within the state's borders. Moreover, the Court has stated that specific jurisdiction attaches in cases identical to this one—when a company cultivates a market for a product in the forum state and the product malfunctions there. Here, Ford (D) advertises and markets its vehicles in Montana and Minnesota, including the two models that allegedly malfunctioned in those states. Apart from sales, the company works hard to foster ongoing connections to its cars' owners. All such Montana- and Minnesota-based conduct relates to the claims in these cases, brought by state residents in the states' courts. Thus, because Ford (D) had systematically served a market in Montana and Minnesota for the very vehicles that the plaintiffs allege malfunctioned and injured them in those states, there is a strong relationship among the defendant, the forum, and the litigation—the "essential foundation" of specific jurisdiction. Allowing jurisdiction in these circumstances both treats Ford (D) fairly and serves principles of "interstate federalism." Contrary to Ford's (D) argument, *Bristol-Myers* reinforces this conclusion, rather than undermining it. In *Bristol-Myers*, although the Court found jurisdiction improper, it did so because the forum state, and the defendant's activities there, lacked any connection to the plaintiffs' claims. That is not true of the cases at bar, where the plaintiffs are residents of the forum states, used the allegedly defective products in the forum states, and suffered injuries when those products malfunctioned there. Accordingly, there is a sufficient relationship between the plaintiffs' claims, the defendant, the forums, and the litigation to support specific jurisdiction in each state. The judgments of the Montana and Minnesota Supreme Courts are therefore affirmed.

ANALYSIS

A key takeaway from this decision is that a defendant's showing that a plaintiff's claim does not arise out of or is not causally linked to the defendant's conduct in the forum state may not be enough to establish that a court lacks personal jurisdiction if a plaintiff can show that the claim sufficiently "relates to" the defendant's conduct in the state. The Court emphasized that when a company like Ford (D) serves a market for a product in a state and that product causes injury in the state to a state resident, the state's courts may entertain the resulting suit. What this might mean is that plaintiffs bringing claims in certain industries, such as pharmaceuticals and medical and health devices, who purchased and used medical devices outside a forum state can now rely on the Court's decision in *Ford* to suggest that in-state business activities other than a defendant's manufacture and sale of a product can support jurisdiction. Thus, for example, specific jurisdiction over brand-name manufacturers for alleged injuries caused by generic drugs could now be available in an action for innovator liability, on the theory that the Court has rejected a strict but-for causation requirement for relatedness. Although this may provide courts with jurisdiction over claims relating to such industries, or involving very large companies, the Court expressly limited the scope of its holding by disclaiming any intent to address e-commerce or Internet contacts, and noting that "[n]one of this is to say that any person using any means to sell any good in a State is subject to jurisdiction there if the product malfunctions after arrival."

Continued on next page.

Quicknotes

FORUM STATE The state in which a court, or other location in which a legal remedy may be sought, is located.

GENERAL JURISDICTION The authority of a court to hear and determine all cases of a particular type.

PERSONAL JURISDICTION The court's authority over a person or parties to a lawsuit.

SPECIFIC JURISDICTION A type of personal jurisdiction that authorizes a court to hear and declare judgment in respect to a particular matter based on the defendant's minimum contacts with the forum state that does not require a causal connection between the defendant's in-state activities and the plaintiff's claims.

Burnham v. Superior Court

Husband and father (P) v. Court (D)

495 U.S. 604 (1990)

NATURE OF CASE: Appeal from denial of motion to quash service of process in dissolution action on the grounds that the court lacked personal jurisdiction.

FACT SUMMARY: Dennis Burnham (P) and his wife were living in New Jersey when they decided to separate. Mrs. Burnham moved with the children to California, filed for divorce in that state and served Mr. Burnham (P) while he was visiting.

RULE OF LAW

State courts have jurisdiction over nonresidents who are physically present in the state.

FACTS: Dennis Burnham (P) and his wife were living in New Jersey when they decided to separate. Mrs. Burnham moved with the children to California and filed for divorce in that state. Mr. Burnham (P) visited his children in January of 1988, at which time he was served with a California court summons and a copy of his wife's divorce petition. He made a special appearance in the California Superior Court (D) moving to quash the service of process on the ground that the Court (D) lacked personal jurisdiction over him because his only contacts with California were a few short visits to the state for the purpose of conducting business and visiting his children. The Superior Court (D) denied the motion, and the California Court of Appeals denied mandamus relief. The court held it to be a valid jurisdictional predicate for in personam jurisdiction that Mr. Burnham (P) was present in the forum state and personally served with process. The United States Supreme Court granted certiorari.

ISSUE: Do state courts have jurisdiction over nonresidents who are physically present in the state?

HOLDING AND DECISION: (Scalia, J.) Yes. State courts have jurisdiction over nonresidents who are physically present in the state. Jurisdiction based on physical presence alone constitutes due process because it is one of the continuing traditions of our legal system that define the due process standard of traditional notions of fair play and substantial justice. That standard was developed by analogy to physical presence, and it would be perverse to say it could now be turned against that touchstone of jurisdiction. Affirmed.

CONCURRENCE: (Brennan, J.) History is an important factor in establishing whether a jurisdictional rule satisfies due process requirements, but it is not the only factor such that all traditional rules of jurisdiction are, ipso facto, forever constitutional.

CONCURRENCE: (Stevens, J.) It is sufficient to note that the historical evidence and consensus identified by Justice Scalia, the considerations of fairness identified by Justice Brennan, and the common sense displayed by Justice White, all combine to demonstrate that this is, indeed, a very easy case.

ANALYSIS

In a footnote to the above case, Justice Scalia explained that in *Helicopteros Nacionales de Colombia v. Hall*, 466 U.S. at 414 (1984), the Supreme Court held that due process is not offended by a state's subjecting a corporation to its jurisdiction when there are sufficient contacts between the state and the foreign corporation. However, the only holding supporting that statement involved regular service of summons upon a corporate president while in the forum state acting in that capacity. See *Perkins v. Benguet Consolidated Mining Co.*, 342 U.S. 437 (1952). It may be whatever special rule exists permitting continuous and systematic contacts to support jurisdiction with respect to matters unrelated to activity in the forum applied only to corporations, which have never fitted comfortably within a jurisdictional regime based primarily upon de facto power over the defendant's person.

Quicknotes

PERSONAL JURISDICTION The court's authority over a person or parties to a lawsuit.

SERVICE OF PROCESS The communication of reasonable notice of a court proceeding to a defendant in order to provide him with an opportunity to be heard.

Carnival Cruise Lines, Inc. v. Shute

Cruise company (D) v. Customers (P)

499 U.S. 585 (1991)

NATURE OF CASE: Review of denial of defense motion for summary judgment in personal injury action.

FACT SUMMARY: Shute (P), an injured cruise ship passenger, filed suit in her home state despite a stipulation in her passenger ticket requiring all suits to be filed in Florida.

RULE OF LAW

Reasonable forum-selection clauses contained in passenger tickets are presumptively valid.

FACTS: The Shutes (P), residents of Washington State, purchased passage for a seven-day cruise on a ship owned by Carnival Cruise Lines, Inc. (Carnival Cruise) (D). The cruise tickets they received contained a forum-selection clause setting the State of Florida as the forum where any disputes arising from the cruise would be litigated. Carnival Cruise (D) had its principal place of business in Florida, and many of its cruises departed from there. During the cruise, Mrs. Shute (P) was injured in a slip-and-fall accident. The Shutes (P) filed a negligence action in Washington. Carnival Cruise (D) moved for summary judgment, contending that the forum clause in the Shutes's (P) ticket required them to bring their suit in a Florida court. The U.S. Court of Appeals for the Ninth Circuit denied its motion on the ground that the clause was not a product of negotiation, and the United States Supreme Court granted certiorari.

ISSUE: Are reasonable forum-selection clauses contained in passenger tickets presumptively valid?

HOLDING AND DECISION: (Blackmun, J.) Yes. Reasonable forum-selection clauses contained in passenger tickets are presumptively valid. They are permissible because a cruise line has a special interest in limiting the fora in which it potentially could be subject to suit. Such a clause also dispels any confusion about where a suit must be brought, thereby sparing litigants and courts the time and expense of litigating the issue. Finally, the passengers themselves benefit from forum clauses because fares are reduced commensurate with the money saved by the cruise line in limiting the fora where it may be sued. Since in this case there is no bad-faith motive apparent in Carnival Cruise's (D) forum provision, and the Shutes (P) have conceded that they had notice of the provision, the Ninth Circuit erred in refusing to enforce the clause. Reversed.

DISSENT: (Stevens, J.) The prevailing rule is that forum-selection clauses are not enforceable if they were not freely bargained for, create additional expense for one party, or deny one party a remedy.

ANALYSIS

Besides forum-selection clauses, a contract may contain a choice of law clause, stipulating which jurisdiction's substantive law will govern, or an arbitration clause, requiring parties to use arbitration as their exclusive forum. The most extreme example of a contract provision limiting a defendant's right to appeal or to even raise a defense to an action is the "cognovit." A cognovit note is written authority of a debtor for entry of a judgment against him or her if the obligation set forth in the note is not paid when due. Such agreements are prohibited in many states.

Quicknotes

COGNOVIT NOTE A note signed by a debtor authorizing an attorney to enter judgment against him or her if payment is not made thereon.

FORUM-SELECTION CLAUSE Provision in a contract setting forth the particular forum in which the parties would resolve a matter if a dispute were to arise.

Mullane v. Central Hanover Bank & Trust Co.

Guardian of trust beneficiaries (P) v. Bank (D)

339 U.S. 306 (1950)

NATURE OF CASE: Constitutional challenge of the sufficiency of the notice provision of the New York Banking Law relating to beneficiaries of common-trust funds.

FACT SUMMARY: Central Hanover Bank & Trust Co. (D) pooled a number of small trust funds, and beneficiaries (some of whom lived out of state) were notified by publication in a local newspaper.

RULE OF LAW

Notice by publication is not sufficient to satisfy due process challenges where the parties to be informed reside out of state and an alternative means better calculated to give actual notice is available.

FACTS: A New York statute allowed corporate trustees to pool the assets of numerous small trusts administered by them. This allowed more efficient and economical administration of the funds. Each participating trust shared ratably in the common fund, but the trustees held complete control of all assets. A periodic accounting of profits, losses, and assets was to be submitted to the courts for approval. Beneficiaries were to be notified of the accounting so that they might object to any irregularities in the administration of the common fund. Once approved by the court, their claims would be barred. A guardian would be appointed to protect the interests of principal and income beneficiaries. Central Hanover Bank & Trust Co. (D) established a common fund by consolidating the corpus of 113 separate trusts under their control. Notice of the common fund was sent to all interested parties along with the relevant portions of the statute. Notice of accountings was by publication in a local New York newspaper. Mullane (P) was the appointed guardian for all parties known and unknown who had an interest in the trust's income. He objected to the sufficiency of the statutory notice provisions claiming that they violated the Due Process Clause of the Fourteenth Amendment. Notice by publication was not a reasonable method of informing interested parties that their rights were being affected, especially with regard to out-of-state beneficiaries. Mullane's (P) objections were overruled in state courts and Mullane (P) brought the present federal appeal.

ISSUE: Is notice by publication sufficient to satisfy due process challenges where the parties to be informed reside out of state and an alternative means better calculated to give actual notice is available?

HOLDING AND DECISION: (Jackson, J.) No. Notice by publication is not sufficient to satisfy due process challenges where the parties to be informed reside out of state and an alternative means, better calculated to give actual notice is available. The purpose of a notice requirement is to inform parties that their rights are being affected. Therefore, the method chosen should, if at all possible, be reasonably designed to accomplish this end. Notice in a New York legal paper is not reasonably calculated to provide out-of-state residents with the desired information. While the state has a right to discharge trustees of their liabilities through the acceptance of their accounting, it must also provide beneficiaries with adequate notice so that their rights to contest the accounting are not lost. In cases where the identity or whereabouts of beneficiaries or future interest holders is unknown, then publication is the most viable alternate means available for giving notice. Publication is only a supplemental method of giving notice. However, the Court will approve its use where alternative methods are not reasonably possible or practical. Where alternative methods, better calculated to give actual notice, are available, publication is an impermissible means of providing notice. Notice to known beneficiaries via publication is inadequate, not because it in fact fails to inform everyone, but, because under the circumstances, it is not readily calculated to reach those who could easily be informed by other means at hand. Since publication to known beneficiaries is ineffective, the statutory requirement violates the Due Process Clause of the Fourteenth Amendment. These parties have, at least potentially, been deprived of property without due process of law. With respect to remote future interest holders and unknown parties, publication is permissible. Reversed and remanded.

ANALYSIS

Ineffective notice provisions violate procedural due process rights. As in all due process challenges, there must be a legitimate state interest and the means selected must be reasonably adapted to accomplish the state's purpose. While in *Mullane* the state's ends were permissible, the method of giving notice was unreasonable as it pertained to known parties. Publication is normally used in conjunction with other means when personal service by hand is unavailable or impractical. *Mullane*

Continued on next page.

has been applied to condemnation cases where a known owner of property was never personally served. *Schroeder v. City of New York*, 371 U.S. 208 (1962). Factors considered by the Court involve the nature of the action, whether the party's whereabouts or identity are known or unknown, whether he or she is a resident and whether or not he or she has attempted to avoid personal service. If an attempt to avoid service is made, then constructive service by publication in conjunction with substitute service by mail is permitted. Finally, foreign corporations are generally required to appoint resident agents authorized to accept service of process.

Quicknotes

DUE PROCESS The constitutional mandate requiring the courts to protect and enforce individuals' rights and liberties consistent with prevailing principles of fairness and justice and prohibiting the federal and state governments from such activities that deprive its citizens of life, liberty, or property interest.

NOTICE Communication of information to a person by one authorized or by an otherwise proper source.

Baidoo v. Blood-Dzraku

Spouse (P) v. Spouse (D)

N.Y. Sup. Ct., 5 N.Y.S.3d 709 (2015)

NATURE OF CASE: Ex parte application in action for marital dissolution to serve spouse with divorce summons exclusively through private message on social networking website.

FACT SUMMARY: Baidoo (P) wanted a divorce from Blood-Dzraku (D), but the only way Baidoo (P) had of contacting Blood-Dzraku (D) was by private message on Facebook, a social networking website, and by telephone. Baidoo (P) sought to serve Blood-Dzraku (D) with the divorce summons exclusively via such private message.

RULE OF LAW

Where a plaintiff in a divorce action cannot physically locate the defendant and does not have an email address for the defendant, and the only means the plaintiff has of reaching the defendant is by private message on a social networking website, service of the divorce summons exclusively by such private message is reasonably calculated to inform the defendant that the defendant is being sued for divorce where it is possible to verify that the network account belongs to the defendant, the defendant regularly checks the account, and it is possible to reach the defendant by telephone to alert the defendant to check the account, thereby satisfying due process concerns.

FACTS: Baidoo (P) wanted a divorce from Blood-Dzraku (D), but the only way Baidoo (P) had of contacting Blood-Dzraku (D) was by private message on Facebook, a social networking website, and by telephone. Accordingly, she applied ex parte to the court asking the court to find as a matter of first impression that service of the divorce summons via private message on Facebook constituted an appropriate form of alternative service and that this judicially crafted method of service be designated the only means by which notice of the divorce action was to be given. In support of her application, Baidoo (P) averred that she and Blood-Dzraku (D) never resided together, even after being married; that she had spoken with Blood-Dzraku (D) by telephone on occasion and he had informed her that he had no fixed address and no place of employment; that he refused to make himself available to be served with divorce papers; that the investigative firms that Baidoo (P) hired to assist in locating Blood-Dzraku (D) had all been unsuccessful in their efforts to locate him; that the post office had no forwarding address for him; that there was no billing address linked to his pre-paid cell phone; and that the Department of Motor Vehicles had no record of Blood-Dzraku (D). Additionally, to show that the Facebook account belonged to Blood-Dzraku (D), Baidoo (P) submitted an affidavit, to which she annexed copies of the exchanges that took place between her and Blood-Dzraku (D) when she contacted him through his Facebook page, and in which she identified him as the subject of the photographs that appeared on that page. The affidavit and its attachments also demonstrated that Blood-Dzraku (D) regularly checked his Facebook account. Finally, because Blood-Dzraku (D) had a cell phone, Baidoo (P) and her attorney could speak to him or leave a voicemail message, or else send him a text message alerting him that a divorce action has been commenced and that he should check his account. The court considered the application.

ISSUE: Where a plaintiff in a divorce action cannot physically locate the defendant and does not have an email address for the defendant, and the only means the plaintiff has of reaching the defendant is by private message on a social networking website, is service of the divorce summons exclusively by such private message reasonably calculated to inform the defendant that the defendant is being sued for divorce where it is possible to verify that the network account belongs to the defendant, the defendant regularly checks the account, and it is possible to reach the defendant by telephone to alert the defendant to check the account, thereby satisfying due process concerns?

HOLDING AND DECISION: (Cooper, J.) Yes. Where a plaintiff in a divorce action cannot physically locate the defendant and does not have an email address for the defendant, and the only means the plaintiff has of reaching the defendant is by private message on a social networking website, service of the divorce summons exclusively by such private message is reasonably calculated to inform the defendant that the defendant is being sued for divorce where it is possible to verify that the network account belongs to the defendant, the defendant regularly checks the account, and it is possible to reach the defendant by telephone to alert the defendant to check the account, thereby satisfying due process concerns. The standard method, and the method of first resort, for serving the summons in a divorce action is personal delivery to a defendant. Ordinarily, this method ensures that a person who is being sued for divorce—a proceeding that can have immeasurable financial and familial consequences—be made aware of and afforded

Continued on next page.

the opportunity to appear in the action. The problem with personal service is that for it to be accomplished, a plaintiff must be able to locate the defendant. Even where a defendant's whereabouts are known, there are times when it is logistically difficult, if not impossible, for a process server to gain the close proximity necessary for personal delivery. Fortunately, the law recognizes this limitation and permits alternative forms of service, whereby a plaintiff: can request permission to (1) deliver the complaint and summons to a person of "suitable age and discretion" at the person's home or business, i.e., "substitute service"; (2) use "nail and mail" service, attaching the summons and complaint to the door of the person's home or business and mailing a copy to their last known address or place of business; (3) publication service, where the summons is printed in a newspaper, allowed only if the plaintiff can show that "service cannot be made by another prescribed method with due diligence"; or (4) an alternative method of service approved by the court that fits the particular circumstances of the case if other available forms of service are impracticable. Here, to prevail on her request, Baidoo (P) must show that the first three of these alternative service methods are unavailable, and she also must show that sending the summons through Facebook can reasonably be expected to give Blood-Dzraku (D) actual notice that he is being sued for divorce, so as to satisfy due process concerns. Because Baidoo (P) has attested that she cannot physically locate Blood-Dzraku (D) despite diligent efforts, it would be an exercise in futility to attempt "substitute service" and "nail and mail" service, both of which require knowledge of the defendant's "actual place of business, dwelling or usual place of abode" (Civil Practice Law & Rules 308[2]). As to service by publication, which is still the most often used means of service permitted in divorce actions when the defendant cannot be served by other means, it is almost guaranteed not to provide a defendant with notice of the action for divorce, or any other law suit for that matter. As a practical matter, the chance of Blood-Dzraku (D) ever seeing the summons in print, either in a daily newspaper of large circulation, or in a newspaper intended for the legal profession or a niche readership, is infinitesimal. The dangers of allowing somebody to be divorced and not know it are simply too great to allow notice to be given by publication, a form of service that, while neither novel or unorthodox, is essentially statutorily authorized non-service. Moreover, the cost of running a notice for a week, buried in an obscure section of a paper and printed in small type, is prohibitive, and in any event likely will yield no results. For these reasons, Baidoo (P) has demonstrated a sound basis for seeking alternative service fashioned by the court. However, she must also show that the method she proposes is one that the court can endorse as being reasonably calculated to apprise defendant that he is being sued for divorce. This hurdle poses a number of challenges. First, there are only a handful of reported decisions, mostly from federal district courts, that have addressed the issue of service of process being accomplished through social media, with there being an almost even split between those decisions approving it and those rejecting it. However, the few courts that have approved it have done so only on condition that the papers commencing the lawsuit be served on the defendant by another method as well. Therefore, the court must be guided by constitutional principles of due process. Here, by showing that the Facebook account belongs to Blood-Dzraku (D), that he regularly checks it, and that he can be contacted by cell phone so he can be told to check the account, Baidoo (P) has satisfied the court that using the Facebook account to effect service of the divorce summons is reasonably calculated to provide Blood-Dzraku (D) with notice that he's being sued for divorce. For these reasons, Baidoo (P) is granted permission to serve Blood-Dzraku (D) with the divorce summons using a private message through Facebook. Specifically, because litigants are prohibited from serving other litigants, Baidoo's (P) attorney must log into Baidoo's (P) Facebook account and message Blood-Dzraku (D) by first identifying himself, and then including either a web address of the summons or attaching an image of the summons. This transmittal must be repeated by the attorney once a week for three consecutive weeks or until acknowledged by Blood-Dzraku (D). Additionally, after the initial transmittal, Baidoo (P) and her attorney are to call and text message Blood-Dzraku (D) to inform him that the summons for divorce has been sent to him via Facebook.

ANALYSIS

As the court notes, as recently as ten years before this case arose, it was considered a cutting-edge development in civil practice for a court to allow the service of a summons by email. Since then, email has all but replaced ordinary mail as a means of written communication, and courts are now routinely permitting it as a form of alternative service. Since courts first started permitting email service, there has been the advent and ascendency of social media, with websites such as Facebook and Twitter occupying a central place in the lives of millions of people. Thus, it would appear that the next frontier in the developing law of the service of process over the Internet is the use of social media sites as forums through which a summons can be delivered. Having practically no precedent to guide it, the court here addressed service-of-process issues specific to social media. The court noted that is well known that a Facebook profile somebody views online may very well belong to someone other than whom the profile

Continued on next page.

purports it to be, and that this has led courts to observe that anyone can make a Facebook profile using real, fake, or incomplete information, and thus there is no way for a court to confirm whether the Facebook page belongs to the defendant to be served. As a result, the court here required Baidoo (P) to submit a supplemental affidavit to verify that the Facebook account she referenced was indeed that of Blood-Dzraku (D). The court noted that although it is true that Baidoo's (P) attested statements were not absolute proof that the account belonged to Blood-Dzraku (D)—it being conceivable that if she herself or someone at her behest created the Facebook page, she could fabricate exchanges and post photographs—she nevertheless persuaded the court that the account in question did indeed belong to Blood-Dzraku (D). Thus, for the time being, this case represents the cutting edge of contemporary service of process.

Quicknotes

DUE PROCESS The constitutional mandate requiring the courts to protect and enforce individuals' rights and liberties consistent with prevailing principles of fairness and justice and prohibiting the federal and state governments from such activities that deprive its citizens of life, liberty, or property interest.

SERVICE OF PROCESS The communication of reasonable notice of a court proceeding to a defendant in order to provide him or her with an opportunity to be heard.

Gibbons v. Brown

Automobile passenger (D) v. Fellow passenger (P)

Fla. Dist. Ct. App., 716 So. 2d 868 (1998)

NATURE OF CASE: Appeal from dismissal of a personal-injury action.

FACT SUMMARY: Mrs. Brown (P) filed a suit against Gibbons (D), a Texas resident, in Florida two years after Gibbons (D) had sued Mr. Brown in a Florida case involving the same auto accident.

RULE OF LAW

A prior decision to file a lawsuit in a state does not qualify as sufficient activity in the state to confer personal jurisdiction.

FACTS: Mr. Brown was driving a car in Canada, in which Mrs. Brown (P) and Gibbons (D) were passengers. After a collision, Gibbons (D), a Texas resident, sued Mr. Brown in Florida. Two years later, Mrs. Brown (P) filed suit against Gibbons (D) in Florida for allegedly causing the accident by giving faulty directions. The trial court dismissed the action based on a lack of personal jurisdiction over Gibbons (D). Mrs. Brown (P) appealed.

ISSUE: Does a prior decision to file a lawsuit in a state qualify as sufficient activity in the state to confer personal jurisdiction?

HOLDING AND DECISION: (Per curiam) No. A prior decision to file a lawsuit in a state does not qualify as sufficient activity in the state to confer personal jurisdiction. Obtaining personal jurisdiction over a nonresident defendant requires a two-pronged showing. First, there must be sufficient jurisdictional facts to bring the defendant within the long-arm statute. Then, there must be sufficient minimum contacts between the defendant and forum state such that jurisdiction would not violate due process. Florida requires that nonresident defendants engage in substantial and not isolated activity within the state in order to be subject to personal jurisdiction. There is no doubt that when an out-of-state plaintiff brings an action in Florida, he or she is subject to jurisdiction in subsequent actions regarding the same subject matter. However, in the present case, there were two years separating Gibbons's (D) suit against Mr. Brown and Mrs. Brown's (P) current action. Additionally, Mrs. Brown (P) was not a party to the first suit. Given these facts, and the lack of any other contact between Gibbons (D) and Florida, the grounds for personal jurisdiction do not meet the state's requirements. Complaint dismissal ordered.

ANALYSIS

The court acknowledged that Florida does not allow jurisdiction to the full range allowed by the United States Constitution. Thus, in the present case, it is possible that another state would have allowed the case against Gibbons (D) to proceed. However, the court never reached the issue of whether the minimum contacts required by due process had been met.

Quicknotes

LONG-ARM STATUTE A state statute conferring personal jurisdiction to state courts over a defendant not residing in the state, when the cause of action arises as a result of activities conducted within the state or affecting state residents.

PERSONAL JURISDICTION The court's authority over a person or parties to a lawsuit.

PROCEDURAL DUE PROCESS The constitutional mandate that if the state or federal government acts so as to deny a citizen of a life, liberty, or property interest, the individual is first entitled to notice and the right to be heard.

Thompson v. Greyhound Lines, Inc.

Passenger (P) v. Bus line (D)

2012 WL 6213792 (S.D. Ala. 2012)

NATURE OF CASE: Motion to dismiss on the grounds, inter alia, of improper venue.

FACT SUMMARY: Thompson (P) brought suit in federal court in Alabama against Greyhound Lines, Inc. (Greyhound) (D) on several state-law claims arising from his having fallen asleep on a bus and missing a court appearance in Mississippi because the bus driver did not wake him and took him back to Alabama. Greyhound (D) moved to dismiss on grounds, inter alia, of improper venue.

RULE OF LAW

Where venue is improper in a federal district, but would be proper in a different district, a case will be transferred to the proper district instead of being dismissed where doing so serves the interests of justice.

FACTS: Thompson (P) on March 14 bought from Greyhound Lines, Inc. (Greyhound) (D) in Pensacola, Florida, a one-way ticket to Tunica, Mississippi, to arrive at 5:05 p.m. on March 15. A Greyhound (D) bus delivered Thompson (P) from Pensacola to Mobile, Alabama, just after midnight on March 15. Seven hours later, Greyhound (D) personnel directed Thompson (P) to board a Colonial Trailways (D) bus. The driver, Reeves (D)—a Florida resident—announced that the bus was traveling only to Jackson, Mississippi, and would thereafter return to Mobile. Reeves (D) also announced that his bus was scheduled to arrive in Jackson at 12:05 p.m. and that a bus would depart Jackson at 12:30 p.m., arriving in Tunica at 5:05 p.m. Thompson (P), upon hearing this, decided it was time for a nap. Thompson (P) awoke at 2:30 p.m., finding himself heading back to Mobile. Reeves (D) refused to change course. Thompson (P) then remained in Mobile for over nine hours before his brother sent him a pre-paid ticket back to Pensacola. Because of these events, Thompson (P) "missed his court-date and was found guilty in absentia." He sued Greyhound (D), Colonial Trailways (D), and Reeves (D) on several state law causes of action, basing subject matter jurisdiction on diversity of citizenship. Greyhound (D) moved to dismiss on grounds of improper venue, as well as for failure to state a claim.

ISSUE: Where venue is improper in a federal district, but would be proper in a different district, will a case be transferred to the proper district instead of being dismissed where doing so serves the interests of justice?

HOLDING AND DECISION: (Steele, J.) Yes. Where venue is improper in a federal district, but would be proper in a different district, a case will be transferred to the proper district instead of being dismissed where doing so serves the interests of justice. As a threshold matter, challenges to venue should be considered before motions to dismiss for failure to state a claim. Thus, it is proper to consider Greyhound's (D) motion to dismiss for improper venue. A plaintiff has the burden of showing that venue in the forum is proper, but where there has been no evidentiary hearing, the plaintiff need present only prima facie showing that venue is proper. Thompson (P) has failed to make such a showing. Venue can be established in a judicial district in which any defendant resides, if all defendants are residents of the state in which the district is located. Because Reeves (D) was a Florida resident, venue is improper under 28 U.S.C. § 1391(b)(1). Under 28 U.S.C. § 1391(b)(2), venue is also proper in a judicial district in which a substantial part of the events or omissions giving rise to the claim occurred. Here, the only event that occurred in this district was that Thompson (P) changed buses here, and that event did not "directly give rise to a claim." The mere fact that Thompson (P) passed through this district and changed buses here is not a "part of the events or omissions giving rise to the claim," much less a "substantial" part. Accordingly, venue is not proper under § 1391(b)(2). However, a substantial part of the events or omissions giving rise to Thompson's (P) claims certainly occurred in the Southern District of Mississippi. Where a case has been improperly filed in the wrong district, the court in that district has the discretion to dismiss the case, or, if the interests of justice would be served, to transfer the case to the proper district, provided that district has jurisdiction over the matter. Here, the Southern District of Mississippi would have specific personal jurisdiction since the key events giving rise to Thompson's (P) claims occurred there. Generally, the interests of justice favor transferring a case to the appropriate judicial district rather than dismissing it. Because Greyhound (D) has failed to articulate any reasons why dismissal should be preferred over transferring the case, the case should be transferred to the Southern District of Mississippi. Greyhound's (D) motion to dismiss is, therefore, denied.

Continued on next page.

ANALYSIS

Although the court here notes that the transferee court must have personal jurisdiction over the parties, the court must also have subject matter jurisdiction. Thompson's (P) action in the Southern District of Mississippi was dismissed because that court determined that Thompson (P) was a Florida citizen at the time he filed that action. Because Reeves (D) was also a Florida citizen, the court lacked diversity jurisdiction under 28 U.S.C. § 1332, and no federal question was asserted under 28 U.S.C. § 1331. Thus, the defendants were able to prevail without ever reaching the issue of whether Thompson (P) failed to state a claim.

Quicknotes

DIVERSITY OF CITIZENSHIP Parties are citizens of different states, or one party is an alien; a factor, along with a statutorily set dollar value of the matter in controversy, that allows a federal district court to exercise its authority to hear a lawsuit based on diversity jurisdiction.

DIVERSITY JURISDICTION The authority of a federal court to hear and determine cases involving parties who are of different states and an amount in controversy greater than a statutorily set amount.

PERSONAL JURISDICTION The court's authority over a person or parties to a lawsuit.

SUBJECT MATTER JURISDICTION The authority of the court to hear and decide actions involving a particular type of issue or subject.

VENUE The specific geographic location over which a court has jurisdiction to hear a suit.

Piper Aircraft v. Reyno

Aircraft company (D) v. Crash victims' representative (P)

454 U.S. 235 (1981)

NATURE OF CASE: Appeal from dismissal on the basis of forum non conveniens.

FACT SUMMARY: Reyno (P), the representative of five victims of an air crash, brought suit in California, even though the location of the crash and the homes of the victims were in Scotland.

RULE OF LAW

A plaintiff may not defeat a motion to dismiss for forum non conveniens merely by showing that the substantive law that would be applied in the alternative forum is less favorable to him or her than that of the present forum.

FACTS: Reyno (P) was the representative of five air crash victims' estates and brought suit for wrongful death in United States district court in California, even though the accident occurred and all the victims resided in Scotland. Piper Aircraft (D) moved to dismiss for forum non conveniens, contending that Scotland was the proper forum. Reyno (P) opposed the motion on the basis that the Scottish laws were less advantageous to her position than American laws. The district court granted the motion, while the court of appeals reversed. The United States Supreme Court granted certiorari.

ISSUE: May a plaintiff defeat a motion to dismiss for forum non conveniens merely by showing that the substantive law that would be applied in the alternative forum is less favorable to him or her than that of the present forum?

HOLDING AND DECISION: (Marshall, J.) No. A plaintiff may not defeat a motion to dismiss for forum non conveniens merely by showing that the substantive law of the alternative forum is less favorable to him or her than that of the present forum. In this case, all the evidence, witnesses, and interests were in Scotland. Thus, the most convenient forum was there. As a result, the motion was properly granted. Reversed.

ANALYSIS

The Court in this case specifically noted that under some circumstances, the fact that the chosen state's laws are less attractive to the defendant could be used to defeat a motion to dismiss for forum non conveniens. If the state chosen by the plaintiff has the only adequate remedy for the wrong alleged, then the motion may be denied.

Quicknotes

FORUM NON CONVENIENS An equitable doctrine permitting a court to refrain from hearing and determining a case when the matter may be more properly and fairly heard in another forum.

MOTION TO DISMISS Motion to terminate an action based on the adequacy of the pleadings, improper service or venue, etc.

Atlantic Marine Construction Co. v. United States District Court

Party to a contract containing a forum-selection clause (P) v. Federal district court (D)

571 U.S. 49 (2013)

NATURE OF CASE: Appeal from affirmance of denial of motions to dismiss or to transfer an action involving a contract containing a forum-selection clause.

FACT SUMMARY: Notwithstanding that Atlantic Marine Construction Co. (Atlantic Marine) (P) and J-Crew Management, Inc. (J-Crew) had a contract that contained a forum-selection clause providing that all disputes between the parties would be litigated in Virginia, J-Crew brought suit in the District Court for the Western District of Texas (District Court) (D). The District Court denied Atlantic Marine's (P) motions to either dismiss the action or transfer it to a district court in Virginia, finding that Atlantic Marine (P) had not carried its burden under 28 U.S.C. § 1404(a) for a transfer, which it concluded was the only mechanism for enforcing a forum-selection clause that points to a federal district. Atlantic Marine (P) challenged the District Court's (D) rulings.

RULE OF LAW

A forum-selection clause may be enforced in a civil action by a motion to transfer under 28 U.S.C. § 1404(a), but not under 28 U.S.C. § 1406(a) or Fed. R. Civ. P. 12(b)(3).

FACTS: Atlantic Marine Construction Co. (Atlantic Marine) (P), a Virginia corporation, entered a subcontract with J-Crew Management, Inc. (J-Crew), a Texas corporation, for work on a construction project. The subcontract included a forum-selection clause, which stated that all disputes between the parties would be litigated in Virginia. When a dispute arose, however, J-Crew filed suit in the Western District of Texas. Atlantic Marine (P) moved to dismiss, arguing that the forum-selection clause rendered venue "wrong" under 28 U.S.C. § 1406(a) and "improper" under Fed. R. Civ. P. 12(b)(3). In the alternative, Atlantic Marine (P) moved to transfer the case to the Eastern District of Virginia under 28 U.S.C. § 1404(a). The District Court for the Western District of Texas (D) denied both motions. It concluded that § 1404(a) is the exclusive mechanism for enforcing a forum-selection clause that points to another federal forum; that Atlantic Marine (P) bore the burden of establishing that a transfer would be appropriate under § 1404(a); and that the court would consider both public- and private-interest factors, only one of which was the forum-selection clause. After weighing those factors, the court held that Atlantic Marine (P) had not carried its burden. The court of appeals affirmed, agreeing with the District Court (D) that § 1404(a) is the exclusive mechanism for enforcing a forum-selection clause that points to another federal forum; that dismissal under Rule 12(b)(3) would be the correct mechanism for enforcing a forum-selection clause that pointed to a nonfederal forum; and that the District Court (D) had not abused its discretion in refusing to transfer the case after conducting the balance-of-interests analysis required by § 1404(a). The United States Supreme Court granted certiorari.

ISSUE: May a forum-selection clause be enforced in a civil action by a motion to transfer under 28 U.S.C. § 1404(a), but not under 28 U.S.C. § 1406(a) or Fed. R. Civ. P. 12(b)(3)?

HOLDING AND DECISION: (Alito, J.) Yes. A forum-selection clause may be enforced in a civil action by a motion to transfer under 28 U.S.C. § 1404(a), but not under 28 U.S.C. § 1406(a) or Fed. R. Civ. P. 12(b)(3). Section 1406(a) and Rule 12(b)(3) allow dismissal only when venue is "wrong" or "improper." Whether venue is "wrong" or "improper" depends exclusively on whether the court in which the case was brought satisfies the requirements of federal venue laws. 28 U.S.C. § 1391, which governs venue generally, states that "[e]xcept as otherwise provided by law...this section shall govern the venue of all civil actions brought in" federal district courts. Section 1391(a)(1). It then defines districts in which venue is proper in § 1391(b). If a case falls within one of § 1391(b)'s districts, venue is proper; if it does not, venue is improper, and the case must be dismissed or transferred under § 1406(a). Whether the parties' contract contains a forum-selection clause has no bearing on whether a case falls into one of the specified districts. Although a forum-selection clause does not render venue in a court "wrong" or "improper" under § 1406(a) or Rule 12(b)(3), the clause may be enforced through a motion to transfer under § 1404(a), which permits transfer to any other district where venue is proper or to any district to which the parties have agreed by contract or stipulation. Section 1404(a), however, governs transfer only within the federal court system. When a forum-selection clause points to a state or foreign forum, the clause may be enforced through the doctrine of forum non conveniens. Section 1404(a) is a codification of that doctrine for the subset of cases in which the transferee forum is another federal court. For all other cases, parties may still invoke the residual forum non conveniens doctrine. Because both § 1404(a) and the forum non conveniens doctrine from which it derives entail the same balancing-of-interests standard, courts should evaluate a

Continued on next page.

forum-selection clause pointing to a nonfederal forum in the same way that they evaluate a forum-selection clause pointing to a federal forum. Although the court of appeals correctly identified § 1404(a) as the appropriate provision to enforce the forum-selection clause in this case, it erred in failing to make the adjustments required in a § 1404(a) analysis when the transfer motion is premised on a forum-selection clause. When the parties have agreed to a valid forum-selection clause, a district court should ordinarily transfer the case to the forum specified in that clause, as only under extraordinary circumstances unrelated to the convenience of the parties should a § 1404(a) motion be denied. Although no such exceptional factors appear to be present in this case, the case is remanded for the lower court to make that determination. Reversed and remanded.

ANALYSIS

In the typical case not involving a forum-selection clause, a district court considering a § 1404(a) motion (or a forum non conveniens motion) must evaluate both the convenience of the parties and various public-interest considerations. Ordinarily, the district court would weigh the relevant factors and decide whether, on balance, a transfer would serve "the convenience of parties and witnesses" and otherwise promote "the interest of justice." The Court here noted that this calculus changes when the parties' contract contains a valid forum-selection clause. The Court reasoned that when parties have contracted in advance to litigate disputes in a particular forum, courts should not unnecessarily disrupt the parties' settled expectations, since a forum-selection clause may have figured centrally in the parties' negotiations and may have affected how they set monetary and other contractual terms; it may, in fact, have been a critical factor in their agreement to do business together in the first place. Thus, the Court concluded that in all but the most unusual cases, "the interest of justice" is served by holding parties to their bargain.

Quicknotes

FORUM NON CONVENIENS An equitable doctrine permitting a court to refrain from hearing and determining a case when the matter may be more properly and fairly heard in another forum.

FORUM-SELECTION CLAUSE Provision contained in a contract setting forth the particular forum in which the parties would resolve a matter if a dispute were to arise.

CHAPTER 3

Subject Matter Jurisdiction of the Federal Courts

Quick Reference Rules of Law

Louisville & Nashville Railroad v. Mottley

Railroad company (D) v. Injured passengers (P)

211 U.S. 149 (1908)

NATURE OF CASE: Appeal of a decision overruling a demurrer in an action for specific performance of a contract.

FACT SUMMARY: Mottley (P) was injured on a train owned by Louisville & Nashville Railroad (D), which granted Mottley (P) a lifetime free pass, which he sought to enforce.

RULE OF LAW

An allegation in the complaint that a constitutional defense will be raised in the answer does not raise a federal question that would give a federal court jurisdiction if no diversity of citizenship is alleged.

FACTS: In 1871, Mottley (P) and his wife were injured while riding on the Louisville & Nashville Railroad (D). The Mottleys (P) released their claims for damages against the Louisville & Nashville Railroad (D) upon receiving a contract,granting free transportation during the remainder of their lives. In 1907, the Louisville & Nashville Railroad (D) refused to renew the Mottleys' (P) passes, relying upon an act of Congress that forbade the giving of free passes or free transportation. The Mottleys (P) filed an action in a Circuit Court of the United States for the Western District of Kentucky. The Mottleys (P) and the Louisville & Nashville Railroad (D) were both citizens of Kentucky. Therefore, the Mottleys (P) attempted to establish federal jurisdiction by claiming that the Louisville & Nashville Railroad (D) would raise a constitutional defense in their answer, thus raising a federal question. The Louisville & Nashville Railroad (D) filed a demurrer to the complaint for failing to state a cause of action. The demurrer was denied. On appeal, the Supreme Court did not look at the issue raised by the litigants, but on their own motion raised the issue of whether the federal courts had jurisdiction to hear the case.

ISSUE: Does an allegation in the complaint that a constitutional defense will be raised in the answer raise a federal question that would give a federal court jurisdiction if no diversity of citizenship is alleged?

HOLDING AND DECISION: (Moody, J.) No. An allegation in the complaint that a constitutional defense will be raised in the answer does not raise a federal question that would give a federal court jurisdiction if no diversity of citizenship is alleged. The Supreme Court reversed the lower court's ruling and remitted the case to that court with instructions to dismiss the suit for want of jurisdiction. Neither party to the litigation alleged that the federal court had jurisdiction in this case, and neither party challenged the jurisdiction of the federal court to hear the case. Because the jurisdiction of the circuit court is defined and limited by statute, the Supreme Court stated that it is their duty to see that such jurisdiction is not exceeded. Both parties to the litigation were citizens of Kentucky and so there was no diversity of citizenship. The only way that the federal court could have jurisdiction in this case would be if there was a federal question involved. Mottley (P) did allege in his complaint that the Louisville & Nashville Railroad (D) based their refusal to renew the free pass on a federal statute. Mottley (P) then attempted to allege information that would defeat the defense of the Louisville & Nashville Railroad (D). This is not sufficient. The plaintiff's complaint must be based upon the federal laws of the Constitution to confer jurisdiction on the federal courts. Mottley's (P) cause of action was not based on any federal laws or constitutional privileges; it was based on a contract. Even though it is evident that a federal question will be brought up at the trial, plaintiff's cause of action must be based on a federal statute or the Constitution in order to have a federal question that would grant jurisdiction to the federal courts. Reversed and remanded.

ANALYSIS

If Mottley (P) could have alleged that he was basing his action on a federal right, it would have been enough to have given the federal court jurisdiction. The federal court would have had to exercise jurisdiction at least long enough to determine whether there actually was such a right. If the federal court ultimately concludes that the claimed federal right does not exist, the complaint would be dismissed for failure to state a claim upon which relief can be granted rather than for lack of jurisdiction. The court has the power to determine the issue of subject matter jurisdiction on its own motion as it did in this case. Subject matter jurisdiction can be challenged at any stage of the proceeding.

Quicknotes

DIVERSITY OF CITIZENSHIP Parties are citizens of different states, or one party is an alien; a factor, along with a

Continued on next page.

statutorily set dollar value of the matter in controversy, that allows a federal district court to exercise its authority to hear a lawsuit based on diversity jurisdiction.

DIVERSITY JURISDICTION The authority of a federal court to hear and determine cases involving parties who are of different states and an amount in controversy greater than a statutorily set amount.

FEDERAL QUESTION The authority of the federal courts to hear and determine in the first instance matters pertaining to the federal Constitution, federal law, or treaties of the United States.

SUBJECT MATTER JURISDICTION The authority of the court to hear and decide actions involving a particular type of issue or subject.

Redner v. Sanders

[Parties not identified.]

2000 WL 1161080 (S.D.N.Y. 2000)

NATURE OF CASE: Motion to dismiss for lack of diversity jurisdiction.

FACT SUMMARY: When plaintiff claimed he was a "resident" of France, defendants argued that only plaintiff's "citizenship" in France would satisfy federal diversity jurisdictional requirements.

RULE OF LAW

For purposes of diversity jurisdiction under 28 U.S.C. § 1332(a)(2), the controversy must be between citizens of a state and citizens or subjects of a foreign state, not merely "residents."

FACTS: Plaintiff filed a complaint in federal court, alleging that he was at all times mentioned "a citizen of the United States residing in France," and that defendants are residents of the State of New York. Defendants moved to dismiss for lack of subject matter jurisdiction, arguing that mere residency in a foreign country does not equate with citizenship of a foreign country as required by 28 U.S.C. § 1332(a)(2).

ISSUE: For purposes of diversity jurisdiction under 28 U.S.C. § 1332(a)(2), must the controversy be between citizens of a state and citizens or subjects of a foreign state, not merely "residents?"

HOLDING AND DECISION: (Griesa, J.) Yes. For purposes of diversity jurisdiction under 28 U.S.C. § 1332(a)(2), the controversy must be between citizens of a state and citizens or subjects of a foreign state, not merely "residents." Here, plaintiff's complaint speaks of his "residing" in France, whereas the statute speaks of citizenship. The two are not synonymous. It appears in fact that defendants are citizens of the State of New York. However, for jurisdiction to exist under (a)(2), plaintiff would need to be a citizen of a foreign state, not merely a resident, and the complaint itself actually alleges that plaintiff is a citizen of the United States. Thus, the case does not involve an action between citizens of the United States and a citizen of a foreign state. Accordingly, there is no jurisdiction under § 1332(a)(2). Motion granted, and suit dismissed.

ANALYSIS

In *Redner*, the court noted that plaintiff's affidavit was entirely lacking in details what his living in France involved. Plaintiff provided no information about exactly where he lived, what kind of a residence he had, whether he had any family in France, or what professional activities he carried out in France.

Quicknotes

28 U.S.C. § 1332 Provides for original jurisdiction in federal district court for all civil actions between citizens of different states.

Hertz Corp. v. Friend

Rental car company (D) v. Employees (P)

559 U.S. 77 (2010)

NATURE OF CASE: Appeal from state supreme court.

FACT SUMMARY: [Hertz Corp. (D) tried to remove a class action against it to federal court on the basis of diversity jurisdiction. The employees (P) objected, arguing that because Hertz (D) derived more revenue from California than any other state, and because the plurality of its business activities occurred there, California was its principal place of business.]

RULE OF LAW

The phrase "principal place of business" in the federal diversity jurisdiction statute refers to the place where the corporation's high-level officers direct, control, and coordinate the corporation's activities.

FACTS: [California-based employees (P) of Hertz Corp. (D) claimed in a class action that Hertz (D) violated California's wage and hours laws. Hertz (D) tried to remove to federal court on the basis of diversity jurisdiction. The federal diversity jurisdiction statute provides that "a corporation shall be deemed to be a citizen of any state by which it has been incorporated and of the state where it has its principal place of business." The employees (P) objected, arguing that because Hertz (D) derived more revenue from California than any other state, and because the plurality of its business activities occurred there, California was its principal place of business.]

ISSUE: Does the phrase "principal place of business" in the federal diversity jurisdiction statute refer to the place where the corporation's high-level officers direct, control, and coordinate the corporation's activities?

HOLDING AND DECISION: (Breyer, J.) Yes. The phrase "principal place of business" in the federal diversity jurisdiction statute refers to the place where the corporation's high-level officers direct, control, and coordinate the corporation's activities. Some courts refer to this test as the "nerve center" test. Normally, this would be where the corporation maintains its headquarters, provided headquarters is not simply an office where the corporation holds its board meetings. This interpretation is supported by the statute's language. The statute uses the word "place" in the singular form of the word, not the plural. This interpretation is also supported by its advancement of administrative simplicity, which demands that courts be provided straightforward rules under which they can readily assure themselves of their power to hear a case. And it is supported by the statute's legislative history, which suggests that the words "principal place of business" should be interpreted to be no more complex than the initial test put forth by the Judicial Conference, the "half of gross income" test, a test the Conference rejected as too impractical to apply. A "nerve center" test offers greater simplicity. There may be no perfect test that satisfies all administrative and purposive criteria, but some complication must be accepted in view of the necessity of having a clearer rule. Reversed.

ANALYSIS

Remember that the nerve center is a single place within a state and not a measure of corporate activity statewide. In the Court's view, this aspect of the nerve center test makes it relatively easy to apply, will promote greater predictability, and is consistent with legislative history suggesting that determining corporate citizenship should not be a complex and impractical task. *Hertz* should promote predictability and uniformity in determining corporate citizenship, particularly in circuits that previously applied multifactor tests or compared corporate activity within multiple states to determine a company's principal place of business.

Quicknotes

DIVERSITY JURISDICTION The authority of a federal court to hear and determine cases involving a statutory sum and in which the parties are citizens of different states, or in which one party is an alien.

In re Ameriquest Mortgage Co. Mortgage Lending Practices Litigation

Real estate appraiser (D) v. Mortgager (P)

2007 U.S. Dist. LEXIS 70805 (N.D. Ill. 2007)

NATURE OF CASE: Motion to dismiss state law claims that were based on the court's supplemental jurisdiction.

FACT SUMMARY: Barbara Skanes (P) claimed that house appraiser Douglas Trevino (D) inflated the value of Skanes's (P) property to increase the loan amount for which she could qualify and increase Ameriquest's (D) potential profit.

RULE OF LAW

Supplemental jurisdiction is proper where there is a sufficient nexus between state and federal claims, and statutory discretionary factors do not weigh in favor of a decision to decline to exercise supplemental jurisdiction.

FACTS: Barbara Skanes (P) claimed that house appraiser Douglas Trevino (D) inflated the value of Skanes's (P) property to increase the loan amount for which she could qualify and to increase Ameriquest's (D) potential profit. She filed a federal claim under the Truth in Lending Act, seeking rescission of the mortgage and statutory damages. She also claimed that at the time of her closing Ameriquest (D) gave her improper and misleading disclosures of her right to cancel her mortgage. In the second and third counts of her claim, she alleged state law fraud claims against Ameriquest (D) and Trevino (D). Trevino (D) moved to dismiss the state law claims.

ISSUE: Is supplemental jurisdiction proper where there is a sufficient nexus between state and federal claims, and statutory discretionary factors do not weigh in favor of a decision to decline to exercise supplemental jurisdiction?

HOLDING AND DECISION: (Aspen, J.) Yes. Supplemental jurisdiction is proper where there is a sufficient nexus between state and federal claims, and statutory discretionary factors do not weigh in favor of a decision to decline to exercise supplemental jurisdiction. Where a court already has jurisdiction over some federal claim, it also has supplemental jurisdiction over state claims that are factually connected to the federal claim. The factual connection is sufficient as long as the facts are common and operative. To determine whether the federal and state law claims are connected by common and operative facts, the facts necessary to prove the federal claim are compared with those necessary to the success of the state claim. In this case, Skanes (P) explicitly connected her federal and state claims. She did not fully know of her right to cancel her mortgage, she paid too much during the life of the loan because the mortgage was overstated, and she has not been able to refinance the mortgage due to the overstatement. The connection is operative, in that if the court were to dismiss the state law claims, it may not be able to grant the rescission of the mortgage under the federal Truth in Lending Act (TILA). Because the court cannot conclude that the resolution of one of her state claims will have no effect on the resolution on her federal claims, supplemental jurisdiction is proper. In addition, there is no reason to choose not to exercise that jurisdiction under discretionary powers. Motion to dismiss denied.

ANALYSIS

In this case, the court says that the factual bases for the federal and state claims are essentially the same, and the resolution of one claim affects the other. But the connection between the facts need not be as tight as they are in this case to support a finding that supplemental jurisdiction is proper.

Quicknotes

SUPPLEMENTAL JURISDICTION A doctrine granting authority to a federal court to hear a claim that does not invoke diversity jurisdiction if it arises from the same transaction or occurrence as the primary action.

Szendrey-Ramos v. First Bancorp

Employee (P) v. Employer (D)

512 F. Supp. 2d 81 (D.P.R. 2007)

NATURE OF CASE: Motion to dismiss employment discrimination claim.

FACT SUMMARY: A bank's general counsel was fired after finding that some bank officials violated the bank's code of ethics. She sued under Title VII of the 1964 Civil Rights Act for discrimination and retaliation, and under Puerto Rican law for wrongful discharge, defamation, tortious interference with contract, and violations of the Puerto Rican Constitution.

RULE OF LAW

A court may decline to exercise supplemental jurisdiction where (1) the state law claims raise complex or novel issues, or (2) the state law claims substantially predominate over the federal claim.

FACTS: Carmen Szendrey-Ramos (P) was general counsel for First Bancorp (D) in Puerto Rico. When an outside law firm sent Szendrey (P) a report alleging possible ethical and legal violations by bank officials, Szendrey (P) conducted an investigation. Szendrey (P) found that there were some violations of the bank's (D) code of ethics. The bank (D) fired Szendrey (P), blaming her for some of the events she had investigated. She sued under the federal Title VII of the 1964 Civil Rights Act for discrimination and retaliation, and under Puerto Rican law for wrongful discharge, defamation, tortious interference with contract, and violations of the Puerto Rican Constitution.

ISSUE: May a court decline to exercise supplemental jurisdiction where (1) the state law claims raise complex or novel issues, or (2) the state law claims substantially predominate over the federal claim?

HOLDING AND DECISION: (Casellas, J.) Yes. A court may decline to exercise supplemental jurisdiction where (1) the state law claims raise complex or novel issues, or (2) the state law claims substantially predominate over the federal claim. Here, the state law claims exceed the federal claims in number and scope. Some of the state claims mimic the federal claims, but most—including wrongful discharge, tortious interference with contracts, and defamation—are distinct and have their own elements of proof, which is not necessary to establish the Title VII claims. The predominance of the state claims over the federal claims is enough to decline to exercise supplemental jurisdiction. But Puerto Rican law claims require a more probing analysis of Szendrey's (P) performance as general counsel, and any shortcomings she may have had, and this leads to another reason for declining to exercise supplemental jurisdiction, which is the presence of complex or novel issues of state law. The interpretation of the relevant Puerto Rico laws is usually the province of the Puerto Rico Supreme Court. The laws at issue in this case are silent on the issue of a lawyer's claim against her former client, and the possibility of divulging confidential information in order to pursue such a claim, and Puerto Rican courts have not yet addressed the issue. Therefore, the Puerto Rico law claims will be dismissed without prejudice, so they may be refiled in Puerto Rican courts.

ANALYSIS

Note that the court could have declined to exercise supplemental jurisdiction on the basis of the predominance of the Puerto Rican claims alone. But the court considered it significant that neither Puerto Rican statutes nor Puerto Rican courts had addressed the issues underlying the non-federal claims. Given that the Puerto Rican claims presented issues of first impression, the federal court declined to exercise jurisdiction on that point as well.

Quicknotes

SUPPLEMENTAL JURISDICTION A doctrine granting authority to a federal court to hear a claim that does not invoke diversity jurisdiction if it arises from the same transaction or occurrence as the primary action.

Keller Logistics Group, Inc. v. Navistar, Inc.

Commercial truck purchaser and leaser (P) v. Commercial truck manufacturer (D)

391 F. Supp. 3d 774 (N.D. Ohio 2019)

NATURE OF CASE: Plaintiff's motion for remand in action removed from state court to federal court after the statutory one-year limit on removal expired.

FACT SUMMARY: In 2016, Keller Logistics Group, Inc., and related companies (collectively, "Keller" (P)), all Ohio corporations, sued Navistar, Inc., a Delaware company with its principal place of business in Illinois, along with Defiance Truck Sales & Service, Inc. (the Dealer (D)), which was based in Ohio. In 2019, after Keller (P) voluntarily dismissed the Dealer (D), Navistar (D) removed the case to federal district court. Keller (P) moved to remand to state court, on the ground that the one-year statute of limitations for removal had passed. Navistar (D) opposed by asserting that the bad-faith exception to the one-year limit for removal had been triggered because Keller (P) had named the Dealer (D) in the suit principally to prevent Navistar (D) from removing the case.

RULE OF LAW

Where a plaintiff has engaged in intentional conduct to deny the defendant the chance to remove the plaintiff's case to federal court, the bad-faith exception to the statutory one-year limit for removal is triggered under 28 U.S.C. § 1446(c)(1), thus preventing remand to state court.

FACTS: Keller Logistics Group, Inc., and related companies (collectively, "Keller" (P)), all Ohio corporations, owned, operated, and leased a fleet of commercial trucks. Keller (P) bought and leased some of its trucks from dealers, including Defiance Truck Sales & Service, Inc. (the Dealer (D)), also an Ohio corporation. In 2011 and 2012, Keller (P) purchased or leased from the Dealer (D) 65 trucks manufactured by Navistar, Inc. (D), a truck manufacturer incorporated in Delaware with its principal place of business in Illinois. Allegedly, many of these trucks malfunctioned, and in 2016, Keller (P) brought suit against Navistar (D) and the Dealer (D) in Ohio state court. Apparently, however, the main reason Keller (P) named the Dealer (D) in the action was to prevent removal of the case to federal court, since the Dealer (D), being from the same state as Keller (P), defeated diversity jurisdiction and, hence, removal. For close to two-and-a-half years, the case endured a motion for judgment on the pleadings, discovery, and a motion for summary judgment. In March 2019, as the summary judgment motion was pending in state court, Keller (P) voluntarily dismissed the Dealer (D), leaving Navistar (D) as the only defendant. Navistar (D) removed to federal district court, citing the court's diversity jurisdiction, and Keller (P) moved to remand, citing the one-year limit for removal under 28 U.S.C. § 1446(c). Although the statute of limitations for removal is one year, Navistar (D) contended it was entitled to the bad-faith exception found in 28 U.S.C. § 1446(c)(1) based on Keller's (P) conduct, which Navistar (D) alleged was designed to prevent Navistar (D) from removing the case. In support of its entitlement to the bad-faith exception, Navistar (D) adduced facts that Keller (P) kept the Dealer (D) in the litigation on the advice of Keller's (P) lawyers, to keep the litigation in Ohio, rather than federal court, and not because Keller (P) had a genuine intention of pursuing damages against the Dealer (D). In fact, Keller (P) admitted as much. Keller's (P) admission was further supported by a lack of active litigation against the Dealer (D) and Keller's (P) lack throughout the litigation of justifying the Dealer's (D) presence in the case. During discovery, Keller (P) did not depose any Dealer (D) employee or representative, and although Keller (P) issued 279 requests for production to Navistar (D), Keller (P) issued only 34 requests to the Dealer (D), the majority of which targeted evidence of Navistar's (D) behavior, not that of the Dealer (D). Additionally, in Keller's (P) extensive response to Navistar's (D) motion for summary judgment, Keller (P) barely mentioned the Dealer (D). It was only when the defendant's reply brief focused on Keller's (P) failure to attribute misconduct to the Dealer (D), thereby for the first time holding Keller (P) to account for the Dealer's (D) presence in the case, that Keller (P) voluntarily dismissed the Dealer (D). Finally, throughout nearly two-and-a-half years in state court, Keller (P) never once engaged the Dealer (D) in settlement discussions. The federal district court considered Keller's (P) motion to remand.

ISSUE: Where a plaintiff has engaged in intentional conduct to deny the defendant the chance to remove the plaintiff's case to federal court, is the bad-faith exception to the statutory one-year limit for removal triggered under 28 U.S.C. § 1446(c)(1), thus preventing remand to state court?

HOLDING AND DECISION: (Zouhary, J.) Yes. Where a plaintiff has engaged in intentional conduct to deny the defendant the chance to remove the plaintiff's case to federal court, the bad-faith exception to the statutory one-year limit for removal is triggered under 28 U.S.C. § 1446(c)(1), thus preventing remand to state court. Here, all the facts adduced by Navistar (D) support

Continued on next page.

its contention that Keller (P) intentionally kept the Dealer (D) in the litigation beyond a year for the purpose of preventing Navistar (D) from removing the case to federal court, not for pursuing the Dealer (D) to judgment. Notwithstanding that Keller (P) contended that they joined the Dealer (D) in the case because the claims against it were valid, the bad-faith exception focuses not on the validity of a plaintiff's claim against a non-diverse party at the time the action was filed, but on whether the plaintiff has acted in bad faith to prevent a defendant from removing the action. Stating a valid claim against the non-diverse defendant does not immunize the plaintiff from a finding of bad faith, which exists where the plaintiff has no intention of pursuing judgment against the non-diverse defendant and instead joins and keeps that defendant in the case for the purpose of thwarting removal. Keller's (P) admission and the facts presented undisputedly are probative of Keller's (P) bad faith for purposes of the bad-faith exception to the one-year limit on removal. Accordingly, Keller's (P) Motion to Remand is denied.

ANALYSIS

In this case, the evidence of Keller's (P) motive for joining the Dealer (D) in the litigation was direct and undisputed, so that Navistar (D), which had the burden of proof on the bad-faith exception, had no difficulty in meeting its burden, even if a high evidentiary standard, such as "clear and convincing," was applied. However, most cases do not involve such obvious bad-faith conduct, and it is not clear what the appropriate evidentiary standard should be. Some district courts apply a clear-and-convincing-evidence standard, whereas others have found that a lower standard applies. A lower standard may be appropriate for several reasons. First, Congress added the bad-faith exception to protect access to a federal forum. Given that direct evidence of bad faith will rarely be available even when bad faith is actually involved, imposing too high a standard would defeat the exception's purpose. Second, when the amount in controversy is at issue, the burden of proof is only a preponderance of the evidence, and, unlike the amount in controversy, which is a jurisdictional requirement, the one-year removal limit is an "excusable" procedural rule. Therefore, imposing a higher burden to circumvent a procedural time limit, when the jurisdictional requirements are not in question, makes little sense.

Quicknotes

BAD FAITH Conduct that is intentionally misleading or deceptive.

DISCOVERY Pretrial procedure during which one party makes certain information available to the other.

DIVERSITY JURISDICTION The authority of a federal court to hear and determine cases involving parties who are of different states and an amount in controversy greater than a statutorily set amount.

MOTION FOR SUMMARY JUDGMENT A request to the court by one of the parties, claiming that the lack of a genuine question of material fact in respect to an issue warrants disposition of the issue as a matter of law in the requesting party's favor, without consideration by the trier of fact (judge or jury) at a trial.

PLEADING A statement setting forth the plaintiff's cause of action or the defendant's defenses to the plaintiff's claims.

PROBATIVE Tending to establish proof.

REMAND To send back for additional scrutiny or deliberation.

STATUTE OF LIMITATIONS A law prescribing the period in which a legal action may be commenced.

CHAPTER 4

State Law in Federal Courts: *Erie* and Choice of Law

Quick Reference Rules of Law

Erie Railroad v. Tompkins

Railroad company (D) v. Pedestrian (P)

304 U.S. 64 (1938)

NATURE OF CASE: Action to recover damages for personal injury allegedly caused by negligent conduct.

FACT SUMMARY: In a personal-injury suit, a federal district court trial judge refused to apply applicable state law because such law was "general" (judge-made) and not embodied in any statute.

RULE OF LAW

Although the 1789 Rules of Decision Act left federal courts unfettered to apply their own rules of procedure in common-law actions brought in federal court, state law governs substantive issues. State law includes not only statutory law, but also case law.

FACTS: Tompkins (P) was walking in a right of way parallel to some railroad tracks when an Erie Railroad (Erie) (D) train came by. Tompkins (P) was struck and injured by what he would, at trial, claim to be an open door extending from one of the rail cars. Under Pennsylvania case law (the applicable law since the accident occurred there), state courts would have treated Tompkins (P) as a trespasser in denying him recovery for other than wanton or willful misconduct on Erie's (D) part. Under "general" law, recognized in federal courts, Tompkins (P) would have been regarded as a licensee and would have been obligated only to show ordinary negligence. Because Erie (D) was a New York corporation, Tompkins (P) brought suit in a federal district court in New York, where he won a judgment for $30,000. Upon appeal to a federal circuit court, the decision was affirmed.

ISSUE: Although the 1789 Rules of Decision Act left federal courts unfettered to apply their own rules of procedure in common-law actions brought in federal court, does state law govern substantive issues? Does state law include not only statutory law, but also case law?

HOLDING AND DECISION: (Brandeis, J.) Yes. Although the 1789 Rules of Decision Act left federal courts unfettered to apply their own rules of procedure in common-law actions brought in federal court, state law governs substantive issues. State law includes not only statutory law, but case law as well. The trial court was in error in refusing to recognize state case law as the proper rule of decision in deciding the substantive issue of liability. The Court's opinion is in four parts: (1) *Swift v. Tyson*, 41 U.S. (16 Pet.) 1 (1842), which held that federal courts exercising jurisdiction on the ground of diversity of citizenship need not, in matters of general jurisprudence, apply the unwritten law of the state as declared by its highest court, is overruled. Section 34 of the Federal Judiciary Act of 1789, c. 20, 28 U.S. § 725 requires that federal courts in all matters, except those where some federal law is controlling, apply as their rules of decision the law of the state, unwritten as well as written. Up to this time, federal courts had assumed the power to make "general law" decisions even though Congress was powerless to enact "general law" statutes. (2) *Swift* had numerous political and social defects. The hoped-for uniformity among state courts had not occurred; and there was no satisfactory way to distinguish between local and general law. In addition, *Swift* introduced grave discrimination by noncitizens against citizens. The privilege of selecting the court for resolving disputes rested with the noncitizen who could pick the more favorable forum. The resulting far-reaching discrimination was due to the broad province accorded "general law" in which many matters of seemingly local concern were included. Furthermore, local citizens could move out of the state and bring suit in a federal court if they were disposed to do so; corporations, similarly, could simply reincorporate in another state. More than statutory relief is involved here; the unconstitutionality of *Swift* is clear. (3) Except in matters governed by the federal Constitution or by acts of Congress, the law to be applied in any case is the law of the state. There is no federal common law. The federal courts have no power derived from the Constitution or by Congress to declare substantive rules of common law applicable in a state whether they are "local" or "general" in nature. (4) The federal district court was bound to follow the Pennsylvania case law, which would have denied recovery to Tompkins (P). Reversed.

CONCURRENCE: (Reed, J.) It is unnecessary to go beyond interpreting the meaning of "laws" in the Rules of Decision Act. Article III and the Necessary and Proper Clause of Article I of the Constitution might provide Congress with the power to declare rules of substantive law for federal courts to follow.

ANALYSIS

Erie can fairly be characterized as the most significant and sweeping decision on civil procedure ever handed down by the United States Supreme Court. As interpreted in subsequent decisions, *Erie* held that while federal courts may apply their own rules of procedure, issues of substantive law must be decided in accord with the applicable state law, usually the state in which

Continued on next page.

the federal court sits. Note, however, how later Supreme Court decisions have made inroads into the broad doctrine enunciated here.

Quicknotes

DIVERSITY OF CITIZENSHIP Parties are citizens of different states, or one party is an alien; a factor, along with a statutorily set dollar value of the matter in controversy, that allows a federal district court to exercise its authority to hear a lawsuit based on diversity jurisdiction.

DIVERSITY JURISDICTION The authority of a federal court to hear and determine cases involving parties who are of different states and an amount in controversy greater than a statutorily set amount.

FEDERAL JURISDICTION The authority of federal courts to hear and determine cases of a particular nature derived from the United States Constitution and rules promulgated by Congress pursuant thereto.

SUBJECT MATTER JURISDICTION The authority of the court to hear and decide actions involving a particular type of issue or subject.

Guaranty Trust Co. v. York

Trustee (D) v. Note holder (P)

326 U.S. 99 (1945)

NATURE OF CASE: Class action alleging fraud and misrepresentation.

FACT SUMMARY: York (P), barred from filing suit in state court because of the state statute of limitations, brought an equity action in federal court based upon diversity of citizenship jurisdiction.

RULE OF LAW

A state statute of limitations that would bar a suit in state court, may also act as a bar to the same action if the suit is brought in equity in federal court and jurisdiction is being based on diversity of citizenship.

FACTS: York (P) sued Guaranty Trust Co. (D) in a federal diversity action. New York substantive law governed. Guaranty Trust (D) asserted the defense of the statute of limitations. York (P) argued that the statute of limitations did not bar the suit because it was on the "equity side" of federal court. The federal court of appeals ruled the suit was not barred, and Guaranty Trust (D) appealed.

ISSUE: Does a state statute of limitations that would bar a suit in state court, also act as a bar to the same action if the suit is brought in equity in federal court and jurisdiction is being based on diversity of citizenship?

HOLDING AND DECISION: (Frankfurter, J.) Yes. A state statute of limitations that would bar a suit in state court, may also act as a bar to the same action if the suit is brought in equity in federal court and jurisdiction is being based on diversity of citizenship. *Erie Railroad Co. v. Tompkins*, 304 U.S. 64 (1938), overruled a particular way of looking at law after its inadequacies had been laid bare. The question is not whether a statute of limitations is deemed a matter of "procedure" in some sense. The question is whether such a statute concerns merely the manner and the means by which a right to recover, as recognized by the state, is enforced, or whether such statutory limitation is a matter of substance in the aspect that alone is relevant to the problem, namely, whether it significantly affects the result of a litigation for a federal court to disregard a law of a state that would be controlling in an action upon the same claim by the same parties in a state court. In essence, the intent of *Erie* was to insure that in all cases where a federal court is exercising jurisdiction solely because of the diversity of citizenship of the parties, the outcome of the litigation in the federal court should be substantially the same, so far as legal rules determine the outcome of a litigation, as it would be if tried in a state court. Reversed and remanded.

ANALYSIS

While clarifying *Erie*, the legal foundation supporting *Guaranty Trust* may be undergoing a process of slow erosion by contemporary courts. *Hanna v. Plumer*, 380 U.S. 460 (1965), held that where state law conflicts with the Federal Rules of Civil Procedure, the latter prevails regardless of the effect on the outcome of the litigation. And in *Byrd v. Blue Ridge Electric Cooperative*, 356 U.S. 525 (1958), the Court suggested that some constitutional doctrines (there, the right to a jury trial in federal court) are so important as to be controlling over state law, regardless of whether application of such constitutional doctrines would result in an outcome different than that which would result under the law of the state in which the federal court sits.

Quicknotes

COMITY A rule pursuant to which courts in one state give deference to the statutes and judicial decisions of another.

DIVERSITY OF CITIZENSHIP Parties are citizens of different states, or one party is an alien; a factor, along with a statutorily set dollar value of the matter in controversy, that allows a federal district court to exercise its authority to hear a lawsuit based on diversity jurisdiction.

DIVERSITY JURISDICTION The authority of a federal court to hear and determine cases involving parties who are of different states and an amount in controversy greater than a statutorily set amount.

***ERIE* DOCTRINE** Federal courts must apply state substantive law and federal procedural law.

Byrd v. Blue Ridge Rural Electric Cooperative

Injured employee (P) v. Electric utility (D)

356 U.S. 525 (1958)

NATURE OF CASE: Negligence action for damages.

FACT SUMMARY: Byrd (P) was injured while connecting power lines for a subcontractor of Blue Ridge Electric Cooperative, Inc. (D).

RULE OF LAW

The *Erie* doctrine requires that federal courts in diversity cases must respect the definitions of rights and obligations created by state courts, but state laws cannot alter the essential characteristics and functions of the federal courts, and the jury function is such an essential function (provided for in the Seventh Amendment).

FACTS: Byrd (P) was injured while on a construction job for Blue Ridge Electric Cooperative, Inc. (Blue Ridge) (D) and sued Blue Ridge (D) in tort. Although Byrd (P) was employed by an independent contractor, Blue Ridge (D) argued that Byrd (P) was performing the same work as Blue Ridge's (D) regular employees and was therefore a "statutory" employee whose exclusive remedy was under the South Carolina workers' compensation legislation. Blue Ridge (D) contended that despite the *Erie* doctrine, [*Erie Railroad Co. v. Tompkins*, 304 U.S. 64 (1938)], South Carolina law could not be allowed to preclude his right to a jury.

ISSUE: Do *Erie* doctrine considerations require that all state determinations of rights be upheld regardless of their intrusions into federal determinations?

HOLDING AND DECISION: (Brennan, J.) No. The *Erie* doctrine requires that federal courts in diversity cases must respect the definitions of rights and obligations created by state courts, but state laws cannot alter the essential characteristics and functions of the federal courts, and the jury function is such an essential function (provided for in the Seventh Amendment). The South Carolina determination here that immunity is a question of law to be tried by a judge is merely a determination of the form and mode of enforcing immunity. It does not involve any essential relationship or determination of right created by the state. Of course, the *Erie* doctrine will reach even such form and mode determinations where no affirmative countervailing considerations can be found. Here, however, the Seventh Amendment makes the jury function an essential factor in the federal process protected by the Constitution. Reversed and remanded.

ANALYSIS

This case points up a major retreat by the Court in its interpretation of the *Erie* doctrine. The *Guaranty Trust* case, 326 U.S. 99 (1945), had stated that the *Erie* doctrine required that federal courts not tamper with state remedies for violations of state-created rights. In *Byrd*, the Court retreats, stating that questions of mere "form and mode" of remedy (i.e., trial by jury or judge) is not necessarily the province of the states where essential federal rights (i.e., Seventh Amendment) are involved. Note that the Court does not abandon the *Guaranty Trust* rationale, however (that the outcome of a case should not be affected by the choice of court in which it is filed). The Court expresses doubt that the permitting of trial by jury here will make any difference in the final determination of the case. Note the inconsistency of argument here since the Court first states that trial by jury is an essential right, and then states that it is really insignificant after all.

Quicknotes

***ERIE* DOCTRINE** Federal courts must apply state substantive law and federal procedural law.

Hanna v. Plumer

Injured claimant (P) v. Executor of defendant (D)

380 U.S. 460 (1965)

NATURE OF CASE: Appeal of dismissal in federal diversity tort action.

FACT SUMMARY: Hanna (P) filed tort action in federal court in Massachusetts, where Plumer (D) resided, for an auto accident that occurred in South Carolina.

RULE OF LAW

The *Erie* doctrine mandates that federal courts are to apply state substantive law and federal procedural law, and where matters fall roughly between the two and are rationally capable of classification as either, the Constitution grants the federal court system the power to regulate their practice and pleading (procedure).

FACTS: In this diversity suit for personal injuries, Plumer (D) represented the estate of one of the drivers involved. Massachusetts law provided that suits required personal service of process on the estate's executor. Process was instead served under Fed. R. Civ. P. 4[(e)(2)(B)], which allowed for the summons and complaint to be left with a competent adult at the defendant's residence. The federal circuit court agreed with the federal district court that the claim should be dismissed because of Hanna's (P) failure to comply with the state's method of serving process within the applicable limitations period. Hanna (P) appealed.

ISSUE: Does the *Erie* doctrine mandate that federal courts are to apply state substantive law and federal procedural law, and where matters fall roughly between the two and are rationally capable of classification as either, the Constitution grants the federal court system the power to regulate their practice and pleading (procedure)?

HOLDING AND DECISION: (Warren, C.J.) Yes. The *Erie* doctrine, *Erie Railroad Co. v. Tompkins*, 304 U.S. 64 (1938), mandates that federal courts are to apply state substantive law and federal procedural law, and where matters fall roughly between the two and are rationally capable of classification as either, the Constitution grants the federal court system the power to regulate their practice and pleading (procedure). It is well settled that the Enabling Act for the Federal Rules of Civil Procedure requires that a procedural effect of any rule on the outcome of a case be shown to actually "abridge, enlarge, or modify" the substantive law in a case for the *Erie* doctrine to come into play. Where, as here, the question only goes to procedural requirements (i.e., service of summons, a dismissal for improper service here would not alter the substantive right of Hanna [P] to serve Plumer [D] personally and refile or effect the substantive law of negligence in the case), Article III and the Necessary and Proper Clause provide that the Congress has a right to provide rules for the federal court system such as Fed. R. Civ. P. 4[(e)(2)(B)]. "Outcome determination analysis was never intended to serve as a talisman" for the *Erie* doctrine. The judgment of the appellate court must be reversed.

CONCURRENCE: (Harlan, J.) I agree with the result of the Court and its rejection of the outcome-determination test. However, the Court was wrong in stating that anything arguably procedural is constitutionally placed within the province of the federal government to regulate. The test for "substantive" would be whether "the choice of rule would substantially affect those primary decisions respecting human conduct which our constitutional system leaves to state regulation."

ANALYSIS

This case points a return to the basic rationales of *Erie R. Co. v. Tompkins*, 304 U.S. 64 (1938). First, the Court asserts that one important consideration in determining how a particular question should be classified (substantive or procedural) is the avoidance of "forum shopping" (the practice of choosing one forum such as federal, to file in, in order to gain the advantages of one), which permits jurisdictions to infringe on the substantive law-defining powers of each other. Second, the Court seeks to avoid inequitable administration of the laws that would result from allowing jurisdictional considerations to determine substantive rights. Justice Warren here, in rejecting the "outcome determination" test, asserts that any rule must be measured ultimately against the Federal Rules Enabling Act and the Constitution.

Quicknotes

PROCEDURAL LAW Law relating to the process of carrying out a lawsuit and not to the substantive rights asserted by the parties.

SUBSTANTIVE LAW Law that pertains to the rights and interests of the parties and upon which a cause of action may be based.

Mckesson v. Doe

Demonstration organizer (D) v. Unidentified police officer (P)

141 S. Ct. 48 (2020)

NATURE OF CASE: Appeal from reversal of dismissal of negligence action brought by unidentified police officer injured by an unidentified demonstrator.

FACT SUMMARY: During a demonstration organized by DeRay Mckesson (Mckesson) (D) in front of police headquarters, an unidentified demonstrator threw an object at an unidentified police officer, Officer John Doe (P), and severely injured the officer. Officer Doe (P) sued Mckesson (D) under state law for negligence under the theory that Mckesson (D) was liable because of the way he organized the demonstration; Mckesson (D) asserted the First Amendment as a defense.

RULE OF LAW

In exceptional circumstances, where the resolution of unsettled state law through certification of a question or questions to the state's highest court can obviate the need by a federal court to address a constitutional issue, the federal court should certify the question or questions of state law to the state's highest court.

FACTS: DeRay Mckesson (Mckesson) (D) organized a demonstration in a city in Louisiana to protest a shooting by a local police officer. The protesters, allegedly at Mckesson's (D) direction, occupied the highway in front of the police headquarters. As officers began making arrests to clear the highway, an unknown individual threw a piece of concrete or a similar rock-like object, striking a police officer, Officer John Doe (Doe) (P) in the face, causing devastating injuries. Though the culprit remained unidentified, Officer Doe (P) sought to recover damages from Mckesson (D) on the theory that he negligently staged the protest in a manner that caused the assault. The U.S. District Court dismissed the negligence claim as barred by the First Amendment. A divided panel of the Court of Appeals for the Fifth Circuit reversed. As the Fifth Circuit recognized at the outset, Louisiana law generally imposes no duty to protect others from the criminal activities of third persons. Nevertheless, the panel majority held that a jury could plausibly find that pursuant to Louisiana law, Mckesson (D) breached his "duty not to negligently precipitate the crime of a third party" because a violent confrontation with a police officer was a foreseeable effect of directing a protest onto the highway. The United States Supreme Court granted certiorari.

ISSUE: In exceptional circumstances, where the resolution of unsettled state law through certification of a question or questions to the state's highest court can obviate the need by a federal court to address a constitutional issue, should the federal court certify the question or questions of state law to the state's highest court?

HOLDING AND DECISION: (Per curiam) Yes. In exceptional circumstances, where the resolution of unsettled state law through certification of a question or questions to the state's highest court can obviate the need by a federal court to address a constitutional issue, the federal court should certify the question or questions of state law to the state's highest court. The question presented here is whether the theory of personal liability adopted by the Fifth Circuit violates the First Amendment. However, the Fifth Circuit's interpretation of state law is too uncertain a premise on which to address the question presented. The constitutional issue, though undeniably important, is implicated only if Louisiana law permits recovery under these circumstances in the first place. The dispute thus could be greatly simplified by guidance from the Louisiana Supreme Court on the meaning of Louisiana law. Louisiana permits federal courts to certify questions of law to the Louisiana Supreme Court where there is an absence of "clear controlling precedents in the decisions" of that court. Whether to certify is left to a federal court's discretion. In exceptional instances, however, certification is advisable before addressing a constitutional issue. Two aspects of this case, taken together, should have led the Fifth Circuit to have certified to the Louisiana Supreme Court the novel questions of state law as to: (1) whether Mckesson (D) could have breached a duty of care in organizing and leading the protest and (2) whether Officer Doe (P) had alleged a particular risk within the scope of protection afforded by the duty, provided one exists. To impose a duty under Louisiana law, courts must consider various moral, social, and economic factors, among them the fairness of imposing liability, the historical development of precedent, and the direction in which society and its institutions are evolving. Speculation by a federal court about how a state court would weigh, for instance, the moral value of protest against the economic consequences of withholding liability is particularly gratuitous when the state courts stand willing to address questions of state law on certification. Second, certification would ensure that any conflict in this case between state law and the First Amendment is not purely hypothetical. Although the Louisiana Supreme Court may announce the same duty as the Fifth Circuit, under the

Continued on next page.

unusual circumstances presented here, the Fifth Circuit should not have ventured into so uncertain an area of tort law—one laden with value judgments and fraught with implications for First Amendment rights—without first seeking guidance on potentially controlling Louisiana law from the Louisiana Supreme Court. Accordingly, the Fifth Circuit's judgment is vacated, and the case is remanded to the Fifth Circuit for further proceedings consistent with this opinion. Vacated and remanded.

DISSENT: (Thomas, J.) [Justice Thomas dissented without writing an opinion.]

ANALYSIS

The great majority of states permit federal courts to certify questions of unsettled state law to their highest courts. However, those state courts may decline the federal courts' certification requests. Also, federal courts rarely certify questions of unsettled state law to the state courts, because, as the Court in its decision noted, doing so can prolong the dispute and increase the expenses incurred by the parties. In any event, the United States' system of "cooperative judicial federalism" presumes that both federal and state courts are competent to apply federal and state law, so that the need for federal courts to certify unsettled questions of state law to the state courts is greatly diminished, except in the most exceptional of circumstances.

Quicknotes

CERTIFIED QUESTION A question of law previously unaddressed by the highest court for a jurisdiction that is submitted to that court to answer how it would rule on the question; questions can be certified from lower courts within the same state, from state courts outside the state, from federal courts to state courts, and from federal courts of appeals to the United States Supreme Court.

DUTY OF CARE A principle of negligence requiring an individual to act in such a manner as to avoid injury to a person to whom he or she owes a duty.

CHAPTER 5

Incentives to Litigate

Quick Reference Rules of Law

Troupe v. C & S Wholesale Grocers, Inc.

Slip and fall victim (P) v. Grocery store operator (D)

2009 WL 1938787 (M.D. Ga. 2009)

NATURE OF CASE: Motion to remand in action for negligence.

FACT SUMMARY: Troupe's (P) negligence case against C & S Wholesale Grocers, Inc. (C & S Wholesale) (D) was removed to federal court. Troupe (P) moved to remand the case to state court, claiming that her medical expenses were in the neighborhood of $14,000. C & S Wholesale (D) countered that if Troupe (P) prevailed, her recovery would be greater than $75,000—the minimum amount needed to establish amount-in-controversy jurisdiction.

RULE OF LAW

A case will not be remanded to state court where, if the plaintiff prevails on its claims, the plaintiff will recover more than the minimum amount in controversy needed to establish jurisdiction.

FACTS: After slipping and falling at C & S Wholesale Grocers, Inc.'s (C & S Wholesale's) (D) store, Troupe (P) brought suit in state court, asserting claims for negligence, and seeking damages for severe physical injuries and distress, punitive damages, special and general damages, and costs. Troupe's (P) medical records showed that she suffered severe pain that was not alleviated by pain medications and other interventions, including physical therapy, chiropractic manipulation, and spinal blocks, and that her condition remained unabated a year after the fall. The records also indicated that she lived alone, was self-employed, and owned her own house cleaning service. She had informed her physicians that her pain was exacerbated by lifting, bending, stooping, and prolonged standing—all of which were required in her profession as a house cleaner. She also told her physicians that she was forced to reduce the number of houses she could clean because of her back condition and that she had to discontinue personal activities such as exercising, which also aggravated her pain. C & S Wholesale (D) removed to federal court, asserting that if Troupe (P) prevailed, her recovery would be greater than $75,000—the amount needed to establish amount in controversy jurisdiction. Troupe (P), claiming her medical expenses were only around $14,000, moved to remand the case to state court.

ISSUE: Will a case be remanded to state court where, if the plaintiff prevails on its claims, the plaintiff will recover more than the minimum amount in controversy needed to establish jurisdiction?

HOLDING AND DECISION: (Royal, J.) No. A case will not be remanded to state court where, if the plaintiff prevails on its claims, the plaintiff will recover more than the minimum amount in controversy needed to establish jurisdiction. The issue presented is whether the court has original jurisdiction on the basis of the amount in controversy. Where, as here, the amount of damages is unspecified, the defendant only need show by a preponderance of the evidence that the amount of damages is likely to exceed the minimum amount in controversy necessary to establish subject matter jurisdiction. Here, the amount in controversy is not apparent from the face of the complaint, which specified only Troupe's (P) medical expenses. There is no way to determine from the complaint whether Troupe (P) has been so badly injured as to make an award of over $75,000 more likely than not. However, given the additional evidence presented in Troupe's (P) medical records, it is likely that if Troupe (P) proves the assertions she made to her physicians, she would be able to prevail on claims for unspecified damages for long-term medical expenses, loss of wages and earning capacity, mental and physical pain and suffering, and loss of enjoyment of life in addition to her specified claim for medical expenses and her claim for punitive damages. Accordingly, C & S Wholesale (D) has satisfied its burden of establishing that the special, general, and punitive damages in this case, if proven, will "more likely than not" exceed the minimum jurisdictional amount. Troupe's (P) motion to remand is denied.

ANALYSIS

The burden of proving any jurisdictional fact rests upon the party seeking to invoke the jurisdiction of the federal courts. Thus, in this case, C & S Wholesale (D) bore the burden of establishing that the requisite jurisdictional amount had been met. This burden may be a heavy one. Some circuits hold that when a plaintiff makes a specific demand for judgment for less than the jurisdictional amount, the defendant is required to prove to "a legal certainty" that the amount in controversy actually exceeds the jurisdictional minimum. Under this standard, a defendant may be permitted to remain in federal court only if he or she shows that the case is clearly worth more than the jurisdictional threshold. However, where a plaintiff has made an unspecified demand for damages in state court, as was the case here, a removing defendant must prove only the amount in controversy by a preponderance of the evidence. Thus, if the damages are unspecified in the complaint,

Continued on next page.

the defendant's burden is to prove only that the actual damages will more likely than not exceed the minimum jurisdictional amount. Here, C & S Wholesale (D) was able to meet this less stringent standard.

Quicknotes

AMOUNT IN CONTROVERSY The value of a claim sought by a party to a lawsuit.

PREPONDERANCE OF THE EVIDENCE A standard of proof requiring the trier of fact to determine whether the fact sought to be established is more probable than not.

SUBJECT MATTER JURISDICTION The authority of the court to hear and decide actions involving a particular type of issue or subject.

Lucy Webb Hayes Natl. Training School v. Geoghegan

Hospital (P) v. Patient (D)

281 F. Supp. 116 (D.D.C. 1967)

NATURE OF CASE: Motion to dismiss an action for an injunction to remove a trespasser.

FACT SUMMARY: Lucy Webb Hayes Natl. Training School, which ran the Sibley Memorial Hospital (collectively, the "Hospital") (P), sought an injunction to remove Geoghegan (D) from the Hospital (P). Geoghegan (D) moved to dismiss, asserting that money damages would adequately compensate the Hospital (P).

RULE OF LAW

An action for an injunction will not be dismissed where money damages are inadequate to satisfy the plaintiff's claims.

FACTS: Geoghegan (D) had been a patient for a long time at Sibley Memorial Hospital, a private hospital run by Lucy Webb Hayes Natl. Training School (collectively, the "Hospital") (P). The Hospital (P) determined at some point that Geoghegan (D) no longer needed to be hospitalized and that her medical needs could be met at a nursing facility. The Hospital (P) demanded that Geoghegan (D) depart the Hospital (P), but she refused. The Hospital (P) then brought suit seeking an injunction to have Geoghegan (D) removed as a trespasser. Geoghegan's (D) husband (D) wanted her to stay in the Hospital (P) for the remainder of her life and was willing to pay the Hospital (P) for her to stay. Accordingly, the Geoghegans (D) moved to dismiss on the grounds that money damages would be adequate to compensate the Hospital (P).

ISSUE: Will an action for an injunction be dismissed where money damages are inadequate to satisfy the plaintiff's claims?

HOLDING AND DECISION: (Holtzoff, J.) No. An action for an injunction will not be dismissed where money damages are inadequate to satisfy the plaintiff's claims. Here an action for damages would be an inadequate remedy. A private hospital has a right to accept or decline any patient, and it has a moral duty to reserve its accommodations for persons who actually need medical and hospital care. It would be a deviation from its purposes to act as a nursing home for aged persons who do not need constant medical care but who need nursing care, which can be provided in nursing homes and similar institutions. Hospitals have a duty not to permit their facilities to be diverted to the uses for which hospitals are not intended. It is also well established that equity will enjoin a continuing trespass where an action for damages would not be an adequate remedy. Because an action for damages would not solve the problem faced by the Hospital (P), and is an inadequate remedy, the Geoghegans' (D) motion to dismiss is denied.

ANALYSIS

Ordinarily, money damages are considered an adequate remedy for a single trespass, whereas such damages may not be considered an adequate remedy for continuous or multiple trespasses. If it is not clear that a legal remedy will be adequate, as was the case here, the court will explore policy considerations (here, the court looked at the public interest served by the Hospital (P)), which ordinarily do not come into play in a legal damages context.

Quicknotes

DAMAGES Monetary compensation that may be awarded by the court to a party who has sustained injury or loss to his or her person, property, or rights due to another party's unlawful act, omission, or negligence.

INJUNCTION A court order requiring a person to do, or prohibiting that person from doing, a specific act.

TRESPASSERS Persons present on the land of another without the knowledge or express permission of the owner, and to whom only a minimum duty of care is owed for injuries incurred while on the premises.

Detroit Will Breathe v. City of Detroit

Demonstrators (P) v. Municipality (D)

484 F. Supp. 3d 511 (E.D. Mich. 2020)

NATURE OF CASE: Motion for temporary restraining order in action brought by demonstrators against municipality and its police force alleging violations of their constitutional rights arising from the police force's use of excessive force and other constitutionally impermissible law enforcement tactics.

FACT SUMMARY: Detroit Will Breathe (P) and a number of individuals (P) (collectively "Plaintiffs" (P)) who were protesting police brutality and racism in the City of Detroit (D) on an ongoing basis alleged that the Detroit Police Department (DPD) and its officers violated their constitutional rights by using excessive force and other constitutionally impermissible law enforcement tactics. The Plaintiffs (P) sought a temporary restraining order to enjoin such force and tactics.

RULE OF LAW

A temporary restraining order (TRO) will issue where plaintiffs are able to establish (1) that there is a likelihood of success on their claims of violations of their constitutional rights by the government, (2) that they are likely to suffer irreparable injury from ongoing constitutional violations of their rights without a TRO, and (3) that it is in the public interest to enjoin such ongoing constitutional violations.

FACTS: Detroit Will Breathe (P) and a number of individuals (P) (collectively "Plaintiffs" (P)) were involved in ongoing daily protest activities in the City of Detroit (D) in response to the killing of George Floyd, a Black man, by police in Minneapolis. The Plaintiffs (P) brought suit in federal district court alleging that the Detroit Police Department (DPD) and its officers had from the start responded to peaceful demonstrations with beatings, tear gas, pepper spray, rubber bullets, sound cannons, flash grenades, chokeholds, and mass arrests without probable cause, thus violating their First and Fourth Amendment rights, and those of bystanders and medical personnel. The Plaintiffs (P) moved for a temporary restraining order (TRO) to enjoin the City of Detroit (D) and its law enforcement agents from using such tactics against demonstrators and bystanders for 14 days until the court could decide whether a longer injunction was required. The U.S. District Court considered the motion.

ISSUE: Will a temporary restraining order (TRO) issue where plaintiffs are able to establish (1) that there is a likelihood of success on their claims of violations of their constitutional rights by the government, (2) that they are likely to suffer irreparable injury from ongoing constitutional violations of their rights without a TRO, and (3) that it is in the public interest to enjoin such ongoing constitutional violations?

HOLDING AND DECISION: (Michelson, J.) Yes. A temporary restraining order (TRO) will issue where plaintiffs are able to establish (1) that there is a likelihood of success on their claims of violations of their constitutional rights by the government, (2) that they are likely to suffer irreparable injury from ongoing constitutional violations of their rights without a TRO, and (3) that it is in the public interest to enjoin such ongoing constitutional violations. A TRO is an extraordinary remedy reserved only for cases where it is necessary to preserve the status quo until trial. In considering a request for a TRO, the court must consider and weigh four factors: (1) plaintiffs' likelihood of success on the merits, (2) whether plaintiffs will suffer irreparable injury without an injunction, (3) whether granting the injunction will cause substantial harm to others, and (4) whether the public interest would be served by the injunction. In doing so here, the court recognizes that although demonstrators have a right to protest the actions of the police and other members of the government without fear of government retaliation, police officers, especially in their duty to protect person and property, have difficult and often dangerous jobs that require them to make split-second decisions. Also, just as not all protestors seek destruction, not all officers seek violence. The court must thus balance the need to protect the sacred rights of speech and assembly from interference and retaliation with that of police to respond appropriately when the safety of the officers and citizens are threatened. The court will keep these principles in mind when considering and balancing the TRO factors. The first factor, likelihood of success on the merits, is the most important factor in the case of an alleged constitutional violation and is typically determinative. The Plaintiffs (P) are likely to succeed on the merits of their Fourth Amendment claims, as they have alleged excessive force, unreasonable detention conditions, and false arrest, and have adduced facts supporting those allegations. The Plaintiffs (P) have also alleged violations of their First Amendment rights to speech and assembly, and have also adduced support for these allegations, thus likely succeeding on their claims that an ordinary person would be deterred from participating in the protests by the actions of the Detroit Police Department (D) and its officers (D).

Continued on next page.

As to the second factor, irreparable harm, because the loss of First Amendment freedoms, for even minimal periods of time, unquestionably constitutes irreparable injury, irreparable injury has likely already occurred. Without a TRO, there is nothing in the record that indicates that the Plaintiffs (P) will not experience further constitutional deprivations and even physical harm at the hands of the police (D) during the ongoing, daily demonstrations. Therefore, the second factor weighs in favor of a TRO. When considering the third factor, balance of equities, the court balances the competing claims of injury and considers the effect on each party of the granting or withholding of the requested TRO. Because police officers are often faced with dangerous and rapidly evolving situations while trying to enforce the law and maintain the safety of the public, it is important that police officers have non-lethal options to use to protect themselves and the public when necessary. Here, the relief that the Plaintiffs (P) request leaves open all lawful options for police to use reasonable force when necessary to defend against a threat and to make arrests when supported by probable cause. Thus, any possible benefit police officers could gain from deploying chemical agents, projectiles, or striking weapons against demonstrators who pose no threat and are not resisting lawful commands is outweighed by the irreparable harm peaceful protestors would face. The final factor, the public interest, also weighs in favor of an injunction, as it is always in the public interest to prevent the violation of a party's constitutional rights. For these reasons, a TRO is warranted, and the Plaintiff's (P) Motion for a Temporary Restraining Order is granted in part.

ANALYSIS

In its effort to draw a line between permitting police officers to use appropriate means in response to violence and destruction of property that would also not chill free speech or abuse those who wished to exercise it, the court issued the temporary restraining order (TRO) for 14 days, with the possibility of its extension for no more than 28 days upon a showing of good cause absent the defendants' consent. The TRO enjoined the City of Detroit (D), the Detroit Police Department (D), and its officers (D) from using striking weapons (including, but not limited to, batons and shields), chemical agents (including, but not limited to, tear gas and pepper spray), or rubber bullets against any individual peacefully engaging in protest or demonstrations who does not pose a physical threat to the safety of the public or police; deploying chemical agents or a sound cannon against persons peacefully engaging in protest or demonstrations without an audible warning and a reasonable amount of time to disperse; placing in a chokehold or ramming with a vehicle any individual attending a demonstration; tightening the zip ties or handcuffs placed on any individual to the point that the restraints cause physical injury, including loss of circulation or change in color; and arresting any demonstrators en masse without probable cause. In issuing this TRO, the court joined the approach taken by sister courts in a number of cities that had analyzed similar claims and issued similar injunctions.

Quicknotes

CHILL Inhibit or discourage.

FIRST AMENDMENT RIGHTS Rights conferred by the First Amendment to the U.S. Constitution prohibiting Congress from enacting any law respecting an establishment of religion or prohibiting the free exercise of religion; abridging freedom of speech or of the press; the right of peaceful assembly; and the right to petition for a redress of grievances.

Fuentes v. Shevin

Owner of chattels (P) v. Court (D)

407 U.S. 67 (1972)

NATURE OF CASE: Constitutional challenge to Florida's prejudgment replevin procedure on due process grounds.

FACT SUMMARY: Margarita Fuentes (P) had her stove and stereo picked up by the sheriff prior to the adjudication of a suit filed by Firestone Tire and Rubber Co. for nonpayment of the installment sales contract.

RULE OF LAW

Procedural due process requires that a party whose rights are being affected be given a meaningful opportunity to be heard; and in order that the party may enjoy that right, the party must be notified.

FACTS: Margarita Fuentes (Fuentes) (P) purchased a gas stove and service policy, and later a stereo, from Firestone Tire and Rubber Co. (Firestone). After a year, there arose a dispute between Fuentes (P) and Firestone over the servicing of the stove. Firestone filed an action for replevin of both the stove and the stereo, claiming Fuentes (P) had defaulted on her installment payments. Before she was served with the complaint, Firestone obtained a writ of replevin and the sheriff seized the stove and stereo. The prejudgment replevin statutes did not require a convincing showing that the goods were wrongfully detained before seizure. A person could merely file a complaint, post a bond, and request a writ. To obtain a hearing, the person whose property was seized had to initiate a suit for a hearing. Fuentes (P) attacked the prejudgment replevin statute as violative of due process. The state court upheld the legislation, and Fuentes (P) appealed.

ISSUE: Does procedural due process require that a party whose rights are being affected be given a meaningful opportunity to be heard; and in order that the party may enjoy that right, the party must be notified?

HOLDING AND DECISION: (Stewart, J.) Yes. Procedural due process requires that a party whose rights are being affected be given a meaningful opportunity to be heard; and in order that the party may enjoy that right, the party must be notified. The constitutional right to be heard is a basic aspect of the duty of government to follow a fair process of decision-making when it acts to deprive a person of his or her possessions. This right to be heard minimizes substantively unfair or mistaken deprivations of property, a danger that is especially great when the state seizes goods simply upon the application of and for the benefit of a private party. Without due process of law, there would be no safeguards to protect a person's property from governmental interference. The right to speak out in one's own defense before an impartial arbitrator is a fundamental right that must be protected. If the right to notice and a hearing is to serve its full purpose, then it is clear that it must be granted at a time when the deprivation can still be prevented. While return of possession and damages can be granted at a later hearing, nothing can undo the fact that a person's property was arbitrarily taken from him or her without procedural due process of law. That the hearing required by due process is subject to waiver, and is not fixed in form, does not affect its root requirement that an individual be given an opportunity for a hearing before he or she is deprived of any significant property interest, except for extraordinary situations where some valid governmental interest is at stake that justifies postponing the hearing until after the event. The statute's requirements of requesting a writ, posting bond, and stating in a conclusory fashion that the property is wrongfully held merely test the applicant's own belief in his or her rights. Since the applicant's private gain is at stake, the danger is all too great that his or her confidence in the cause will be misplaced. While possession may be reinstated by the posting of a counter-bond, it is well settled that a temporary, non-final deprivation of property is nonetheless violative of the Due Process Clause of the Fourteenth Amendment. Moreover, the Due Process Clause encompasses both the possessory rights to property and situations where the title is in dispute. Situations requiring a postponement of notice and hearing are truly unusual. They require an important governmental purpose and a special need for prompt action, and are initiated by and for the benefit of the government as opposed to a private individual (e.g., war effort, economic disaster, etc.). The contention that the parties waived their constitutional rights is also without merit, since waiver requires clear and explicit language indicating exactly the rights to be waived. For the above-mentioned reasons, both Florida's and Pennsylvania's prejudgment replevin statutes violate the Due Process Clause of the Fourteenth Amendment. Vacated and remanded.

ANALYSIS

In California, Michigan, and a large number of other states, the writ of replevin is now referred to as claim and delivery. In California, this action is contained in § 511.010, et seq. of the Code of Civil Procedure.

Continued on next page.

A hearing is required for the granting of a writ of possession (comparable to the prior writ of replevin) under the guidelines set out in § 512.010. Exceptions are made for property feloniously taken, credit cards, and property acquired in the normal course of trade or business for commercial use. It must be alleged that the property is not necessary for the support of the defendant or the defendant's family and that there is a danger that the property will become unavailable to levy, its value will be substantially impaired, and it is necessary to protect the property (§ 512.020). At the hearing, the court will make its determination based on affidavits, pleadings, and other evidence on record. Upon showing of good cause, the court may admit additional evidence or continue the hearing until the new evidence can be obtained (§ 512.050). Finally, with regard to waiver of a hearing requirement, it appears that it is permissible if the parties are acting at arm's length and have equal bargaining power, *D.H. Overmeyer Co. v. Frick Co.*, 405 U.S. 174 (1972); however, if the consumer has no option but to buy on credit, the parties are not equal in bargaining power and the clause is unconscionable, *Kosches v. Nichols*, 327 N.Y.S. 2d 968 (1971). This is but another example of consumer protection. The businessperson can waive his or her constitutional rights, but the consumer cannot.

Quicknotes

GARNISHMENT Satisfaction of a debt by deducting payments directly from the debtor's wages before wages are paid to debtor by his or her employer; due process requires that the debtor be first given notice and an opportunity to be heard.

PROCEDURAL DUE PROCESS The constitutional mandate that if the state or federal government acts so as to deny a citizen of a life, liberty, or property interest, the individual is first entitled to notice and the right to be heard.

REPLEVIN An action to recover personal property wrongfully taken.

Evans v. Jeff D.

State official (D) v. Class representative (P)

475 U.S. 717 (1986)

NATURE OF CASE: In a federal civil rights class action seeking injunctive relief to improve institutional care provided by the state to emotionally and mentally challenged children, appeal challenging the invalidation of a waiver of attorney's fees and costs included in a settlement agreement between the parties.

FACT SUMMARY: The attorney in a federal civil rights class action seeking injunctive relief to improve institutional care provided by Idaho (D) to emotionally and mentally challenged children (P) agreed, as part of a settlement agreement, to waive attorney's fees and costs in exchange for Idaho (D) granting the prospective relief sought. The waiver was invalidated as violating the Civil Rights Attorney's Fees Awards Act of 1976 (Fees Act). Idaho (D) contended that the Fees Act did not require an award of attorney's fees and costs.

RULE OF LAW

The Civil Rights Attorney's Fees Awards Act of 1976 (Fees Act), 42 U.S.C. § 1988, does not prohibit a federal district court, in its discretion, from approving a waiver of attorney's fees and costs as part of a settlement agreement between the parties to certain civil rights actions enumerated in the Fees Act.

FACTS: A civil rights class action was brought in federal district court by the Idaho Legal Aid Society on behalf of emotionally and mentally challenged children (P) against Idaho (D), alleging that Idaho's (D) treatment of the children in state institutions violated the children's (P) constitutional rights as well as other federal and state laws. The suit sought injunctive relief that would improve the treatment of the children (P). Johnson, the attorney representing the class, initially did not have a provision in his representation agreement that covered legal fees. A week before trial, Idaho (D), as part of a settlement proposal, offered all of the injunctive relief sought by the class on condition that the settlement agreement would include a provision for the waiver of any claim to fees or costs. Although the Idaho Legal Aid Society wanted Johnson to reject this offer, Johnson nevertheless accepted it, believing it was his ethical obligation to the children (P) to do so. [The District Court approved the fee waiver, but on appeal, the Court of Appeals invalidated the fee waiver on the grounds that it was prohibited by the Civil Rights Attorney's Fees Awards Act of 1976 (Fees Act), 42 U.S.C. § 1988.] The United States Supreme Court granted certiorari.

ISSUE: Does the Civil Rights Attorney's Fees Awards Act of 1976 (Fees Act), 42 U.S.C. § 1988, prohibit a federal district court, in its discretion, from approving a waiver of attorney's fees and costs as part of a settlement agreement between the parties to certain civil rights actions enumerated in the Fees Act?

HOLDING AND DECISION: (Stevens, J.) No. The Civil Rights Attorney's Fees Awards Act of 1976 (Fees Act), 42 U.S.C. § 1988, does not prohibit a federal district court, in its discretion, from approving a waiver of attorney's fees and costs as part of a settlement agreement between the parties to certain civil rights actions enumerated in the Fees Act. The language of the Fees Act, as well as its legislative history, indicates that Congress bestowed on the "prevailing party" a statutory eligibility for a discretionary award of attorney's fees in specified civil rights actions. Neither the statute nor the legislative history suggests that Congress intended to forbid all waivers of attorney's fees—even those insisted upon by a civil rights plaintiff in exchange for some other relief to which the plaintiff is indisputably not entitled—anymore than it intended to bar a concession on damages to secure broader injunctive relief. To the contrary, a general proscription against the waiver of attorney's fees in exchange for a settlement on the merits would itself impede the vindication of civil rights, at least in some cases, by reducing the attractiveness of settlement. Settlement, rather than ongoing litigation, is in the interests of both plaintiffs and defendants, as it relieves them of the burdens, stress, cost, and time of litigation. Therefore, it is not necessary to construe the Fees Act as embodying a general rule prohibiting settlements conditioned on the waiver of fees in order to be faithful to the purposes of the Fees Act, and there is nothing in the particular circumstances of the case at bar that would warrant an exception to the principle accepting waivers in return for concessions by defendant. Permitting a district court in the exercise of its discretion to accept a fee waiver promotes the Fees Act's objectives by making its fee-shifting provisions "a powerful weapon" in the hands of civil rights plaintiffs. Whether this "weapon" might be even more powerful if fee waivers were prohibited in cases like the one addressed here is a question best left to Congress, which, in any event, has not commanded that fees be paid whenever a case covered by the Fees Act is settled. [Reversed.]

Continued on next page.

ANALYSIS

The dissenters—Justice Brennan joined by Justices Marshall and Blackmun—emphasized that Congress authorized fee shifting in the Civil Rights Attorney's Fees Awards Act of 1976 (Fees Act), 42 U.S.C. § 1988 to improve the enforcement of civil rights legislation by making it easier for victims of civil rights violations to find lawyers willing to take their cases, and argued that the Court's decision would make it more difficult for civil rights plaintiffs to obtain legal assistance, a result contrary to Congress's purpose. The dissenters also contended that the majority's view that the Fees Act was intended merely to give individual victims of civil rights violations another remedy mischaracterized, and was at odds with, the whole thrust of the Fees Act. In addition, the dissenters criticized, as without factual support, the majority's assertion that requiring defendants to pay statutory fee awards would prevent a "significant number" of settlements, and noted that because the parties can negotiate a fee (or a range of fees) that is not unduly high and condition their settlement on the court's approval of this fee, the magnitude of a defendant's liability for fees in the settlement context need be neither uncertain nor particularly great. Against this, the defendant must weigh the risk of a non-negotiated fee to be fixed by the court after a trial, which fee award could be very uncertain and, potentially, of very great magnitude.

Quicknotes

INJUNCTIVE RELIEF A court order issued as a remedy, requiring a person to do, or prohibiting that person from doing, a specific act.

SETTLEMENT AGREEMENT An agreement entered into by the parties to a civil lawsuit agreeing upon the determination of rights and issues between them, thus disposing of the need for judicial determination.

Buckhannon Board and Care Home, Inc. v. West Virginia Department of Health and Human Resources

Declaratory-relief complainant (P) v. State (D)

532 U.S. 598 (2001)

NATURE OF CASE: Appeal of denial of attorney's fees award.

FACT SUMMARY: Buckhannon Board and Care Home, Inc. (Buckhannon) (P) brought suit to declare provisions of a state statute invalid as violating a federal statute. When the state statute was amended to delete the attacked provisions, Buckhannon (P) sought attorney's fees under the federal statute even though its federal court suit was dismissed as moot.

RULE OF LAW

An award of attorney's fees and costs to a "prevailing party" under federal statutes may be awarded only to a party who has secured a judgment on the merits or a court-ordered consent decree.

FACTS: Buckhannon Board and Care Home, Inc. (Buckhannon) (P), which operated care homes and assisted living facilities, ran afoul of a state regulation that required residents to be sufficiently ambulatory to get out of a burning building. After receiving a cease and desist order from the West Virginia Department of Health and Human Resources (D) requiring closure of its residential-care facilities, Buckhannon (P) brought suit against the latter, seeking declaratory and injunctive relief that the self-preservation requirement violated the Fair Housing Amendments Act of 1990. The West Virginia Legislature subsequently enacted legislation eliminating the self-preservation requirement, and the federal district court dismissed Buckhannon's (P) suit as moot. Buckhannon (P) thereupon requested attorney's fees as the "prevailing party" under the Fair Housing Amendments Act. The court denied the motion, the court of appeals affirmed, and Buckhannon (P) appealed.

ISSUE: May an award of attorney's fees and costs to a "prevailing party" under federal statutes be awarded only to a party who has secured a judgment on the merits or a court-ordered consent decree?

HOLDING AND DECISION: (Rehnquist, C.J.) Yes. An award of attorney's fees and costs to a "prevailing party" under federal statutes may be awarded only to a party who has secured a judgment on the merits or a court-ordered consent decree. In designating those parties eligible for an award of litigation costs, Congress employed the term "prevailing party," a legal term of art that indicates one who has been awarded some relief by the court. Enforceable judgments on the merits and court-ordered consent decrees create the "material alteration of the legal relationship of the parties" necessary to permit an award of attorney's fees. However, the "catalyst theory," which would allow an award where there is no judicially sanctioned change in the relationship of the parties, should not give rise to an award of attorney's fees. A defendant's voluntary change in conduct, although perhaps accomplishing what the plaintiff sought to achieve by the lawsuit, lacks the necessary judicial imprimatur on the change. The legislative history on the issue is at best ambiguous as to the availability of the "catalyst" theory for awarding attorney's fees. Particularly in view of the "American Rule" that attorney's fees will not be awarded absent explicit statutory authority, such legislative history is clearly insufficient to alter the accepted meaning of the statutory term. Affirmed.

DISSENT: (Ginsburg, J.) To "prevail" so as to receive attorney's fees, it should not be a requirement that the court enter a judgment on the merits. Nor should there necessarily be any finding of wrongdoing. A court-approved settlement will do. The catalyst rule, as applied by the clear majority of federal circuits, is a key component of the fee-shifting statutes Congress adopted to advance enforcement of civil rights.

ANALYSIS

In *Buckhannon*, the Supreme Court noted that, in addition to judgments on the merits, settlement agreements enforced through a consent decree may serve as the basis for an award of attorney's fees.

Quicknotes

AMERICAN RULE The rule that attorney's fees are not recoverable, unless expressly provided by law or pursuant to a contract.

CONSENT DECREE A decree issued by a court of equity ratifying an agreement between the parties to a lawsuit; an agreement by a defendant to cease illegal activity.

JUDGMENT ON THE MERITS A determination of the rights of the parties to litigation based on the presentation evidence, barring the party from initiating the same suit again.

CHAPTER 6

Pleading

Quick Reference Rules of Law

Haddle v. Garrison (S.D. Ga. 1996)

Employee (P) v. Employer (D)

Unpublished Opinion. Docket No. 96-00029-CV-1 (S.D. Ga. 1996)

NATURE OF CASE: Motion to dismiss for failure to state a claim.

FACT SUMMARY: Haddle (P) sued his former employer for allegedly conspiring to fire him to deter him from testifying at a federal criminal trial.

RULE OF LAW

A 42 U.S.C. § 1985(2) claim requires the plaintiff suffer actual injury, and discharge from at-will employment does not constitute actual injury.

FACTS: Haddle (P), a former employee at Healthmaster Home Health Care, Inc. (Healthmaster) (D), alleged that his employment was terminated in an attempt to deter his participation as a witness at a federal criminal trial. Haddle (P) filed suit in district court for violation of 42 U.S.C. § 1985(2). Healthmaster (D) and their officers (D) moved to dismiss for failure to state a claim upon which relief can be granted. They argued that because Haddle (P) was an at-will employee, there was no actual injury as required by 42 U.S.C. § 1985(2).

ISSUE: Does discharge from at-will employment constitute actual injury for purposes of 42 U.S.C. § 1985(2)?

HOLDING AND DECISION: (Alaimo, J.) No. A 42 U.S.C. § 1985(2) claim requires the plaintiff suffer actual injury, and discharge from at-will employment does not constitute actual injury. Section 1985(2) provides that one or more persons may not engage in a conspiracy to deter, intimidate, or threaten another from attending and testifying at a federal court proceeding and cause an injury. Fed. R. Civ. P. 12(b)(6) permits a defendant to move to dismiss a complaint where the plaintiff has failed to state a claim upon which relief can be granted. This motion attacks the legal sufficiency of the complaint. Consequently, a court must assume that all of the factual allegations of the complaint are true in deciding the motion. In the present case, the U.S. Court of Appeals for the Eleventh Circuit has already ruled that at-will employees have no constitutionally protected property interest in continued employment and thus suffer no actual injury under § 1985(2) when discharged. Accordingly, Haddle (P) has failed to state a federal claim, even if his allegations about the conspiracy to deter him from testifying are true. The motion to dismiss is granted.

ANALYSIS

On appeal, the Eleventh Circuit affirmed this decision in per curiam decision, holding that precedent forecloses Michael A. Haddle's (P) arguments on appeal (unpublished opinion, Docket No. 96-8856 (11th Cir. 1997)). However, the Supreme Court eventually took up the case because it conflicted with the decisions in two other circuits. In the end, Haddle's (P) appeal was upheld and the dismissal reversed.

Quicknotes

FED. R. CIV. P. 12 Allows for successive motions to dismiss for failure to state a claim.

Haddle v. Garrison

[Parties not identified.]

Unpublished Opinion. Docket No. 96-8856 (11th Cir. 1997)

NATURE OF CASE: Appeal from dismissal of a 42 U.S.C. § 1985(2) claim for failure to state a claim.

FACT SUMMARY: [See the brief for *Haddle v. Garrison* (S.D. Ga. 1996) on page 76 in this *Casenote Legal Briefs* book.]

RULE OF LAW

An appeal from a dismissal for failure to state a claim will be denied where the appellant's arguments are foreclosed by prior precedent.

FACTS: [See the brief for *Haddle v. Garrison* (S.D. Ga. 1996) on page 76 in this *Casenote Legal Briefs* book.]

ISSUE: Will an appeal from a dismissal for failure to state a claim be denied where the appellant's arguments are foreclosed by prior precedent?

HOLDING AND DECISION: (Per curiam) Yes. An appeal from a dismissal for failure to state a claim will be denied where the appellant's arguments are foreclosed by prior precedent. Haddle's arguments on appeal are foreclosed by this court's decision in *Morast v. Lance,* 807 F.2d 926 (11th Cir. 1987). The judgment of the district court is therefore affirmed.

ANALYSIS

In *Morast v. Lance,* 807 F.2d 926 (1987), the U.S. Court of Appeals for the Eleventh Circuit held that an at-will employee who is dismissed pursuant to a conspiracy proscribed by 42 U.S.C. § 1985(2) has no cause of action. The *Morast* court explained that to make out a cause of action under § 1985(2) the plaintiff must have suffered an actual injury. Because Morast was an at-will employee, he had no constitutionally protected interest in continued employment. Therefore, Morast's discharge did not constitute an actual injury under this statute. Relying on its decision in *Morast,* the court of appeals affirmed in this extremely short opinion. Haddle appealed again, and the United States Supreme Court granted certiorari to resolve a split among the circuits. The Supreme Court held that Haddle had suffered a harm that could support damages finding, and, accordingly, it reversed.

Haddle v. Garrison

Employee (P) v. Employer (D)

525 U.S. 121 (1998)

NATURE OF CASE: Appeal from dismissal of action under 42 U.S.C. § 1985(2).

FACT SUMMARY: Haddle (P) sued his former employer for allegedly conspiring to fire him to deter him from testifying at a federal criminal trial.

RULE OF LAW

A claim under Civil Rights Act of 1871, Rev. Stat. § 1980, 42 U.S.C. § 1985(2) does not require an injury to a constitutionally protected property interest.

FACTS: Healthmaster Home Health Care, Inc. (Healthmaster) (D) and officers Garrison (D) and Kelly (D) were indicted by a federal grand jury in 1995. Haddle (P), an employee, had cooperated with the investigation and was expected to appear as a witness at the resulting criminal trial. Garrison (D) and Kelly (D) allegedly conspired with the other officers at Healthmaster (D) to terminate Haddle (P) in retaliation. Haddle (P) filed suit in district court for violation of 42 U.S.C. § 1985(2). Healthmaster (D) and the officers (D) moved to dismiss for failure to state a claim upon which relief can be granted. The district court ruled that because Haddle (P) was an at-will employee, there was no actual injury as required by § 1985(2). The dismissal motion was granted and the U.S. Court of Appeals for the Eleventh Circuit affirmed. Since Eleventh Circuit's decision conflicted with the holdings in two other circuits, the United States Supreme Court granted certiorari.

ISSUE: Does a claim under Civil Rights Act of 1871, Rev. Stat. § 1980, 42 U.S.C.§ 1985(2) require an injury to a constitutionally protected property interest?

HOLDING AND DECISION: (Rehnquist, C.J.) No. A claim under Civil Rights Act of 1871, Rev. Stat. § 1980, 42 U.S.C. § 1985(2) does not require an injury to a constitutionally protected property interest. Section 1985(2) provides that one or more persons may not engage in a conspiracy to deter, intimidate, or threaten another from attending and testifying at a federal court proceeding. The Eleventh Circuit held there was no injury to Haddle (P) because he had no property interest in at-will employment that could give rise to damages. However, nothing in the language of § 1985(2) or the remedial provisions establishes this requirement. The section is directed against intimidation or retaliation against witnesses, not the deprivation of property. The fact employment at will is not property does not mean the loss of this employment does not cause injury. Such harm has long been a compensable injury under tort law and is similar to intentional interference with contractual relations. Dismissal of Haddle's (P) complaint for failure to state a claim was in error. Reversed and remanded.

ANALYSIS

The employment term for "at-will employees" is not definite, and when *Haddle* was decided, very few Supreme Court cases addressed the issue of at-will employment. In addition, amici in the case included the National Whistleblowers Association. The Court's reversal arguably could have caused a significant increase in the number of whistleblower cases filed in federal court.

Quicknotes

SUPPLEMENTAL JURISDICTION A doctrine granting authority to a federal court to hear a claim that does not invoke diversity jurisdiction if it arises from the same transaction or occurrence as the primary action.

Ashcroft v. Iqbal

Former U.S. Attorney General (D) v. Pakistani citizen (P)

556 U.S. 662 (2009)

NATURE OF CASE: Certiorari to determine complaint sufficiency in constitutional claim.

FACT SUMMARY: Javaid Iqbal (P), a Pakistani citizen, was arrested in the United States on criminal charges and detained by federal officials soon after the 9/11 terrorist attacks. He claimed his confinement conditions violated his constitutional rights. The federal official defendants moved to dismiss Iqbal's (P) complaint as facially insufficient.

RULE OF LAW

A well-pleaded complaint requires nonconclusory, plausible, factual pleadings.

FACTS: United States officials arrested Javaid Iqbal (P), a Pakistani citizen and Muslim, on criminal charges and detained him after the 9/11 terrorist attacks. Iqbal (P) filed a federal complaint alleging he was deprived of certain constitutional rights while confined. He alleged the deprivations occurred because of his race, religion, or national origin. He named former U.S. Attorney General John Ashcroft (D) and Federal Bureau of Investigation (FBI) Director Robert Mueller (D) in addition to several others. Ashcroft (D) and Mueller (D) moved to dismiss the complaint as facially insufficient and raised the defense of qualified immunity based on their official status at the time of the confinement. The district court denied the motion and Ashcroft (D) and Mueller (D) took an interlocutory appeal to the U.S. Court of Appeals for the Second Circuit. The Second Circuit affirmed, and the United States Supreme Court granted certiorari.

ISSUE: Does a well-pleaded complaint require nonconclusory, plausible, factual pleadings?

HOLDING AND DECISION: (Kennedy, J.) Yes. A well-pleaded complaint requires nonconclusory, plausible, factual pleadings. Iqbal's (P) complaint alleges the federal government had a policy of detaining Arab Muslims after the 9/11 attacks until the individuals were "cleared" by the FBI. Iqbal (P) claimed Ashcroft (D) was the "architect" of this policy and Mueller (D) was instrumental in its "adoption, promulgation, and implementation." This Court held in *Bell Atlantic Corp. v. Twombly*, 550 U.S. 544 (2007), that pleadings required factual content that allows the court to draw the reasonable inference that the defendant is liable for the alleged misconduct. The plausibility standard did not rise to a probability but requires more than conclusions of misconduct. *Twombly* supported the principles that a court accepts factual allegations as true but need not accept conclusory allegations as true. Fed. R. Civ. P. 8 may now permit more flexibility, but it does not permit mere conclusions. Further, only a complaint that states a plausible claim survives a motion to dismiss. The courts may begin their analysis with determining which pleadings include factual allegations that will be entitled to a presumption of truth. Here, Iqbal (P) states only conclusory allegations that Ashcroft (D) was the principal architect and Mueller (D) was the principal implementer of the policies. These conclusory allegations are not entitled to a presumption of truth. Iqbal (P) fails to include factual allegations supporting his conclusions that Ashcroft (D) and Mueller (D) knew of the federal officials' behavior regarding his confinement. The consideration then becomes whether the complaint suggests an entitlement to relief. It does not. Iqbal (P) was plausibly held for reasons other than race, religion, or national origin. Detaining such suspects until cleared does not violate constitutional protections. Iqbal (P) argues *Twombly* should be limited to antitrust pleadings, but nothing supports this theory. *Twombly* is the pleading standard for all civil actions. Iqbal (P) finally argues Fed. R. Civ. P. 9(b) permits him "general" rather than "specific" pleading for an alleged constitutional violation. Rule 9(b) does not override the factual pleading requirements of Rule 8 but merely requires even greater specificity for the enumerated claims. Reversed and remanded.

DISSENT: (Souter, J.) Consistent with *Twombly*, nonconclusory allegations should be taken as true unless they are "sufficiently fantastic to defy reality." The key allegations here are not conclusory and the complaint was facially sufficient.

DISSENT: (Breyer, J.) The lower court expressly rejected minimally intrusive discovery in favor of dismissal. That would have been appropriate because the discovery could have been in anticipation of a summary judgment motion.

ANALYSIS

Pleading requirements have become stricter so general notice is no longer sufficient. The defendant is not merely put on notice of the plaintiff's claim but is entitled to factual allegations informing it of the support for the claim. Some analysts were concerned about the future of litigation because of a fear that pleadings would have to be so specific that most plaintiffs would

Continued on next page.

not be able to proceed. Most courts, however, have required factual pleading for a long time and did not become more stringent after *Iqbal.* The rule stated in *Iqbal* is "plausibility" not "probability" so the allegations do not have to be proven on the face of the complaint, but the facts alleged must be plausible and permit a reasonable inference of defendant's misconduct.

Quicknotes

INTERLOCUTORY APPEAL The appeal of an issue that does not resolve the disposition of the case but is essential to a determination of the parties' legal rights.

McCleary-Evans v. Maryland Department of Transportation, State Highway Administration

African American female job applicant (P) v. Potential employer (D)

780 F.3d 582 (4th Cir. 2015)

NATURE OF CASE: Appeal from dismissal of action alleging violations of Title VII of the Civil Rights Act of 1964, 42 U.S.C. § 2000e-2(a)(1).

FACT SUMMARY: Dawnn McCleary-Evans (McCleary-Evans) (P), an African American female, brought suit against the Maryland Department of Transportation's State Highway Administration (Highway Administration) (D), alleging that the Highway Administration (D) failed or refused to hire her for two positions for which she applied because of her race and her sex, in violation of Title VII of the Civil Rights Act of 1964, 42 U.S.C. § 2000e–2(a)(1). She contended that her allegations that the Highway Administration (D) had a history of hiring White candidates, and that in her case White candidates were in fact hired over her, despite her being highly qualified for the positions for which she applied, were sufficient to state a plausible claim of discrimination that should have entitled her to proceed with her case to at least the discovery stage.

RULE OF LAW

Where a job applicant alleges discrimination in hiring based only on the applicant's race and sex, the employer's history of not hiring those of race and sex similar to that of the job applicant, and that those with hiring authority likewise were not of race or sex similar to that of the job applicant, without more, the job applicant has not stated a plausible case of discrimination in violation of Title VII of the Civil Rights Act of 1964, 42 U.S.C. § 2000e–2(a)(1).

FACTS: Dawnn McCleary-Evans (McCleary-Evans) (P), an African-American female, applied for two positions with the Maryland Department of Transportation's State Highway Administration (Highway Administration) (D) for which she was highly qualified. At her interviews, the decision makers were non-Black, and, ultimately, the Highway Administration (D) hired White candidates over her. McCleary-Evans (P) brought suit in federal district court against the Highway Administration (D), alleging that the decision makers were biased and had "predetermined" that they would select White candidates to fill the positions, in violation of Title VII of the Civil Rights Act of 1964, 42 U.S.C. § 2000e–2(a)(1). She based her allegations, in part, on the Highway Administration's (D) history of hiring Whites. The district court dismissed the case under Fed. R. Civ. P. 12(b)(6), concluding that the complaint failed to allege facts that plausibly support a claim of discrimination, and the U.S. Court of Appeals for the Fourth Circuit granted review.

ISSUE: Where a job applicant alleges discrimination in hiring based only on the applicant's race and sex, the employer's history of not hiring those of race and sex similar to that of the job applicant, and that those with hiring authority likewise were not of race or sex similar to that of the job applicant, without more, has the job applicant stated a plausible case of discrimination in violation of Title VII of the Civil Rights Act of 1964, 42 U.S.C. § 2000e–2(a)(1)?

HOLDING AND DECISION: (Niemeyer, J.) No. Where a job applicant alleges discrimination in hiring based only on the applicant's race and sex, the employer's history of not hiring those of race and sex similar to that of the job applicant, and that those with hiring authority likewise were not of race or sex similar to that of the job applicant, without more, the job applicant has not stated a plausible case of discrimination in violation of Title VII of the Civil Rights Act of 1964, 42 U.S.C. § 2000e–2(a)(1). McCleary-Evans (P) has failed to include adequate factual allegations to support a claim that the Highway Administration (D) discriminated against her because she was African American or female. Her "naked" allegations, merely reciting the necessary elements of her case, were conclusory and did not suffice to state a case of discrimination. She alleged no factual basis for what happened during the course of her interview, and only speculation can fill the gaps in her complaint—speculation as to why two non-Black candidates were selected to fill the positions instead of her. While the allegation that non-Black decision makers hired non-Black applicants instead of the plaintiff is consistent with discrimination, it does not alone support a reasonable inference that the decision makers were motivated by bias. McCleary-Evans (P) can only speculate that the persons hired were not better qualified, or did not perform better during their interviews, or were not better suited based on experience and personality for the positions. In short, her complaint stopped short of the line between possibility and plausibility of entitlement to relief. [Affirmed.]

DISSENT: (Wynn, J.) Contrary to the majority's conclusion, all of McCleary-Evans's (P) allegations, taken together at the early stage of her case and drawing on

Continued on next page.

judicial experience and common sense, sufficiently state a claim of "eminently" plausible discrimination. Therefore, a plausibly meritorious case such as hers should not be prematurely dismissed, especially given that asymmetric discovery burdens are often the byproduct of asymmetric information. The district court faulted McCleary-Evans (P) for failing to allege how much control the Highway Administration (D) decision makers wielded over other members of the hiring committee and failing to identify the qualifications of the selected candidates. However, it is simply unrealistic to expect McCleary-Evans (P) to allege such facts without the benefit of at least some limited discovery. When courts impose unrealistic expectations on plaintiffs at the pleading stage of a lawsuit, they fail to apply "judicial experience and common sense" to the highly context-specific task of deciding whether to permit a lawsuit to proceed to discovery. Moreover, at the early stages of Title VII litigation, borderline conclusory allegations may be all that is available to even the most diligent of plaintiffs, given that the requisite proof of the defendant's discriminatory intent is often in the exclusive control of the defendant, "behind doors slammed shut by an unlawful termination."

ANALYSIS

The district court, and the circuit court, relied on two U.S. Supreme Court decisions in reaching their conclusions in dismissing McCleary-Evans's (P) action: *Ashcroft v. Iqbal*, 556 U.S. 662 (2009) and *Bell Atl. Corp. v. Twombly*, 550 U.S. 544 (2007). Taken together, these cases require a plaintiff under Federal Rule of Civil Procedure 8(a)(2) to state more than labels and conclusions, as a mere "formulaic recitation of the elements of a cause of action will not do." *Twombly*, 550 U.S. at 555. Under these two cases, a complaint must contain factual allegations sufficient to raise a right to relief "above the speculative level." *Id.* As Judge Posner of the Seventh Circuit Court of Appeals noted in his dissent in *Swanson v. Citibank, N.A.*, 614 F.3d 400 (7th Cir. 2010), the Supreme Court in the *Twombly* and *Iqbal* decisions clearly aimed to curb the rising costs of discovery borne by defendants facing meritless lawsuits and to quell the tide of "extortionate litigation" in this country by incentivizing plaintiffs to be more diligent in their pre-litigation investigations, thereby bringing greater balance to the asymmetric discovery burdens that may arise in litigation. However, as Judge Wynn notes in dissent, if litigation costs are to be considered in the application of federal pleading standards, the costs borne by plaintiffs and society as a whole when meritorious discrimination lawsuits are prematurely dismissed likewise should not be ignored—especially given that plaintiffs such as McCleary-Evans (P) often are unable to gain access to the kind of specific factual allegations mandated by *Twombly* and *Iqbal* until after they have had an opportunity to conduct initial discovery.

Quicknotes

DISCOVERY Pretrial procedure during which one party makes certain information available to the other.

DISCRIMINATION Unequal treatment of a class of persons.

Stradford v. Zurich Insurance Co.

Insured (P) v. Insurer (D)

2002 WL 31027517 (S.D.N.Y. 2002)

NATURE OF CASE: Motion to dismiss counterclaim.

FACT SUMMARY: When Dr. Stradford (P) sued his insurer, Zurich Insurance Company (Northern) (D), for property damage, Northern (P) counterclaimed for fraud, contending that Stradford (P) was fully aware the damage had occurred during a period in which the policy had lapsed for nonpayment of premiums. Stradford (P) moved to dismiss the fraud claim.

RULE OF LAW

Under Fed. R. Civ. P. 9(b), the time, place, and nature of alleged misrepresentations must be disclosed to a party accused of fraud.

FACTS: Dr. Stradford (P), a dentist, brought suit against his insurer, Zurich Insurance Company (Northern) (D), for water damage allegedly occurring to his property during a period that Northern (D) claimed was an interim period when the insurance had lapsed because of Stradford's (P) failure to make premium payments. Northern (D), accordingly, counterclaimed against Stradford (P), contending that Stradford (P), by making the claim and filing the suit, knowingly had devised a scheme and artifice to defraud the insurer and obtain money by false pretenses and representations. Stradford (P) moved to dismiss the counterclaim that was based in fraud for failure to state the fraud claim with sufficient particularity.

ISSUE: Under Fed. R. Civ. P. 9(b), must the time, place, and nature of alleged misrepresentations be disclosed to a party accused of fraud?

HOLDING AND DECISION: (Buchwald, J.) Yes. Under Fed. R. Civ. P. 9(b), the time, place, and nature of alleged misrepresentations must be disclosed to a party accused of fraud. Here, Northern's (D) counterclaims simply failed to identify the statement made by Stradford (P) that they claimed to be false. Thus, it is unclear from the face of the counterclaims whether Northern (D) was asserting that Stradford's (P) claimed losses were improperly inflated, that Stradford's (P) office never even flooded, or that the offices flooded, but not during the term of the insurance policy. In essence, Northern (D) claimed that Stradford (P) lied but failed to identify the lie. The primary purpose of Rule 9(b) is to afford a litigant accused of fraud fair notice of the claim and the factual ground upon which it is based. Here, Northern's (D) counterclaims failed to provide Stradford (P) with fair notice of precisely which statement, or which aspect of his claim, Northern (D) alleged to be false. The counterclaims were therefore insufficient under Rule 9(b) and must be dismissed. However, in accordance with the practice of the Second Circuit, Northern (D) is permitted to file an amended pleading, which it has done, that cures the defects found in the counterclaims by making it clear that it was alleging that Stradford's (P) office was flooded at a time when he had permitted the insurance policy to lapse, yet that he misrepresented the date of the loss to try to bring the loss within the coverage period. Defendant's request for permission to move for summary judgment is granted.

ANALYSIS

Fed. R. Civ. P. 9(b) provides that in all averments of fraud or mistake, the circumstances constituting fraud or mistake shall be stated with particularity. Malice, intent, knowledge, and other condition of mind of a person may be averred generally.

Quicknotes

FED. R. CIV. P. 9(b) States that in all averments of fraud or mistake, the circumstances constituting fraud or mistake shall be stated with particularity.

Jones v. Bock

Prisoner (P) v. State (D)

549 U.S. 199 (2007)

NATURE OF CASE: Appeal to Supreme Court on issue of pleading requirements.

FACT SUMMARY: Lorenzo Jones (P) was a prisoner in Michigan. He sued the State (D) after he suffered injuries in custody when the staff refused to reassign him to work he could perform in light of his injuries.

RULE OF LAW

A plaintiff need not plead and demonstrate exhaustion of administrative remedies in the complaint.

FACTS: Lorenzo Jones (P) was a prisoner in Michigan. He sued the State (D) after he suffered injuries in custody when the staff refused to reassign him to work he could perform in light of his injuries.

ISSUE: Must a plaintiff plead and demonstrate exhaustion of administrative remedies in the complaint?

HOLDING AND DECISION: (Roberts, C.J.) No. A plaintiff need not plead and demonstrate exhaustion of administrative remedies in the complaint. The Federal Rules of Civil Procedure do not require that exhaustion be pleaded, and Rule 8(c) identifies a non-exhaustive list of affirmative defenses that must be pleaded in response, leaving room for exhaustion as an affirmative defense. In addition, the Prison Litigation Reform Act, which deals extensively with the subject of exhaustion, is silent on the issue whether exhaustion must be pleaded by the plaintiff or is an affirmative defense. This supports the fact that the usual practice should be followed, and the usual practice under the Federal Rules is to regard exhaustion as an affirmative defense. The reasons behind the decisions of some lower courts to impose a pleading requirement on plaintiffs in this context—which are to separate, when it comes to prisoner suits, those claims that have merit and those that have none and will merely clog the process—are understandable. But the way to establishing higher pleading requirements is to amend the rules, not on a case-by-case basis in courts.

ANALYSIS

The outcome of this case is in keeping with the Roberts Court's general idea that policy considerations and courts should not expand the requirements of the Federal Rules of Civil Procedure. The general belief is that expansion of the Rules should be made through the Rules amendment process.

Quicknotes

AFFIRMATIVE DEFENSE A manner of defending oneself against a claim not by denying the truth of the charge but by the introduction of some evidence challenging the plaintiff's right to bring the claim.

EXHAUSTION REMEDIES Requirement that a party exhaust all administrative remedies available before a court will intervene in the controversy.

Christian v. Mattel, Inc.

Alleged infringed toymaker (P) v. Alleged infringing toymaker (D)

286 F.3d 1118 (9th Cir. 2003)

NATURE OF CASE: Appeal of an award of Fed. R. Civ. P. 11 sanctions.

FACT SUMMARY: When the court awarded Fed. R. Civ. P. 11 sanctions against Claudene Christian (P) and her attorney, Hicks, for a combination of frivolous pleading and improper discovery tactics, Christian (P) and Hicks argued that Rule 11 sanctions must be limited to papers signed in violation of the rule, not to other conduct.

RULE OF LAW

Fed. R. Civ. P. 11 sanctions are limited to papers signed in violation of the rule, not to other conduct.

FACTS: Claudene Christian (P), who created and marketed a cheerleader doll, filed a complaint alleging that the toymaker Mattel, Inc. (D) infringed the copyright on her doll. Mattel (D) proffered evidence that its copyright predated Christian's (P) doll. However, Christian (P), through her attorney, Hicks, refused voluntarily to dismiss the suit. The federal district court granted Mattel's (D) motion for summary judgment and for Fed. R. Civ. P. 11 sanctions, finding that Christian's (P) attorney, Hicks, had filed a meritless claim and that Hicks had demonstrated that his conduct fell far below the proper standards of attorneys, including, among other things, unprofessional behavior during discovery proceedings and misrepresentations to the court during oral arguments. The court awarded Mattel (D) \$501,565 in attorney's fees. Christian (P) and Hicks appealed.

ISSUE: Are Fed. R. Civ. P. 11 sanctions limited to papers signed in violation of the rule, not to other conduct?

HOLDING AND DECISION: (McKeown, J.) Yes. Fed. R. Civ. P. 11 sanctions are limited to papers signed in violation of the rule, not to other conduct. While the laundry list of Hicks's outlandish conduct is a long one and raises questions as to his respect for the judicial process, nonetheless Rule 11 sanctions are limited to papers signed. Conduct in depositions, discovery meetings of counsel, oral representations at hearings, and behavior in prior proceedings do not fall within the ambit of Rule 11. Here, the orders clearly demonstrate that the district court decided, at least in part, to sanction Hicks because he signed and filed a factually and legally meritless complaint, and also, strongly suggest that the court considered "extra-pleadings conduct" as a basis for the Rule 11 sanctions. Because it cannot from the record be determined for certain whether the district court granted Mattel's (P) Rule 11 motion as a result of an impermissible intertwining of its conclusion about the complaint's frivolity and Hicks's extrinsic misconduct, the district court Rule 11 order is vacated, and the matter is remanded to delineate the factual and legal basis for its sanctions orders.

ANALYSIS

In *Christian*, the court emphasized that Fed. R. Civ. P. 11 does not authorize sanctions for "extra-pleadings conduct" such as, for example, discovery abuses or misstatements made to the court during an oral presentation.

Quicknotes

FED. R. CIV. P. 11 Sets forth: the requirement that every pleading or written paper be signed by at least one attorney of record; the representations made by the attorney to the court upon the signing of such document; and the sanctions for violation of the provision.

Zielinski v. Philadelphia Piers, Inc.

Injured forklift operator (P) v. Rival forklift company (D)

139 F. Supp. 408 (E.D. Pa. 1956)

NATURE OF CASE: Action in torts to recover damages for personal injuries.

FACT SUMMARY: Philadelphia Piers (D) was estopped to deny ownership of a forklift and the agency of the operator.

RULE OF LAW

In the federal courts, a defendant who knowingly makes inaccurate statements may be estopped from denying those inaccurate statements at the trial.

FACTS: Zielinski (P) was injured on February 9, 1953, while operating a forklift on Pier 96 for J.A. McCarthy. Zielinski (P) alleged in his complaint that Sandy Johnson was operating a forklift owned by Philadelphia Piers, Inc. (D) and was their agent as well. Because of the negligent manner in which Sandy Johnson operated the forklift, Zielinski (P) was injured. A complaint was served on Philadelphia Piers (D). Actually, Sandy Johnson worked for Carload Contractors, Inc., which had leased the forklift from Philadelphia Piers (D). Sandy Johnson had worked for Philadelphia Piers (D) for the previous 15 years and wasn't aware that he was now working for Carload Contractors. Sandy Johnson testified at a deposition taken August 18, 1953, that he had worked for Philadelphia Piers. (D). As soon as Carload Contractors found out about the accident, they made a report to their insurance company. When Philadelphia Piers (D) received the complaint, they forwarded it on to their insurance company, which was the same insurance company of Carload Contractors, telling them of the mistake and asking them to take care of it. Philadelphia Piers (D) was at the deposition when Sandy Johnson testified that he worked for Philadelphia Piers (D), and by receiving the complaint and the letter they sent to their insurance company, it was clear that they knew of Zielinski's (P) mistake. Zielinski (P) didn't find out that he was suing the wrong party until the pretrial conference held on September 27, 1955. Zielinski (P) requested a ruling that for the purposes of this case the forklift operated by Sandy Johnson was owned by Philadelphia Piers (D), and that Sandy Johnson was its agent acting in the course of his employment. In other words, Philadelphia Piers (D) would be estopped to deny the facts they allowed Zielinski (P) to believe.

ISSUE: In the federal courts, may a defendant who knowingly makes inaccurate statements be estopped from denying those inaccurate statements at the trial?

HOLDING AND DECISION: (Van Dusen, J.) Yes. In the federal courts, a defendant who knowingly makes inaccurate statements may be estopped from denying those inaccurate statements at the trial. Philadelphia Piers (D) made a general denial of the paragraph in the complaint that alleged that Sandy Johnson was an agent of Philadelphia Piers (D) and was driving their forklift. It was clear from interrogatories that they were aware of the accident and the facts involved because they made an investigation and forwarded their report to their insurance company. Philadelphia Piers (D) should have made a specific denial of parts of the complaint they believed and knew to be false and admitted the parts that were true. This would have warned Zielinski (P) that he was suing the wrong party. This case was being tried in the district court sitting in Pennsylvania and there were no federal court decisions on this point, so the Pennsylvania law was used. The Pennsylvania rule is that where an improper and ineffective answer has been filed, an allegation of agency in the complaint requires a statement to the jury that agency is admitted if the time allowed to amend an answer has already passed. Philadelphia Piers (D) was under no duty to advise Zielinski (P) of his error other than by appropriate pleadings, but neither did they have a right, knowing of the mistake, to foster it by its acts of omission. Therefore, Philadelphia Piers (D) will be estopped to deny Sandy Johnson's agency and their ownership of the forklift and the jury will be instructed as Zielinski (P) requested. Philadelphia Piers (D) will not be prejudiced by having to defend this action, because it will be its insurance company who will have to do it and they are the insurance company for the proper defendants. A pre-trial order may be modified at trial if justice so requires.

ANALYSIS

Fed. R. Civ. P. 8(b) requires that denials fairly meet the substance of the averments denied. This requirement, together with the basic requirement of good faith in pleading contained in Fed. R. Civ. P. 11, probably would provide adequate grounds for the decision in this case. Rule 8(b) also requires that the party shall state in short and plain terms his or her defenses to each claim asserted against him or her. If Philadelphia Piers (D) had stated that their defense to the complaint was that they

Continued on next page.

were not the employers or owners of the personnel or machinery involved, Zielinski (P) would have been able to bring this action against the proper party. Philadelphia Piers (D) seemed to lack the good faith the federal rules require because they waited until the time of trial to raise their defense that Zielinski had sued the wrong party.

Quicknotes

COMPLAINT The initial pleading commencing litigation that sets forth a claim for relief.

FED. R. CIV. P. 8 Sets forth the general rules of pleading a claim for relief.

GENERAL DENIAL Type of pleading contradicting all the assertions of a former pleading.

Beeck v. Aquaslide 'N' Dive Corp.

Injured slide user (P) v. Slide manufacturer (D)

562 F.2d 537 (8th Cir. 1977)

NATURE OF CASE: Appeal from grant of leave to amend.

FACT SUMMARY: Beeck (P) was injured on a pool slide alleged to have been manufactured by Aquaslide 'N' Dive Corp. (Aquaslide) (D), and after Aquaslide (D) admitted manufacture in its answer, the district court granted it leave to amend to deny manufacture over Beeck's (P) objection.

RULE OF LAW

The opponent of a motion for leave to amend must show he or she will be prejudiced by the grant of leave under Fed. R. Civ. P. 15(a)[2].

FACTS: Beeck (P) was injured while using the slide at a social gathering at Kimberly Village, Davenport, Iowa. Beeck (P) then brought this action in district court under diversity jurisdiction alleging that Aquaslide 'N' Dive Corp. (Aquaslide) (D) was liable under theories of negligence, strict liability, and breach of implied warranty. Aquaslide (D) answered the complaint, admitting that it manufactured the slide in question in reliance upon the opinions of insurance investigators. The district court then granted Aquaslide (D) leave to amend the answer to deny this assertion and permitted a separate trial on the question of manufacture over the objection of Beeck (P). The jury found for Aquaslide (D) and the court entered summary judgment against Beeck (P). By the time of the amendment, the statute of limitations for Beeck's (P) cause of action had run, and Beeck (P) appealed.

ISSUE: Must the opponent of a motion for leave to amend show he or she will be prejudiced by the grant of leave under Fed. R. Civ. P. 15(a)[2]?

HOLDING AND DECISION: (Benson, J.) Yes. The opponent of a motion for leave to amend must show he or she will be prejudiced by the grant of leave under Fed. R. Civ. P. 15(a)[2]. Fed. R. Civ. P. 15(a)[2] provides that "leave shall be freely given when justice so requires." The grant or denial of such leave to amend is within the sound discretion of the trial judge. The party opposing the motion for leave must show he or she will be prejudiced by the grant of leave under Fed. R. Civ. P. 15(a)[2]. In this case, Aquaslide (D) relied upon the conclusions of three separate insurance companies and their investigators and were thus not negligent in determining the facts in question, and it was not an abuse of discretion to give Aquaslide (D) a chance to correct a fact disputed. Beeck (P) alleged that he was prejudiced because his action was foreclosed by the running of the statute of limitations. This argument required the trial judge to assume that Aquaslide (D) would prevail on the manufacturing issue, and the judge properly refused to so presume. Neither was the grant of separate trials improper. A substantial issue of material fact was raised that would exonerate Aquaslide (D) if resolved in its favor. There was thus no abuse of discretion. Affirmed.

ANALYSIS

Because of the running of the statute of limitations, it would be unlikely, if not impossible, that Beeck (P) would be able to move against any other party. The court had to counterbalance this injustice against that of precluding Aquaslide (D) from proving that it did not manufacture the slide that caused the injury. Since the amendment and the separate trial gave Beeck (P) a chance to disprove Aquaslide's (D) argument, and since the Federal Rules of Civil Procedure technically permitted the amendment and severance, the balance was struck in Aquaslide's (D) favor.

Quicknotes

AMENDMENT TO PLEADING The modification of a pleading either as a matter of course upon motion to the court or by consent of both parties; a party is entitled to change its pleading once as a matter of course before a responsive pleading has been served.

ISSUE OF MATERIAL FACT An issue or dispute regarding a fact that is legally relevant to a claim or cause of action that will, as a matter of substantive law, make a difference to the outcome reached in a given case. Also stated as "material issue of fact."

Moore v. Baker

Patient (P) v. Physician (D)

989 F.2d 1129 (11th Cir. 1993)

NATURE OF CASE: Appeal of denial of motion to amend pleading in nonconsent action.

FACT SUMMARY: Moore (P) initially alleged that Dr. Baker (D) violated the informed-consent law, but then sought to include a claim for medical malpractice.

RULE OF LAW

A claim that does not arise out of the same conduct, transaction, or occurrence as the original claim does not relate back to the original pleading.

FACTS: Moore (P) consulted Dr. Baker (D) to correct a blockage of her carotid artery. Baker (D) recommended surgery and warned Moore (P) of the risks. The operation left Moore (P) permanently disabled. Moore's (P) initial complaint alleged only a violation of Georgia's informed-consent law. The trial court granted Baker's (D) motion for summary judgment. The statute of limitations ran the day after Moore (P) filed the original complaint. Moore (P) then sought to amend the complaint to include a claim for negligence, asserting that the new claim should relate back to the date of the original complaint. The trial court denied Moore's (P) motion, and Moore (P) appealed.

ISSUE: Does a claim that does not arise out of the same conduct, transaction, or occurrence as the original claim relate back to the original pleading?

HOLDING AND DECISION: (Morgan, J.) No. A claim that does not arise out of the same conduct, transaction, or occurrence as the original claim does not relate back to the original pleading. In this case, the new claim arises out of alleged actions that are distinct in time and involve separate and distinct conduct. The failure-to-warn claim focused on actions prior to surgery, while the negligence claim focuses on actions during and post-surgery. Affirmed.

ANALYSIS

Whether the conduct, transaction, or occurrence in the amended complaint relates back to the original complaint to avoid the bar of a statute of limitations is a subjective test open to argument and interpretation. The role of the appellate court is to decide whether the trial court abused its discretion in applying this test to the facts of the case.

Quicknotes

AMENDMENT TO PLEADING The modification of a pleading either as a matter of course upon motion to the court or by consent of both parties; a party is entitled to change its pleading once as a matter of course before a responsive pleading has been served.

RELATION BACK DOCTRINE Doctrine that holds a party may not amend its pleading to set forth a new or different claim or defense unless it involves the subject matter of the original pleading; under Fed. R. Civ. P. 15(c), if a party amends its pleading as a matter of course before a responsive pleading is served, such amendment is said to relate back to the original pleading if it involves the subject matter of the original pleading.

Bonerb v. Richard J. Caron Foundation

Injured basketball player (P) v. Foundation (D)

159 F.R.D. 16 (W.D.N.Y. 1994)

NATURE OF CASE: Motion to amend complaint in personal-injury action.

FACT SUMMARY: After Bonerb (P) filed suit for injuries received on a basketball court while he was being treated at the Richard J. Caron Foundation (Foundation) (D), he sought to amend his complaint to add a cause of action for "counseling malpractice."

RULE OF LAW

When allegations in an amended complaint and the original complaint derive from the same nucleus of operative facts, the amended complaint relates back to the date of the original complaint.

FACTS: Bonerb (P) slipped and fell while playing basketball at the Richard J. Caron Foundation (Foundation) (D) while participating in the Foundation's (D) mandatory exercise program. Bonerb's (P) original complaint alleged the Foundation's (D) basketball court was negligently maintained. Bonerb (P) sought to amend the complaint to include a new claim for counseling malpractice. Bonerb (P) sought to relate back the malpractice claim to the date of the original complaint since the statute of limitations had expired for asserting a malpractice claim.

ISSUE: When allegations in an amended complaint and the original complaint derive from the same nucleus of operative facts, does the amended complaint relate back to the date of the original complaint?

HOLDING AND DECISION: (Heckmann, J.) Yes. When allegations in an amended complaint and the original complaint derive from the same nucleus of operative facts, the amended complaint relates back to the date of the original complaint. The determining factor is whether the facts stated in the original complaint put the defendant on notice of the claim that plaintiff later seeks to add. Here, Bonerb (P) is using the same factual allegations in the amended complaint as in the original complaint. Bonerb (P) has merely changed the legal theory upon which the claim is based. Motion to amend is granted.

ANALYSIS

Amendment to a pleading may occur in an answer as well as a complaint. Fed. R. Civ. P. 15(a) allows relation back for claims and defenses asserted in the original pleading or attempted to be set forth in the original pleading, which arose from the conduct, transaction, or occurrence of the original pleading.

Quicknotes

NUCLEUS OF OPERATIVE FACTS An underlying fact situation common to those pleadings asserting it.

RELATION BACK DOCTRINE Doctrine that holds that a party may not amend its pleading to set forth a new or different claim or defense unless it involves the subject matter of the original pleading; under Fed. R. Civ. P. 15(c), if a party amends its pleading as a matter of course before a responsive pleading is served, such amendment is said to relate back to the original pleading if it involves the subject matter of the original pleading.

CHAPTER 7

Discovery

Quick Reference Rules of Law

Zubulake v. UBS Warburg LLP

Former employee (P) v. Employer (D)

229 F.R.D. 422 (S.D.N.Y. 2003)

NATURE OF CASE: Action for sanctions for destruction of evidence.

FACT SUMMARY: Laura Zubulake (P) moved to sanction UBS Warburg LLP (D) for failure to produce relevant information and for late production of material.

RULE OF LAW

An attorney's duty to produce evidence is not discharged upon notification to the parties and witnesses that all possibly relevant evidence must be preserved for litigation.

FACTS: Laura Zubulake (P) moved to sanction UBS Warburg LLP (UBS) (D) for failure to produce relevant information and for late production of material. UBS (D) employees had deleted some e-mails and other electronic files that were relevant to Zubulake's (P) case against UBS (D). In addition, UBS's (D) lawyers failed to request certain information from one employee and to give the litigation hold instructions to another. They also did not communicate effectively about how the employees should maintain their computer files for litigation and about how to safeguard backup tapes that might have contained some of the deleted e-mails.

ISSUE: Is an attorney's duty to produce evidence discharged upon notification to the parties and witnesses that all possibly relevant evidence must be preserved for litigation?

HOLDING AND DECISION: (Scheindlin, J.) No. An attorney's duty to produce evidence is not discharged upon notification to the parties and witnesses that all possibly relevant evidence must be preserved for litigation. The attorney must issue a "litigation hold" at the outset of litigation and should periodically reissue it so that new employees are aware of it. The attorney should also communicate directly with key players in the litigation. And employees should be instructed by attorneys that they must produce electronic copies of their relevant active files, and that backup media must be identified and stored safely and separate from other, non-relevant backup material. But the attorney's role is still limited, and the ultimate responsibility for preserving evidence rests with the parties. [Here, UBS (D) acted willfully in destroying potentially relevant information, and sanctions were therefore warranted to put Zubulake (P) in the position she would have been in had UBS (D) faithfully discharged its discovery obligations. The jury was instructed to construe the missing e-mails in Zubulake's (P) favor, since most of the existing e-mails support her case.]

ANALYSIS

The court's goal in imposing sanctions was to put the plaintiff in the position where she would have been had the destruction of evidence not occurred. But in this case, there was other evidence that supported the plaintiff's case, and therefore the court instructed the jury to weigh the destroyed evidence against the defendant. A different result would occur, however, if there were not additional evidence supporting the plaintiff's case, even if all of the destroyed evidence would have supported her case.

Quicknotes

EVIDENTIARY FACTS Those facts necessary for the determination of the ultimate facts.

RELEVANT EVIDENCE Evidence having any tendency to prove or disprove a disputed fact.

Favale v. Roman Catholic Diocese of Bridgeport

Former employee (P) v. Former employer (D)

233 F.R.D. 243 (D. Conn. 2005)

NATURE OF CASE: Motions to compel and for a protective order in action for, inter alia, sexual harassment, retaliation, negligent hiring, and negligent supervision.

FACT SUMMARY: Maryann Favale (P), a former employee of the Roman Catholic Diocese of Bridgeport (the Diocese) (D) who claimed that her former supervisor, Sister Stobierski, sexually harassed Favale (P), sought to compel Stobierski to testify as to Stobierski's treatment for anger management, psychological and psychiatric conditions, and sought to compel the Diocese (D) to produce any records it had of any such treatment. The Diocese (D) sought a protective order barring such discovery.

RULE OF LAW

Discovery of highly personal information will not be compelled where it is not relevant to conduct alleged to have caused the plaintiff's harms.

FACTS: Maryann Favale (P) was an administrative assistant at a school run by the Roman Catholic Diocese of Bridgeport (the Diocese) (D). At some point, Sister Stobierski became the school's principal. Favale (P) brought suit alleging that Stobierski had sexually harassed her. She sought damages for sexual harassment, retaliation, defamation, intentional and negligent infliction of emotional distress, negligent hiring, negligent supervision, and other causes of action. Favale (P) moved to compel Stobierski to testify to any prior treatment she may have received for her alleged anger management history and psychological or psychiatric conditions. Favale (P) also move to compel the Diocese (D) to produce any records it had of any such treatment. The Diocese (D), asserting that the discovery sought by Favale (P) was irrelevant and privileged, moved for a protective order barring the discovery. Favale (P) countered that the discovery was relevant to the claims of negligent hiring and negligent supervision.

ISSUE: Will discovery of highly personal information be compelled where it is not relevant to conduct alleged to have caused the plaintiff's harms?

HOLDING AND DECISION: (Squatrito, J.) No. Discovery of highly personal information will not be compelled where it is not relevant to conduct alleged to have caused the plaintiff's harms. To prove a claim for negligent hiring, a plaintiff must show that he or she suffered harm as a result of the defendant's negligence in hiring an employee who was unfit or incompetent to perform the work for which the employee was hired, and that his or her injuries resulted from the employee's unfit or incompetent performance. To prove a negligent supervision claim, the plaintiff must prove that defendant knew or reasonably should have known of the employee's propensity to engage in the type of tortious conduct that caused the plaintiff's injuries. Here, Favale's (P) alleged injuries resulted from Stobierski's alleged repeated acts of sexual harassment—not from anger management or other psychological or psychiatric conditions. Accordingly, Stobierski's testimony as to those conditions would be irrelevant to the defense or claim of either party. Even if the Diocese (D) had been aware of Stobierski's alleged anger management history or psychological or psychiatric conditions, this knowledge would have no bearing on Favale's (P) claims for negligent supervision and negligent hiring, because the wrongful conduct of which the Diocese (D) would have had notice of was not the same type of wrongful conduct that caused Favale (P) harm. For the same reasons, if the Diocese (D) possessed records relating to Stobierski's alleged conditions, these records would not establish Stobierski's propensity for the type of behavior that caused Favale (P) harm, because they would not demonstrate a propensity for sexual harassment. For these reasons, Favale's (P) motion to compel is denied, and the Diocese's (D) motion for a protective order barring the type of discovery sought by Favale (P) is granted, especially since the type of information Favale (P) is seeking is "profoundly personal."

ANALYSIS

This case illustrates the principle that there are boundaries to discovery. A court can limit discovery if it determines, among other things, the discovery (1) is unreasonably cumulative or duplicative; (2) is obtainable from another source that is more convenient, less burdensome, or less expensive; or (3) if the burden or expense of the proposed discovery outweighs its likely benefit. In addition, a district court enjoys broad discretion when resolving discovery disputes. When exercising such discretion, the court should—as the court did here—determine the relevance of discovery requests, assess oppressiveness, and weigh these factors in deciding whether discovery should be compelled.

Quicknotes

DISCOVERY Pretrial procedure during which one party makes certain information available to the other.

Cerrato v. Nutribullet, LLC

Individual (P) v. Corporation (D)

2017 WL 3608266 (M.D. Fla. 2017)

NATURE OF CASE: Consideration of plaintiff's motion to compel production of the prior accident reports relating to the product that allegedly caused injuries to the plaintiff.

FACT SUMMARY: Phyllis Cerrato (P) was allegedly injured when a blender designed by Nutribullet (D) exploded while she was operating it.

RULE OF LAW

Courts will generally find discovery requests that do not include time limitations or do not accurately define the type of information requested to be overbroad and not proportional to the needs of the case.

FACTS: Phyllis Cerrato (P) was allegedly injured when a blender designed by Nutribullet, LLC (D) exploded while she was operating it. The alleged defect in the product was that it could not be turned off. The explosion caused hot liquids to burn Cerrato (P) and caused property damage to Cerrato's (P) kitchen. Cerrato (P) brought a products liability action against Nutribullet (D). During discovery, Cerrato (P) requested any and all documents relating to any injuries caused by the product at any time. She also requested any consumer complaints relating to the product. Nutribullet (D) objected to both requests on the grounds they were overbroad and unduly burdensome. Cerrato (P) filed a motion to compel the discovery.

ISSUE: Will courts generally find discovery requests that do not include time limitations or do not accurately define the type of information requested to be overbroad and not proportional to the needs of the case?

HOLDING AND DECISION: (Sneed, J.) Yes. Courts will generally find discovery requests that do not include time limitations or do not accurately define the type of information requested to be overbroad and not proportional to the needs of the case. In this case, Cerrato's (P) requests are not proportional. They include no time limitations, no limitation on the type of injuries caused in the past by the product or the nature of the defect in those prior cases. Accordingly, the court orders that Nutribullet (D) produce all accident reports and complaints that relate to incidents where the product could not be turned off. The time frame shall be five years prior to the date of the incident to the date of the filing of the complaint. Nutribullet (D) shall be allowed to redact the consumer names on those complaints, as that information is irrelevant to the claims at issue. Motion granted in part and denied in part.

ANALYSIS

Trial court judges at both the federal and state levels have broad discretion to determine the scope of discovery in a case. They are closest to the matter and are familiar with the claims as well as the amount of discovery potentially available in the case. Appellate court judges do not typically overturn trial court judges' rulings on discovery matters, unless there is an abuse of discretion, which is a very difficult standard to prove.

Quicknotes

DISCOVERY Pretrial procedure during which one party makes certain information available to the other.

PRODUCTS LIABILITY The legal liability of manufacturers and sellers for damages and injuries suffered by buyers, users, or bystanders because of defects in goods purchased.

Wagoner v. Lewis Gale Medical Center, LLC

Individual (P) v. Corporation (D)

2016 WL 3893135 (W.D. Va. 2016)

NATURE OF CASE: Consideration of plaintiff's motion to compel production of e-mails from the defendant.

FACT SUMMARY: Lewis Gale Medical Center, LLC (D) terminated Wagoner (P), a security guard, after two months on the job.

RULE OF LAW

Relevant electronically stored information may not be discoverable if the party in possession can show the information is not reasonably accessible because of undue burden or cost.

FACTS: Lewis Gale Medical Center, LLC (Lewis Gale) (D) terminated Wagoner (P), a security guard, after two months on the job. Wagoner (P) filed suit alleging that Lewis Gale (D) wrongfully terminated him in violation of the Americans with Disabilities Act, based upon his dyslexia. During discovery, Wagoner (P) requested four months of documents and e-mails from two other custodians at the hospital. The request sought documents using specific search terms such as "Wagoner," "dyslexia," "reading," and "copying," among others. Lewis Gale (D) objected on the grounds it would cost them almost $45,000 to search its computer systems and then review any documents with those search terms. It alleged there were over 30,000 e-mails that would be responsive to the request. Wagoner (P) filed a motion to compel.

ISSUE: May relevant electronically stored information not be discoverable if the party in possession can show the information is not reasonably accessible because of undue burden or cost?

HOLDING AND DECISION: (Ballou, J.) Yes. Relevant electronically stored information may not be discoverable if the party in possession can show the information is not reasonably accessible because of undue burden or cost. Fed. R. Civ. P. 26(b)(2)(B). Courts also can order cost sharing in particular cases. In this matter, Lewis Gale (D) has not shown that the information Wagoner (P) is seeking is not reasonably accessible. Whether production of documents is unduly burdensome or expensive depends on whether the data is physically accessible. Lewis Gale (D) has not shown the information has to be restored or reconstructed in any manner. The issue here is that Lewis Gale (D) employs a computer system that does not preserve any e-mails beyond three days. This makes it costly for Lewis Gale (D) to search and find e-mails when faced with legal claims. That Lewis Gale (D) chose a system that makes it expensive for them to find the documents should not be held against Wagoner (P). Accordingly, Lewis Gale (D) must produce the records requested. For the same reason, cost shifting is not appropriate and the principle that each party bears the costs of producing its own discovery shall apply. Motion to compel granted.

ANALYSIS

In this matter, the discovery request was limited in time to four months and sought e-mails with a limited set of search parameters. Once the court finds that a request is relevant and proportional, it will be difficult for the other party to claim that cost alone prohibits the production of the documents.

Quicknotes

DISCOVERY Pretrial procedure during which one party makes certain information available to the other.

WRONGFUL TERMINATION Unlawful termination of an individual's employment.

Rengifo v. Erevos Enterprises, Inc.

Former employee (P) v. Former employer (D)

2007 WL 894376 (S.D.N.Y. Mar. 20, 2007)

NATURE OF CASE: Motion for protective order in action to recover unpaid overtime wages.

FACT SUMMARY: Willy Rengifo (P), who brought an action against his former employer, Erevos Enterprises, Inc. (Erevos) (D), to recover unpaid overtime wages, sought a protective order barring discovery related to his immigration status, social security number, and authorization to work in the United States.

RULE OF LAW

In an action to enforce employment rights, a protective order barring discovery related to the plaintiff's immigration status, social security number, and authorization to work in the United States will be granted where, at most, such discovery is related to collateral issues.

FACTS: Willy Rengifo (P), a former employee of Erevos Enterprises, Inc. (Erevos) (D), brought suit against Erevos (D) to recover unpaid overtime wages under federal and state law. Erevos (D) sought discovery related to Rengifo's (P) immigration status, authorization to work in the United States, and social security number, contending that these were relevant to his right to recover unpaid wages, as well as to his credibility. Rengifo (P) sought a protective order, asserting that the discovery sought by Erevos (D) was irrelevant to his right to overtime pay, and that the intimidating effect of requiring disclosure of immigration status was sufficient to establish "good cause" for the protective order since the question of immigration status went only to a collateral issue. Erevos (D) also argued that because (1) Rengifo (P) had failed to produce a complete set of pay stubs that reflected all of the compensation he had received, and (2) he had not produced any records regarding the number of hours he had worked on a weekly basis, discovery of documents containing his tax identification number or social security number, such as tax returns, was necessary and relevant to obtain this information.

ISSUE: In an action to enforce employment rights, will a protective order barring discovery related to the plaintiff's immigration status, social security number, and authorization to work in the United States be granted where, at most, such discovery is related to collateral issues?

HOLDING AND DECISION: (Ellis, J.) Yes. In an action to enforce employment rights, a protective order barring discovery related to the plaintiff's immigration status, social security number, and authorization to work in the United States will be granted where, at most, such discovery is related to collateral issues. As to discovery regarding Rengifo's (P) immigration status, courts have recognized the in terrorem effect of inquiring into a party's immigration status and authorization to work in the U.S. when such inquiry is irrelevant to any material claim, because it presents a danger of intimidation that would inhibit plaintiffs in pursuing their rights. Here, Rengifo's (P) immigration status and authority to work is a collateral issue, so that a protective order is necessary to prevent him from being intimidated to the point where he would rather withdraw from the suit than face potential deportation or criminal charges. Additionally, Rengifo (P) seeks to prevent disclosure of his social security number or tax identification number. These identifying data are irrelevant to Rengifo's (P) claims for unpaid overtime wages, and, in any event, Erevos (D) possesses relevant data on hours and compensation, and there is no reason to assume that its records are less reliable than any records maintained by Rengifo (P). Erevos (D) also argues that by applying for a job and providing his social security number, Rengifo (P) represented that he was a legal resident, and that Erevos (D) is entitled to test the truthfulness of that information. Erevos (D) further argues that if Rengifo (P) filed tax returns, this information would be relevant to his overtime claim, but if he failed to file tax returns, this fact would affect the veracity of statements he would potentially make at trial. Although credibility is always an issue, it seems that Erevos's (D) attempt to discover tax identification numbers on the basis of testing credibility is a back-door attempt to learn of immigration status. The opportunity to test the credibility of a party based on representations made when seeking employment does not outweigh the chilling effect that disclosure of immigration status has on employees seeking to enforce their rights. If an employee is undocumented, allowing an employer to inquire into immigration status in employment cases would allow the employer to implicitly raise threats of deportation or criminal prosecution when a worker reports illegal practices. Even limiting disclosure of immigrant status to the case at bar through a confidentiality agreement would not eliminate the danger of intimidation and of destroying the cause of action. In sum, giving Erevos (D) opportunity to test the credibility of Rengifo does not outweigh the public interest in allowing employees to enforce their rights. For these reasons, Rengifo's (P) application for a protective order is granted.

Continued on next page.

ANALYSIS

According to Rule 26(b)(1) of the Federal Rules of Civil Procedure, a party "may obtain discovery regarding any matter, not privileged, which is relevant to the subject matter involved in the pending action." However, Rule 26(c) authorizes courts, for good cause, to "make any order which justice requires to protect a party or person from annoyance, embarrassment, oppression, or undue burden or expense, including . . . that certain matters not be inquired into, or that the scope of the disclosure or discovery be limited to certain matters . . ." The burden is upon the party seeking non-disclosure or a protective order to show good cause. Thus, in this case, Rengifo (P) carried the burden of showing there was good cause for the protective order he was requesting by showing that the damage and prejudice that would result to him if discovery into his immigration status were permitted far outweighed its probative value.

Quicknotes

DISCOVERY Pretrial procedure during which one party makes certain information available to the other.

PROTECTIVE ORDER Court order protecting a party against potential abusive treatment through use of the legal process.

Hickman v. Taylor

Representative of deceased (P) v. Tug owner (D)

329 U.S. 495 (1947)

NATURE OF CASE: Action for damages for wrongful death.

FACT SUMMARY: Five crew members drowned when a tug sank. In anticipation of litigation, the attorney for Taylor (D), the tug owner, interviewed the survivors. Hickman (P), as representative of one of the deceased, brought this action and tried by means of discovery to obtain copies of the statements Taylor's (D) attorney obtained from the survivors.

RULE OF LAW

A party seeking to discover material obtained by an adverse party's counsel in preparation for possible litigation has a burden to show a justification for such production.

FACTS: Five of nine crew members drowned when a tug sank. A public hearing was held at which the four survivors were examined. Their testimony was recorded and was made available to all interested parties. A short time later, the attorney for Taylor (D), the tug owner, interviewed the survivors, in preparation for possible litigation. He also interviewed other persons believed to have information on the accident. Ultimately, claims were brought by representatives of all five of the deceased. Four were settled. Hickman (P), the fifth claimant, brought this action. He filed interrogatories asking for any statements taken from crew members as well as any oral or written statements, records, reports, or other memoranda made concerning any matter relative to the towing operation, the tug's sinking, the salvaging and repair of the tug, and the death of the deceased. Taylor (D) refused to summarize or set forth the material on the grounds that it was protected by the attorney-client privilege.

ISSUE: Does a party seeking to discover material obtained by an adverse party's counsel in preparation for possible litigation have a burden to show a justification for such production?

HOLDING AND DECISION: (Murphy, J.) Yes. A party seeking to discover material obtained by an adverse party's counsel in preparation for possible litigation has a burden to show a justification for such production. Material obtained by counsel in preparation for litigation is the work product of the lawyer, and while such material is not protected by the attorney-client privilege, it is not discoverable on mere demand without a showing of necessity or justification. The deposition-discovery rules are to be accorded a broad and liberal treatment, since mutual knowledge of all the relevant facts gathered by both parties is essential to proper litigation. But discovery does have ultimate and necessary boundaries. Limitations arise upon a showing of bad faith or harassment or when the inquiry seeks material that is irrelevant or privileged. In this case, the material sought by Hickman (P) is not protected by the attorney-client privilege. However, such material as that sought here does constitute the work product of the lawyer. The general policy against invading the privacy of an attorney in performing his or her various duties is so well recognized and so essential to the orderly working of our legal system that the party seeking work-product material has a burden to show reasons to justify such production. Interviews, statements, memoranda, correspondence, briefs, mental impressions, etc., obtained in the course of preparation for possible or anticipated litigation fall within the work product. Such material is not free from discovery in all cases. Where relevant and nonprivileged facts remain hidden in an attorney's file and where production of those facts is essential to the preparation of one's case, discovery may be had. But there must be a showing of necessity and justification. In this case, Hickman (P) seeks discovery of oral and written statements of witnesses whose identity is well known and whose availability to Hickman (P) appears unimpaired. Here no attempt was made to show why it was necessary that Taylor's (D) attorney produce the material. No reasons were given to justify this invasion of the attorney's privacy. Hickman's (P) counsel admitted he wanted the statements only to help him prepare for trial. That is insufficient to warrant an exception to the policy of protecting the privacy of an attorney's professional activities.

CONCURRENCE: (Jackson, J.) A common-law trial is and always should be an adversary proceeding. Discovery was hardly intended to enable a learned profession to perform its functions either without wits or on wits borrowed from the adversary. I can conceive of no practice more demoralizing to the bar than to require a lawyer to write out and deliver to the adversary an account of what witnesses have told him.

ANALYSIS

The *Hickman* decision left open a number of questions as to the scope of the work product doctrine and the showing needed to discover work product material. In 1970, Fed. R. Civ. P. 26(b)(3) was added to deal with the

Continued on next page.

discovery of work product. It provides that documents and tangible things that were prepared in anticipation of litigation or for trial are discoverable only upon a showing that the party seeking such materials has substantial need of them and that he or she is unable without undue hardship to obtain the substantial equivalent of the materials by other means. The rule states mental impressions, conclusions, opinions, or legal theories of an attorney or other representative of a party are to be protected against disclosure.

Quicknotes

ATTORNEY-CLIENT PRIVILEGE A doctrine precluding the admission into evidence of confidential communications between an attorney and the client made in the course of obtaining professional assistance.

ATTORNEY WORK PRODUCT DOCTRINE A doctrine excluding from discovery work performed by an attorney in preparation for litigation.

DEPOSITION A pretrial discovery procedure whereby oral or written questions are asked by one party of the opposing party or of a witness for the opposing party under oath in preparation for litigation.

DISCOVERY Pretrial procedure during which one party makes certain information available to the other.

Thompson v. The Haskell Co.

Sexually harassed employee (P) v. Employer (D)

65 F. Empl. Prac. Cas. (BNA) 1088 (M.D. Fla. 1994)

NATURE OF CASE: Motion for protective order in sexual-harassment suit.

FACT SUMMARY: Thompson (P) sought to protect her psychologist's report from discovery.

RULE OF LAW

Under exceptional circumstances, if it is impractical for the party seeking discovery to obtain facts or opinions on the same subject by other means, a party may, by interrogatories or by deposition, discover information by an expert who has been retained or specially employed by another party in anticipation of litigation and who is not to be called as a witness.

FACTS: Thompson (P) sued The Haskell Co. (D) and Zona (D), a supervisor of The Haskell Co. (D), alleging sexual harassment and that her employment with The Haskell Co. (D) was terminated when she refused to acquiesce to Zona's (D) advances. Thompson's (P) former counsel employed Dr. Lucas, a psychologist, to perform a diagnostic review and personality profile ten days after Thompson (P) was terminated. Thompson (P) sought an order to protect the psychological records possessed by Dr. Lucas.

ISSUE: Under exceptional circumstances, if it is impractical for the party seeking discovery to obtain facts or opinions on the same subject by other means, may a party, by interrogatories or by deposition, discover information by an expert who has been retained or specially epmployed by another party in anticipation of litigation and who is not to be called as a witness?

HOLDING AND DECISION: (Snyder, J.) Yes. Under exceptional circumstances, if it is impractical for the party seeking discovery to obtain facts or opinions on the same subject by other means, a party may, by interrogatories or by deposition, discover information by an expert who has been retained or specially employed by another party in anticipation of litigation and who is not to be called as a witness. Here, Dr. Lucas's report was made ten days after Thompson (P) was terminated and is the only evidence available that is probative of Thompson's (P) emotional state at that time. Motion denied.

ANALYSIS

Thompson (P) did not file her complaint until several months after she was terminated. Thus, opposing counsel had no opportunity to obtain psychological information from Thompson (P) shortly after her termination that would be probative of her emotional state during that time. This factor provided the exceptional circumstance in the present case.

Quicknotes

DEPOSITION A pretrial discovery procedure whereby oral or written questions are asked by one party of the opposing party or of a witness for the opposing party under oath in preparation for litigation.

DISCOVERY Pretrial procedure during which one party makes certain information available to the other.

EXPERT WITNESS A witness providing testimony at trial who is specially qualified regarding the particular subject matter involved.

INTERROGATORY A method of pretrial discovery in which written questions are provided by one party to another who must respond in writing under oath.

Chiquita International Ltd. v. M/V Bolero Reefer

Shipper (P) v. Cargo carrier (D)

1994 U.S. Dist. LEXIS 5820 (S.D.N.Y. 1994)

NATURE OF CASE: Motion to compel discovery.

FACT SUMMARY: International Reefer Ltd. (D), a carrier, sought to compel discovery of a marine surveyor who had evaluated its loading cranes and side ports.

RULE OF LAW

A nontestifying expert may not be subject to discovery unless exceptional circumstances apply.

FACTS: Shipper Chiquita International Ltd. (Chiquita) (P) sued International Reefer Services, S.A. (D), a cargo carrier, for cargo loss and damage. Chiquita (P) alleged that loading cranes and side ports on International Reefer's (D) carrier failed to function properly, which prevented the carrier from shipping the full load of Chiquita (P) bananas to Germany and unloading them before spoilage in accord with their contract. International Reefer (D) requested an order compelling discovery from Winer, a marine surveyor Chiquita (P) had employed to inspect the carrier upon arrival in Germany. International Reefer (D) asserted that Winer was a fact witness rather than an expert and that even if Winer were a nontestifying expert, exceptional circumstances existed to compel discovery. Chiquita (P) objected.

ISSUE: May a nontestifying expert be subject to discovery if exceptional circumstances do not apply?

HOLDING AND DECISION: (Francis, J.) No. A nontestifying expert may not be subject to discovery unless exceptional circumstances apply. A fact witness is a witness whose information was obtained in the normal course of business; however, a nontestifying expert is a person hired to make an evaluation in connection with expected litigation. Winer was hired by Chiquita (P) to make an observation in anticipation of litigation; thus, he is a nontestifying expert. Because International Reefer (D) could have employed its own expert to examine its carrier, and Chiquita (P) did not prevent another expert from being retained, no exceptional circumstances apply here. Application for Winer's deposition is denied.

ANALYSIS

It is often not clear whether a person is a fact witness or nontestifying expert; thus, this is a favorite topic for law school examinations. Another favorite topic is determining if exceptional circumstances apply that would warrant compelling discovery from a nontestifying expert.

Quicknotes

DEPOSITION A pretrial discovery procedure whereby oral or written questions are asked by one party of the opposing party or a witness for the opposing party under oath in preparation for litigation.

DISCOVERY Pretrial procedure during which one party makes certain information available to the other.

EXPERT WITNESS A witness providing testimony at trial who is specially qualified regarding the particular subject matter involved.

Mueller v. Swift

Individual (P) v. Individuals (D)

2017 WL 3058027 (D. Colo. 2017)

NATURE OF CASE: Consideration of defendants' motion for sanctions against the plaintiff due to plaintiff's alleged spoliation of evidence.

FACT SUMMARY: David Mueller (P), a radio disc jockey, brought claims against Taylor Swift (D) and his employer for tortious interference with his employment contract after the employer terminated him because of allegations Swift (D) made relating to inappropriate touching by Mueller (P) during a photo opportunity.

RULE OF LAW

A court may order sanctions or an adverse inference where a party has a duty to preserve evidence because it knew litigation was imminent and the other party was prejudiced by the destruction or loss of the evidence at issue.

FACTS: Prior to one of her concerts, Taylor Swift (D) attended a backstage photo opportunity with David Mueller (P). Swift (D) later alleged to Mueller's (P) employer, radio station KYGO (D), that Mueller (P) inappropriately touched her buttocks under her dress during the shoot. The following day, Mueller (P) met with his superiors, Eddie Haskell (D) and Robert Call (D), to discuss the allegations. Unbeknownst to them, Mueller (P) recorded the entire two-hour conversation. KYGO (D) terminated Mueller (P) on the grounds that Mueller (P) had changed his version of events that he did not touch Swift (D) as alleged to a new version that it was only incidental. Mueller (P) brought suit against the defendants for tortious interference with his employment contract. Regarding the recording, Mueller (P) edited down the recording and sent only clips of it to his attorney. Mueller (P) then allegedly spilled coffee on the laptop that contained the full recording and it could not be preserved. During discovery, the defendants filed this motion for sanctions based on Mueller's (P) spoliation of evidence by not preserving a copy of the entire recording.

ISSUE: May a court order sanctions or an adverse inference where a party has a duty to preserve evidence because it knew litigation was imminent and the other party was prejudiced by the destruction or loss of the evidence at issue?

HOLDING AND DECISION: (Martínez, J.) Yes. A court may order sanctions or an adverse inference where a party has a duty to preserve evidence because it knew litigation was imminent and the other party was prejudiced by the destruction or loss of the evidence at issue. Two factors are paramount in this scenario: (1) the degree of culpability of the party that did not preserve the evidence; and (2) the actual degree of prejudice to the other parties. Mueller (P) does not dispute he had a duty to preserve the entire recording. He clearly knew or should have known that litigation was imminent. It is very likely Mueller (P) was aware litigation was possible and that is the reason he created the recording. The recording is also relevant to Mueller's (P) claims that Haskell (D) and Call (D) improperly interfered with his employment relationship with KYGO (D). The recording likely contained evidence that would tend to prove or disprove that claim. The recording could also potentially prove whether Mueller (P) did indeed change his story while speaking with Haskell (D) and Call (D). The spoliation of evidence also prejudiced the defendants. If the recording had been preserved, it would have saved time and expense during discovery and allowed for better preparation for trial. Regarding culpability, there is not enough evidence for the court to find that Mueller (P) acted in bad faith, warranting the issuance of an adverse inference instruction at trial. Nor will the court characterize the loss as mere negligence. The court cannot find that Mueller (P) acted in bad faith because the record does not establish that he acted with intent to deprive the other parties of evidence. However, Mueller (P) did alter the recording to preserve evidence that was helpful to his claims. Accordingly, there will [be] no instruction of an adverse inference at trial. To be fair, the defendants will be able to cross examine Muller (P) during trial about his (P) spoliation of the recording. This will allow the jury to make its own assessment of the degree of Mueller's (P) culpability and the prejudice to the defendants. If the jury believes Mueller (P) acted in bad faith, it will draw its own adverse inferences. Mueller's (P) credibility is central to his claims and the credibility of witnesses at trial falls within the province of the jury, not the court. The motion for spoliation of evidence is granted, but the defendants' request for an adverse inference instruction is denied.

ANALYSIS

The adverse inference instruction typically states to a jury it must find that the entirety of a lost or destroyed piece of evidence would have been unfavorable to the party guilty of the spoliation. In extreme cases, courts may even dismiss a plaintiff's entire case if it finds the

Continued on next page.

plaintiff acted in bad faith and the defendants were so prejudiced by the loss of evidence that they are unable to defend the claims.

Quicknotes

ADVERSE INFERENCE A harmful conclusion made by the fact-finder from a party's not producing evidence that the party has within its control.

BAD FAITH Conduct that is intentionally misleading or deceptive.

SANCTIONS A penalty imposed in order to ensure compliance with a statute or regulation.

SPOLIATION OF EVIDENCE When a party has a duty to preserve evidence because it knew litigation was imminent and the other party was prejudiced by the destruction or loss of the evidence at issue.

TORTIOUS INTERFERENCE WITH CONTRACTUAL RELATIONSHIP An intentional tort whereby a defendant intentionally elicits the breach of a valid contract resulting in damages.

Security National Bank of Sioux City v. Abbott Laboratories

[Parties not identified.]

299 F.R.D. 595 (N.D. Iowa 2014) *rev'd sub nom. Security Natl. Bank of Sioux City v. Day,* 800 F.3d 936 (8th Cir. 2015)

NATURE OF CASE: Attorney sanctions for discovery abuses in action for products liability.

FACT SUMMARY: As attorney sanctions for an unwarranted number of "obstructionist" objections and interruptions, as well as coaching, that an attorney made during depositions, the judge ordered the attorney to write and create a video that could serve as a guide to other attorneys for avoiding the obstructionist conduct the attorney had engaged in.

RULE OF LAW

Where a judge has determined that counsel has engaged in discovery abuse, the judge may specially tailor a sanction designed to deter the specific abuses the attorney has engaged in.

FACTS: A district judge who was reviewing depositions in a products liability case determined that one of the attorneys in the case (whom the judge called "Counsel") had engaged in obstructionist conduct by making hundreds of unnecessary and meritless objections and interruptions, as well as coaching. The judge determined that sanctions were appropriate. The judge, while believing that substantial monetary sanctions would be appropriate, felt that these would not serve as well as a specially tailored sanction to deter the attorney, and other attorneys, from engaging in the type of obstructionist conduct the attorney had exhibited. Accordingly, the judge ordered the attorney to write and create a video that could serve as a guide to other attorneys for avoiding the obstructionist conduct the attorney had engaged in. [The judge's holding and decision elaborates the judge's rationale and details the specifics of the sanction.]

ISSUE: Where a judge has determined that counsel has engaged in discovery abuse, may the judge specially tailor a sanction designed to deter the specific abuses the attorney has engaged in?

HOLDING AND DECISION: (Bennett, J.) Yes. Where a judge has determined that counsel has engaged in discovery abuse, the judge may specially tailor a sanction designed to deter the specific abuses the attorney has engaged in. Based on Counsel's deposition conduct, the court would be well within its discretion to impose substantial monetary sanctions on Counsel. However, the court is less interested in negatively affecting Counsel's pocketbook than in positively affecting Counsel's obstructive deposition practices. The court also is interested in deterring others who might be inclined to comport themselves similarly to Counsel. Deterrence is especially important given that so many litigators are trained to make obstructionist objections. In light of this goal, the following sanction is imposed: Counsel must write and produce a training video in which Counsel, or another partner in Counsel's firm, appears and explains the holding and rationale of this opinion, and provides specific steps lawyers must take to comply with its rationale in future depositions in any federal and state court. The lawyer in the video must state that the video is being produced and distributed pursuant to a federal court's sanction order regarding a partner in the firm, but the lawyer need not state the name of the partner, the case the sanctions arose under, or the court issuing this order. Upon completing the video, Counsel must file it with this court, under seal, for the court's review and approval. If and when the court approves the video Counsel must (1) notify certain lawyers at Counsel's firm about the video via e-mail and (2) provide those lawyers with access to the video. The lawyers who must receive this notice and access include each lawyer at Counsel's firm—including branch offices worldwide—who engages in federal or state litigation or who works in any practice group in which at least two of the lawyers have filed an appearance in any state or federal case in the United States. After providing these lawyers with notice of and access to the video, Counsel must file in this court, under seal, (1) an affidavit certifying that Counsel complied with this order and received no assistance (other than technical help or help from the lawyer appearing in the video) in creating the video's content and (2) a copy of the e-mail notifying the appropriate lawyers in Counsel's firm about the video. Failure to comply with this order within 90 days may result in additional sanctions.

ANALYSIS

The Federal Rules of Civil Procedure specifically acknowledge that one function of discovery sanctions should be deterrence. The advisory committee notes (1983 amendments) to Fed. R. Civ. P. 26, state that "Sanctions to deter discovery abuse would be more effective if they were diligently applied not merely to penalize those whose conduct may be deemed to warrant such a sanction, but to deter those who might be tempted to such conduct in the absence of such a deterrent." On appeal, notwithstanding that court of appeals found that the district judge's goal of deterring other attorneys was proper, that the judge had the discretion to raise the matter sua sponte,

Continued on next page.

and that the specially-crafted sanction was not inappropriate, the court of appeals reversed, on the grounds that the judge's sanction—which came almost two years after the depositions at issue—had not been imposed within a time frame that had a nexus to the behavior sought to be deterred, and because the attorney being sanctioned had not been provided with notice of the specially-tailored sanction in a manner that would have enabled the attorney to respond. See *Sec. Natl. Bank of Sioux City v. Abbott Labs.*, 800 F.3d 936 (8th Cir. 2015).

Quicknotes

OBSTRUCTION To interfere with, hinder, or delay.

SUA SPONTE An action taken by the court by its own motion and without the suggestion of one of the parties.

CHAPTER 8

Resolution Without Trial

Quick Reference Rules of Law

Peralta v. Heights Medical Center

Employer/guarantor (P) v. Hospital (D)

485 U.S. 80 (1988)

NATURE OF CASE: Review of summary judgment dismissing bill of review.

FACT SUMMARY: A trial court refused to set aside a default entered after improper service when Peralta (P) could not show a meritorious defense to the action.

RULE OF LAW

A meritorious defense is not required to set aside a default entered after improper service.

FACTS: Heights Medical Center, Inc. (Heights Medical) (D) sued Peralta (P) on a guarantee to pay medical expenses on an employee of Peralta (P). Peralta (P) was improperly served. Heights Medical (D) nonetheless entered a default on Peralta's (P) failure to respond and a judgment lien was placed on certain real estate belonging to Peralta (P). The property was sold at a marshal's sale at a large discount. Peralta (P), upon discovering the sale, filed an action to void the sale and have the default set aside, as the service was invalid. The trial court granted summary judgment, dismissing the action, holding that Peralta (P) had to show meritorious defense to the underlying action, which he could not do. The Texas Court of Appeals affirmed. The United States Supreme Court accepted review.

ISSUE: Is a meritorious defense required to set aside a default entered after improper service?

HOLDING AND DECISION: (White, J.) No. A meritorious defense is not required to set aside a default entered after improper service. It is basic to due process before a judgment can be entered against a person that he or she be given legally sufficient notice of the action and be given an opportunity to defend. It is no defense to a due process claim that the defendant would have lost on the merits. There are avenues that can be employed by a litigant in a losing posture, such as settling or impleading other parties. For a defendant to do this, he or she must have notice of the suit. Here, Peralta (P) was not given such notice, and due process therefore demands that the default be set aside. Reversed.

ANALYSIS

Various avenues exist to challenge a default. The most direct manner is to move for relief in the same action in which the default is entered. However, most states place time limitations on this, as did Texas in this instance. This forced Peralta (P) to file a bill of review, a collateral proceeding.

Quicknotes

DEFAULT JUDGMENT A judgment entered against a defendant due to the defendant's failure to appear in a court or defend him- or herself against the allegations of the opposing party.

SERVICE OF PROCESS The communication of reasonable notice of a court proceeding to a defendant in order to provide the defendant with an opportunity to be heard.

Kalinauskas v. Wong

Former employee (P) v. Employer (D)

151 F.R.D. 363 (D. Nev. 1993)

NATURE OF CASE: Motion for protective order.

FACT SUMMARY: Caesars Palace Hotel & Casino (D) sought to enforce a confidential settlement agreement with a former employee.

RULE OF LAW

A protective order or confidentiality agreement can be modified to place private litigants in a position they would otherwise reach only after repetition of another's discovery if modification would not tangibly prejudice substantial rights of the party opposing modification.

FACTS: Kalinauskas (P) sued Desert Palace, Inc. (D), doing business as Caesars Palace Hotel & Casino (Caesars) (D), for sexual discrimination. She sought to depose Thomas, a former Caesars (D) employee, who had sued Caesars (D) for sexual harassment the previous year. Thomas had settled her claim with Caesars (D) and agreed to a confidential settlement agreement that stated in part that Thomas "shall not discuss any aspect of plaintiff's employment at Caesars other than to state the dates of her employment and her job title." Caesars (D) sought a protective order to enforce the confidential settlement agreement and to bar Thomas's deposition. Kalinauskas (P) opposed the order.

ISSUE: Can a protective order or confidentiality agreement be modified to place private litigants in a position they would otherwise reach only after repetition of another's discovery if modification would not tangibly prejudice substantial rights of the party opposing modification?

HOLDING AND DECISION: (Johnston, J.) Yes. A protective order or confidentiality agreement can be modified to place private litigants in a position they would otherwise reach only after repetition of another's discovery if modification would not tangibly prejudice substantial rights of the party opposing modification. Here, Kalinauskas's (P) claim duplicates Thomas's claim both factually and legally. Thus, to force Kalinauskas (P) to duplicate all of Thomas's work would be wasteful. The protective order is granted to the extent that during the deposition of Thomas no information regarding the settlement itself may be disclosed and is denied as to all other aspects. Protective order granted in part and denied in part.

ANALYSIS

The party seeking to enforce a protective order against a party seeking discovery information has the burden of showing that allowing modification of the order would substantially prejudice that party's rights. As the case above indicates, this burden could be met by showing that an applicable privilege applies to the information sought to be disclosed or that the party would suffer potential injury or prejudice if the information were to be disclosed.

Quicknotes

DISCOVERY Pretrial procedure during which one party makes certain information available to the other.

PROTECTIVE ORDER Court order protecting a party against potential abusive treatment through use of the legal process.

Ferguson v. Countrywide Credit Industries, Inc.

Employee (P) v. Employer (D)

298 F.3d 778 (9th Cir. 2002)

NATURE OF CASE: Appeal of denial of motion to compel arbitration.

FACT SUMMARY: Misty Ferguson (P) sued Countrywide Credit Industries, Inc. (Countrywide) (D) and her supervisor for sexual harassment, retaliation, and hostile work environment, and Countrywide (D) moved to compel the matter to arbitration. The district court denied Countrywide's (D) motion.

RULE OF LAW

An arbitration agreement is unconscionable, and therefore unenforceable, where it is a prerequisite to employment, job applicants are not permitted to modify the terms of the agreement, and the terms are one sided, favoring the employer.

FACTS: Misty Ferguson (P) sued Countrywide Credit Industries, Inc. (Countrywide) (D) and her supervisor for sexual harassment, retaliation, and hostile work environment. Countrywide (D) moved to compel the matter to arbitration pursuant to an employment contract, which required Ferguson (P) to arbitrate her claims. The district court refused to compel arbitration, holding that the arbitration agreement was unenforceable under the doctrine of unconscionability.

ISSUE: Is an arbitration agreement unconscionable, and therefore unenforceable, where it is a prerequisite to employment, job applicants are not permitted to modify the terms of the agreement, and the terms are one-sided, favoring the employer?

HOLDING AND DECISION: (Pregerson, J.) Yes. An arbitration agreement is unconscionable, and therefore unenforceable, where it is a prerequisite to employment, job applicants are not permitted to modify the terms of the agreement, and the terms are one sided, favoring the employer. A contract is unenforceable under the doctrine of unconscionability where there is both procedural and substantive unconscionability. Procedural unconscionability exists here, because the bargaining power of each party is unequal: Ferguson (P) had to sign the agreement, and accept all of its terms, or not get the job applied for. Substantive unconscionability also exists here, because the terms of the agreement are one sided: The agreement compels arbitration of Ferguson's (P) claims but exempts from arbitration the claims of Countrywide (D). In addition, Countrywide's (D) agreement requires Ferguson (P) to pay filing fees for arbitration, which could exceed the costs of litigation. Finally, the agreement includes limitations on the number of subjects Ferguson (P) could raise during discovery. While the discovery provision in the arbitration agreement is not so one sided it alone could be called unconscionable, in the context of an arbitration agreement that overall favors Countrywide (D), it too is unconscionable. Affirmed.

ANALYSIS

The outcome of this case, decided in California, stands in direct contrast to *Carter v. Countrywide Credit Industries, Inc.*, 362 F.3d 294 (5th Cir. 2004). *Carter* was decided in Texas, which is generally much more lenient on arbitration agreements.

Quicknotes

SUBSTANTIVE UNCONSCIONABILITY Rule of law whereby a court may excuse performance of a contract, or of a particular contract term, if it determines that such terms are unduly oppressive or unfair to one party to the contract and violate the subordinate party's reasonable expectations.

AT&T Mobility LLC v. Concepcion

Cell phone service provider (D) v. Consumer (P)

563 U.S. 333 (2011)

NATURE OF CASE: Appeal from affirmance of denial of motion to compel arbitration in a consumer class action.

FACT SUMMARY: AT&T Mobility LLC (AT&T) (D) contended the enforceability of the arbitration provision in its cell phone service agreement could not be conditioned by the states on the availability of classwide arbitration procedures, since the states were preempted by the Federal Arbitration Act from so doing.

RULE OF LAW

The Federal Arbitration Act prohibits states from conditioning the enforceability of arbitration agreements on the availability of classwide arbitration procedures.

FACTS: The cell phone service contract between the Concepcions (P) and AT&T Mobility LLC (AT&T) (D) provided for arbitration of all disputes, but did not permit classwide arbitration. After the Concepcions (P) were charged sales tax on the retail value of phones provided free under their service contract, they sued AT&T (D) in a California federal district court. Their suit was consolidated with a class action alleging, inter alia, that AT&T (D) had engaged in false advertising and fraud by charging sales tax on "free" phones. The District Court for the Southern District of California denied AT&T's (D) motion to compel arbitration under the Concepcions's (P) contract. Relying on the California Supreme Court's decision in *Discover Bank v. Superior Court*, 36 Cal. 4th 148, 30 Cal. Rptr. 3d 76, 113 P. 3d 1100 (2005), it found the arbitration provision unconscionable because it disallowed classwide proceedings, and AT&T (D) had failed to show that bilateral arbitration adequately substituted for the deterrent effects of class actions. The Ninth Circuit Court of Appeals agreed that the provision was unconscionable under California law, and held that the Federal Arbitration Act, which in Section 2 makes arbitration agreements "valid, irrevocable, and enforceable, save upon such grounds as exist at law or in equity for the revocation of any contract," did not preempt its ruling because the *Discover Bank* rule was simply a refinement of the unconscionability analysis applicable to contracts generally in California. The United States Supreme Court granted certiorari.

ISSUE: Does the Federal Arbitration Act prohibit states from conditioning the enforceability of arbitration agreements on the availability of classwide arbitration procedures?

HOLDING AND DECISION: (Scalia, J.) Yes. The Federal Arbitration Act (FAA) prohibits states from conditioning the enforceability of arbitration agreements on the availability of classwide arbitration procedures. The FAA was enacted in 1925 in response to widespread judicial hostility to arbitration agreements. The FAA's Section 2, which is the FAA's primary substantive provision, reflects a "liberal federal policy favoring arbitration," *Moses H. Cone Memorial Hospital v. Constr. Corp.*, 460 U.S. 1, 24, and the "fundamental principle that arbitration is a matter of contract," *Rent-A-Centr, West, Inc. v. Jackson*, 561 ___, ___ (2010 (slip op., at 3). Thus, courts must place arbitration agreements on an equal footing with other contracts and enforce them according to their terms. Section 2's saving clause permits agreements to be invalidated by "generally applicable contract defenses," such as fraud, duress or unconscionability, but not by defenses that apply only to arbitration or derive their meaning from the fact that an agreement to arbitrate is at issue. *Doctor's Associates, Inc. v. Casarotto*, 518 U.S. 618, 687 (1996). Under *Discover Bank*, class waivers in consumer arbitration agreements are unconscionable if the agreement is in an adhesion contract, disputes between the parties are likely to involve small amounts of damages, and the party with inferior bargaining power alleges a deliberate scheme to defraud. The Concepcions (P) claim that the *Discover Bank* rule is a ground that "exist[s] at law or in equity for the revocation of any contract" under FAA § 2. Moreover, they argue that even if the *Discover Bank* rule is construed as a prohibition on collective-action waivers rather than simply an application of unconscionability, the rule would still be applicable to all dispute-resolution contracts, since California prohibits waivers of class litigation as well. When state law prohibits outright the arbitration of a particular type of claim, the FAA displaces the conflicting rule. However, the inquiry is more complex when a generally applicable doctrine is alleged to have been applied in a fashion that disfavors or interferes with arbitration. Thus, the Court previously noted that the FAA's preemptive effect might extend even to grounds traditionally thought to exist at law or in equity for the revocation of any contract, and said that a court may not rely on the uniqueness of an agreement to arbitrate as a basis for a state-law holding that enforcement would be unconscionable, because this would enable the court to effect what the state legislature cannot. Although § 2's saving clause preserves

Continued on next page.

generally applicable contract defenses, it does not suggest an intent to preserve state-law rules that stand as an obstacle to the accomplishment of the FAA's objectives. The Concepcions (P) agree that rules aimed at destroying arbitration, or demanding procedures incompatible with arbitration, would be preempted by the FAA because they cannot sensibly be reconciled with § 2. The FAA's overarching purpose is to ensure the enforcement of arbitration agreements according to their terms so as to facilitate informal, streamlined proceedings, with expeditious results. Parties may agree to limit the issues subject to arbitration, to arbitrate according to specific rules, and to limit with whom they will arbitrate. Class arbitration, to the extent it is manufactured by *Discover Bank* rather than being consensual, interferes with fundamental attributes of arbitration. The switch from bilateral to class arbitration sacrifices arbitration's informality and makes the process slower, more costly, and more likely to generate procedural morass than final judgment. In fact, class arbitration requires procedural formality, as it is modeled on the Federal Rules of Civil Procedure for class litigation. Also, class arbitration greatly increases risks to defendants. The absence of multilayered review makes it more likely that errors will go uncorrected. That risk of error may become unacceptable when damages allegedly owed to thousands of claimants are aggregated and decided at once. Faced with even a small chance of devastating loss, defendants such as AT&T (D) will be pressured into settling questionable claims. Arbitration is poorly suited to these higher stakes. In litigation, a defendant may appeal a certification decision and a final judgment, but FAA § 10 limits the grounds on which courts can vacate arbitral awards. In sum, because *Discover Bank* impedes Congress's objectives, it is preempted by the FAA. Reversed and remanded.

DISSENT: (Breyer, J.) The rule enunciated by *Discover Bank* does not conflict with the FAA and is consistent with its language and primary objective. Where the circumstances articulated by that rule are met, class action waivers in any type of contract are unconscionable under state law. The rule thus sets forth a general principle of unconscionability that is not limited to all class action waivers in the consumer context. Because it applies equally to class action litigation waivers in contracts without arbitration agreements as it does to class arbitration waivers in contracts with such agreements, the rule falls directly within the scope of the FAA's exception permitting courts to refuse to enforce arbitration agreements on grounds that exist "for the revocation of any contract." 9 U.S.C. § 2. That is true linguistically, and as a matter of legal principle. The majority is wrong in finding that the *Discover Bank* rule stands as an obstacle to achievement of the FAA's objectives, and the majority provides no support for its belief that individual, rather than class, arbitration is a fundamental attribute of arbitration. Moreover, the majority fails to explain where it gets this notion, which is a key premise of its rationale. Because California applies the same legal principles to address the unconscionability of class arbitration waivers as it does to address the unconscionability of any other contractual provision, the merits of class proceedings should not factor into the Court's decision. For example, if California had applied its law of duress to void an arbitration agreement, it would be irrelevant for FAA preemption analysis whether the procedures in the coerced agreement were efficient. Moreover, class proceedings have well-known countervailing advantages, such as encouraging the bringing of small claims—and the acceptance of them by attorneys. No rational attorney would have accepted the Concepcion's (P) case where recovery would be limited to $30.22. Instead, *Discover Bank* sets forth circumstances in which the California courts believe that the terms of consumer contracts can be manipulated to insulate an agreement's author from liability for its own frauds by deliberately cheating large numbers of consumers out of individually small sums of money. Why is this kind of decision—weighing the pros and cons of all class proceedings alike—not California's to make? Under the Nation's federalist system, states are considered sovereigns; here, California is entitled to weigh the pros and cons of all class proceedings alike, and, in respecting federalist ideals, its law should be upheld, not preempted. Federalist principles should not be honored "in their breach."

ANALYSIS

Since almost all class actions occur between parties who are in transactional relationships with one another, such as shareholders and corporations, consumers and merchants, employees and employers, etc., it is arguable that this decision will permit the party with greater bargaining power in any particular transaction to force the weaker parties to accept class waivers with no recourse – other than not entering into the transaction at all. Thus, the majority's emphasis on the Federal Arbitration Act's promotion of *consensual* arbitration agreements rings hollow.

Quicknotes

ARBITRATION An alternative resolution process where a dispute is heard and decided by a neutral third party, rather than through legal proceedings.

ARBITRATION AGREEMENT A mutual understanding entered into by parties wishing to submit to the decision-making authority of a neutral third party, selected by the parties and charged with rendering a decision.

Continued on next page.

CLASS ACTION A suit commenced by a representative on behalf of an ascertainable group that is too large to appear in court, shares a commonality of interests, and will benefit from a successful result.

INTER ALIA Among other things.

Celotex Corp. v. Catrett

Asbestos product manufacturer (D) v. Wife of decedent (P)

477 U.S. 317 (1986)

NATURE OF CASE: Appeal from reversal of summary judgment denying damages for asbestos exposure.

FACT SUMMARY: In Catrett's (P) action against Celotex Corp. (D) for the death of her husband as a result of his exposure to asbestos manufactured by Celotex (D), Celotex (D) moved for summary judgment, contending that Catrett (P) had failed to identify, in answering interrogatories specifically requesting such information, any witnesses who could testify about the decedent's exposure to Celotex's (D) asbestos.

RULE OF LAW

The plain language of Fed. R. Civ. P. 56(c) mandates the entry of summary judgment, after adequate time for discovery, against a party who fails to make a showing sufficient to establish the existence of an element essential to that party's case.

FACTS: Catrett (P) sued Celotex Corp. (D), alleging that the death of her husband resulted from his exposure to products containing asbestos manufactured by Celotex (D). At trial, Celotex (D) moved for summary judgment, contending that Catrett (P) had failed to identify, in answering interrogatories specifically requesting such information, any witnesses who could testify about the decedent's exposure to Celotex's (D) asbestos products. The district court granted Celotex's (D) motion because there was no showing that the decedent was exposed to Celotex's (D) product within the statutory period. Catrett (P) appealed.

ISSUE: Does the plain language of Fed. R. Civ. P. 56(c) mandate the entry of summary judgment, after adequate time for discovery, against a party who fails to make a showing sufficient to establish the existence of an element essential to that party's case?

HOLDING AND DECISION: (Rehnquist, J.) Yes. The plain language of Fed. R. Civ. P. 56(c) mandates the entry of summary judgment, after adequate time for discovery, against a party who fails to make a showing sufficient to establish the existence of an element essential to that party's case. In such a situation, there can be "no genuine issue as to any material fact," since a complete failure of proof concerning an essential element of the nonmoving party's case necessarily renders all other facts immaterial. Here, Catrett (P) failed to identify any witnesses who could testify about her husband's exposure to Celotex's (D) asbestos products. There was also no showing that the decedent was exposed to Celotex's (D) product within the statutory period. Catrett's (P) failure to show sufficient evidence to establish essential elements of her case makes summary judgment proper. Reversed and remanded.

CONCURRENCE: (White, J.) If respondent Catrett (P) had named a witness to support her claim, summary judgment could not have been granted without Celotex (D) somehow showing that the named witness's testimony raised no genuine issue of material fact.

ANALYSIS

Celotex is an important case in two ways. First, it integrates the burden of proof borne by the parties at trial with the corresponding burdens on a summary judgment motion. Second, it hints at a larger, more significant role for summary judgment in deciding cases.

Quicknotes

MATERIAL FACT A fact without the existence of which a contract would not have been entered.

SUMMARY JUDGMENT Judgment rendered by a court in response to a motion by one of the parties, claiming that the lack of a question of material fact in respect to an issue warrants disposition of the issue without consideration by the jury.

Tolan v. Cotton

Police shooting victim (P) v. Police officer (D)

572 U.S. 650 (2014)

NATURE OF CASE: Appeal from affirmance of summary judgment for defendant in action brought under 42 U.S.C. § 1983.

FACT SUMMARY: Robert Tolan (P), who claimed that police officer Jeffrey Cotton (D) shot him using excessive force, contended that the U.S. Court of Appeals for the Fifth Circuit improperly failed to credit evidence he presented that contradicted Cotton's (D) evidence, so that the court erroneously weighed the evidence and resolved disputed factual issues in favor of Cotton (D).

RULE OF LAW

In ruling on a motion for summary judgment, a court must credit the evidence of the nonmovant and draw all justifiable inferences in the nonmovant's favor, so that if it fails to do so, it erroneously weighs the evidence and resolves disputed issues in favor of the moving party.

FACTS: Police officer John Edwards incorrectly entered the license plate number of a car, which led to the car being identified as stolen, when in fact it was not. Edwards ordered the two men who had just exited the car—Robert Tolan (P) and his cousin Cooper—to the ground on the porch of Tolan's (P) house. Tolan's (P) parents, hearing the commotion, exited the house, and, like Tolan (P) before them, assured Edwards that the car was not stolen, and that this was where Tolan (P) lived and that they owned the house. In the meantime, officer Jeffrey Cotton (D) appeared on the scene, with his gun drawn. He ordered Tolan's (P) mother to stand against the garage door. The parties disputed what happened next. The Tolans claimed that Cotton (D) slammed Ms. Tolan against the garage door with extreme force. Cotton (D) claimed that when he escorted Ms. Tolan to the garage, she flipped her arms up and told him to get his hands off her. Tolan (P) claimed that upon seeing his mother being pushed, he rose to his knees. The officers claimed he rose to his feet. Both parties agreed that Tolan (P) then exclaimed, from roughly 15 to 20 feet away, "[G]et your fucking hands off my mom." The parties also agreed that Cotton (D) then drew his pistol and fired three shots at Tolan (P). Tolan (P) and his mother testified that these shots came with no verbal warning. One of the bullets entered Tolan's (P) chest, collapsing his right lung and piercing his liver. Tolan (P) filed suit against Cotton (D) under 42 U.S.C. § 1983 claiming that Cotton (D) had used excessive force in contravention of Tolan's (P) Fourth Amendment rights. Cotton (D) moved for summary judgment, which the district court granted, determining that Cotton's (D) use of force was not unreasonable. The U.S. Court of Appeals for the Fifth Circuit affirmed. It held that even if Cotton's (D) conduct did violate the Fourth Amendment, Cotton (D) was entitled to qualified immunity because he did not violate a clearly established right. In reaching this conclusion, the Fifth Circuit relied on the following facts: the front porch had been dimly lit; Tolan's (P) mother had refused orders to remain quiet and calm; and Tolan's (P) words had amounted to a verbal threat. Most critically, the court also relied on the purported fact that Tolan (P) was moving to intervene in Cotton's (D) handling of his mother, and that Cotton (D) therefore could reasonably have feared for his life. The United States Supreme Court granted certiorari.

ISSUE: In ruling on a motion for summary judgment, must a court credit the evidence of the nonmovant and draw all justifiable inferences in the nonmovant's favor, so that if it fails to do so, it erroneously weighs the evidence and resolves disputed issues in favor of the moving party?

HOLDING AND DECISION: (Per curiam) Yes. In ruling on a motion for summary judgment, a court must credit the evidence of the nonmovant and draw all justifiable inferences in the nonmovant's favor, so that if it fails to do so, it erroneously weighs the evidence and resolves disputed issues in favor of the moving party. In holding that Cotton's (D) actions did not violate clearly established law, the Fifth Circuit failed to view the evidence at summary judgment in the light most favorable to Tolan (P) with respect to the central facts of this case. By failing to credit evidence that contradicted some of its key factual conclusions, the court improperly weighed the evidence and resolved disputed issues in favor of the moving party. The Fifth Circuit ignored evidence that contradicted Cotton's (D) testimony that the porch was dimly lit. The court also ignored evidence that Tolan's (P) mother was not agitated or aggravated when she spoke to Cotton (D)—which contradicted the evidence presented by Cotton (D). The court also concluded that Tolan (P) was "shouting," and "verbally threatening" the officer, but the court ignored directly contradictory evidence from which a jury could conclude that Tolan (P) was not being threatening but instead was pleading with Cotton (D) to cease assaulting his mother. Finally, the court concluded that Tolan (P) was moving towards Cotton (D) at the time of the shooting, but it failed to credit evidence that Tolan (P) was on his knees and not

Continued on next page.

going anywhere. Considered together, these facts lead to the inescapable conclusion that the court below credited the movant's evidence and failed properly to acknowledge key evidence offered by the nonmovant. The disputed factual issues should have been resolved by a jury, instead of on summary judgment. Vacated and remanded.

ANALYSIS

This case illustrates the rule that courts may not resolve genuine disputes of fact in favor of the party seeking summary judgment. This rule is simply an application of the more general rule that a judge's function at summary judgment is not to weigh the evidence and determine the truth of the matter but to determine whether there is a genuine issue for trial. Summary judgment is appropriate only if the movant shows that there is no genuine issue as to any material fact and the movant is entitled to judgment as a matter of law. In making that determination, a court must view the evidence in the light most favorable to the opposing party.

Quicknotes

QUALIFIED IMMUNITY An affirmative defense relieving officials from civil liability for the performance of activities within their discretion so long as such conduct is not in violation of an individual's rights pursuant to law as determined by a reasonable person standard.

SUMMARY JUDGMENT Judgment rendered by a court in response to a motion made by one of the parties, claiming that the lack of a question of material fact in respect to an issue warrants disposition of the issue without consideration by the jury.

Scott v. Harris

Law enforcement officer (D) v. Speeding motorist injured by law enforcement officer (D)

550 U.S. 372 (2007)

NATURE OF CASE: Appeal from affirmance of denial of summary judgment to defendant in action brought under 42 U.S.C. § 1983 alleging, inter alia, the use of excessive force resulting in an unreasonable seizure under the Fourth Amendment.

FACT SUMMARY: Harris (P), who initiated a high-speed car chase, was rendered a quadriplegic when his car was hit by the police cruiser being driven by Timothy Scott (Deputy Scott) (D), a county deputy, and crashed. Harris (P) sued Deputy Scott (D), alleging that Deputy Scott (D) violated his constitutional rights. Deputy Scott (D) contended he was entitled to qualified immunity, and, therefore, summary judgment.

RULE OF LAW

Where a trial record blatantly contradicts the plaintiff's version of events so that no reasonable jury could believe it, a court may not adopt that version of the facts for purposes of ruling on a summary judgment motion.

FACTS: A Georgia county deputy clocked Harris's (P) vehicle traveling at 73 miles per hour on a road with a speed limit of 55 miles per hour. The deputy activated his blue flashing lights indicating that Harris (P) should pull over. Instead, Harris (P) sped away, initiating a chase down what is in most portions a two-lane road, at speeds exceeding 85 miles per hour. The deputy radioed his dispatch to report that he was pursuing a fleeing vehicle. Deputy Timothy Scott (Deputy Scott) (D), heard the radio communication and joined the pursuit along with other officers. In the midst of the chase, Harris (P) pulled into the parking lot of a shopping center and was nearly boxed in by the various police vehicles. Harris (P) evaded the trap by making a sharp turn, colliding with Deputy Scott's police car, exiting the parking lot, and speeding off once again down a two-lane highway. Deputy Scott (D) then took over as the lead pursuit vehicle. Deputy Scott (D) initially decided to attempt to terminate the episode by employing a maneuver that causes the fleeing vehicle to spin to a stop, but then decided against that and, instead, applied his push bumper to the rear of Harris's (P) vehicle. As a result, Harris (P) lost control of his vehicle, which left the roadway, ran down an embankment, overturned, and crashed. Harris (P) was badly injured and was rendered a quadriplegic. Harris (P) filed suit in federal district court against Deputy Scott (D) and others under 42 U.S.C. § 1983, alleging, inter alia, a violation of his federal constitutional rights, through the use of excessive force resulting in an unreasonable seizure under the Fourth Amendment. In response, Deputy Scott (D) filed a motion for summary judgment based on an assertion of qualified immunity. The District Court denied the motion, finding that "there are material issues of fact on which the issue of qualified immunity turns which present sufficient disagreement to require submission to a jury." The United States Court of Appeals for the Eleventh Circuit affirmed, concluded that Deputy Scott's (D) actions could constitute "deadly force," and that the use of such force in this context would violate Harris's (P) constitutional right to be free from excessive force during a seizure. The United States Supreme Court granted certiorari.

ISSUE: Where a trial record blatantly contradicts the plaintiff's version of events so that no reasonable jury could believe it, may a court adopt that version of the facts for purposes of ruling on a summary judgment motion?

HOLDING AND DECISION: (Scalia, J.) No. Where a trial record blatantly contradicts the plaintiff's version of events so that no reasonable jury could believe it, a court may not adopt that version of the facts for purposes of ruling on a summary judgment motion. Ordinarily, at this stage of the proceedings, there are no factual findings by a judge or jury, and a court is required to view the facts and draw reasonable inferences in the light most favorable to the party opposing the summary judgment motion. In qualified immunity cases, this usually means adopting (as the Court of Appeals did here) the plaintiff's version of the facts. Here, however, there was a videotape of the events, and that videotape contradicts Harris's (P) version of events adopted by the Court of Appeals. For example, the Court of Appeals agreed that during the chase there was little, if any, actual threat to pedestrians or other motorists, as the roads were mostly empty and Harris (P) remained in control of his vehicle. The Court of Appeals agreed, too, that Harris (P) slowed for turns and intersections, and typically used his indicators for turns; that he did not run any motorists off the road; that he was not a threat to pedestrians in the shopping center parking lot, which was free from pedestrian and vehicular traffic as the center was closed; and that, by the time the parties were back on the highway and Deputy Scott (D) rammed Harris's (P) vehicle, the motorway had been cleared of motorists and pedestrians allegedly because of police blockades of the nearby intersections. The video tells a different story, of Harris (P) traveling shockingly fast, swerving around other

Continued on next page.

vehicles, running multiple red lights, forcing other vehicles to the shoulder of the road, and forcing the police to engage in dangerous maneuvers just to keep up. Far from being the cautious and controlled driver the lower court depicts, what the video shows more closely resembles a "Hollywood-style car chase" of the most frightening sort, placing police officers and innocent bystanders alike at great risk of serious injury. At the summary judgment stage, facts must be viewed in the light most favorable to the nonmoving party only if there is a genuine dispute as to those facts. However, where the record taken as a whole could not lead a rational trier of fact to find for the nonmoving party, there is no genuine issue for trial. When opposing parties tell two different stories, one of which is blatantly contradicted by the record, so that no reasonable jury could believe it, a court should not adopt that version of the facts for purposes of ruling on a motion for summary judgment. That was the case here with regard to the factual issue whether respondent was driving in such fashion as to endanger human life. Harris's (P) version of events is so utterly discredited by the record that no reasonable jury could have believed him. The Court of Appeals should not have relied on such visible fiction; it should have viewed the facts in the light depicted by the videotape. Reversed.

DISSENT: (Stevens, J.) The factual determinations made by the majority should have been left to be decided by a jury, especially since the lower courts, which were more familiar with the facts and circumstances of the case, came to a conclusion counter to that of the majority, thus demonstrating that reasonable minds could disagree about how to characterize the factual events in the case. The answer to the general question asked by the Court, whether an officer may take actions that place a fleeing motorist at risk of serious injury or death in order to stop the motorist's flight from endangering the lives of innocent bystanders, depends on the circumstances involved. Relying on a de novo review of a videotape of a portion of a nighttime chase on a lightly traveled road in Georgia where no pedestrians or other "bystanders" were present, buttressed by uninformed speculation about the possible consequences of discontinuing the chase, eight of the "jurors" on this Court reach a verdict that differs from the views of the judges on both the District Court and the Court of Appeals, who are surely more familiar with the hazards of driving on Georgia roads than they are. The Court's justification for this unprecedented departure from the Court's well-settled standard of review of factual determinations made by a district court and affirmed by a court of appeals is based on its mistaken view that the Court of Appeals' description of the facts was "blatantly contradicted by the record" and that respondent's version of the events was "so utterly discredited by the record that no reasonable jury could have believed him." Contrary to the majority's appraisal of the facts, the video confirms the lower courts' conclusions. More importantly, the majority's use of the video does not provide a principled basis for depriving Harris (P) of his right to have a jury evaluate the question whether Deputy Scott's (D) decision to use deadly force to bring the chase to an end was reasonable. The majority omitted from its description of the initial speeding violation the fact that Harris (P) was on a four-lane portion of a highway when the officer clocked him speeding. More significantly—and contrary to the majority's assumption that Harris's (P) vehicle "force[d] cars traveling in both directions to their respective shoulders to avoid being hit,"—a fact unmentioned in the text of the opinion explains why those cars pulled over prior to being passed by respondent. The sirens and flashing lights on the police cars following Harris (P) gave the same warning that a speeding ambulance or fire engine would have provided. The 13 cars that Harris (P) passed on his side of the road before entering the shopping center, and both of the cars that he passed on the right after leaving the center, no doubt had already pulled to the side of the road or were driving along the shoulder because they heard the police sirens or saw the flashing lights before Harris (P) or the police cruisers approached. A jury could certainly conclude that those motorists were exposed to no greater risk than persons who take the same action in response to a speeding ambulance, and that their reactions were fully consistent with the evidence that Harris (P), though speeding, retained full control of his vehicle. Further, the video shows clearly—and contrary to the majority's characterization—that Harris (P) did not pass slower vehicles in his lane when there were vehicles approaching in the opposite lane, and only overtook vehicles in his lane when there were no approaching vehicles in the opposite lane. Thus, the video does not reveal any incidents that could even be remotely characterized as "close calls." Accordingly, the factual statements made by the Court of Appeals were entirely accurate, and at no point did Harris (P) lose control of his vehicle. That court also correctly concluded that Harris (P) did not pose risk to pedestrians or other vehicles in the shopping center parking lot, given that at the time the center was closed and police had closed off intersections so Harris (P) could not enter residential neighborhoods. Whether a person's actions have risen to a level warranting deadly force is a question of fact best reserved for a jury. Here, the majority has usurped the jury's factfinding function and, in doing so, has implicitly labeled the four other judges to review the case unreasonable. If two groups of judges can disagree so vehemently about the nature of the pursuit and the circumstances surrounding that pursuit, it seems

Continued on next page.

eminently likely that a reasonable juror could disagree with this Court's characterization of events.

ANALYSIS

In this case, the availability of the video to the Court – and the majority's and dissent's very different reactions thereto – make clear the highly fact-dependent nature of the constitutional issue presented and underscores how reasonable minds can sometimes vehemently disagree about how to characterize a given set of facts. The case also illustrates how important a certain characterization of facts can be to the outcome of the legal issues in a case. The judges on the Court of Appeals panel apparently viewed the video, which was entered into the record, and, along with Supreme Court Justice Stevens, described a very different version of events than did the majority. Accordingly, the Court of Appeals judges and Justice Stevens reached different conclusions than did the majority. Although the majority claimed only to have drawn factual inferences in Harris's (P) favor "to the extent supportable by the record," it seems that its own view of the record clearly precluded it from doing so to the same extent as the two courts through which the case had already traveled.

Quicknotes

DEADLY FORCE That degree of force that is likely to result in death or great bodily injury.

DE NOVO REVIEW The review of a lower court decision by an appellate court, which is hearing the case as if it had not been previously heard and as if no judgment had been rendered.

EXCESSIVE FORCE Force that is unreasonable or unnecessary given the circumstances.

FOURTH AMENDMENT Provides that persons be secure as to their person and private belongings against unreasonable searches and seizures.

INTER ALIA Among other things.

MATERIAL ISSUE OF FACT Frequently stated as "issue of material fact"; an issue or dispute regarding a fact that is legally relevant to a claim or cause of action that will, as a matter of substantive law, make a difference to the outcome reached in a given case.

QUALIFIED IMMUNITY An affirmative defense relieving officials from civil liability for the performance of activities within their discretion so long as such conduct is not in violation of an individual's rights pursuant to law as determined by a reasonable person standard.

SEIZURE Under the Fourth Amendment, the application of physical force to the body of a person, or a show of force or authority, intended to restrain a person's liberty. Only "unreasonable" seizures by the government are prohibited by the Fourth Amendment.

SUMMARY JUDGMENT Judgment rendered by a court in response to a motion made by one of the parties, claiming that the lack of a question of material fact in respect to an issue warrants disposition of the issue without consideration by the jury.

CHAPTER 9

The Trier and the Trial

Quick Reference Rules of Law

Caperton v. A.T. Massey Coal Co.

Business associate (P) v. Coal company (D)

556 U.S. 868 (2009)

NATURE OF CASE: Grant of writ of certiorari.

FACT SUMMARY: A judge in a state court who was elected to the bench after receiving $3 million from a donor refused to recuse himself when the court heard a case in which a verdict had been entered against that donor for $50 million. The plaintiff in the case objected that he did not receive a fair trial.

RULE OF LAW

It is unconstitutional for a state court judge to hear a case involving the financial interests of a major backer of the judge's election campaign.

FACTS: Hugh Caperton (P) brought suit against A.T. Massey Coal Co. (Massey) (D) for unlawfully cancelling a contract that bankrupted Caperton (P). A West Virginia jury returned a verdict that found Massey (D) and its affiliates liable for fraudulent misrepresentation, concealment, and tortious interference with existing contractual relations. The jury awarded Caperton (P) the sum of $50 million in compensatory and punitive damages. After the verdict but before the appeal, West Virginia held its 2004 judicial elections, and Don Blankenship, Massey's (D) chairman, chief executive officer, and president, supported Brent Benjamin in the election. He contributed the $1,000 statutory maximum to Benjamin's campaign committee, donated almost $2.5 million to a political organization that supported Benjamin, and just over $500,000 on independent expenditures to support Benjamin. Blankenship's $3 million in contributions were more than the total amount spent by all other Benjamin supporters and three times the amount spent by Benjamin's own committee. Benjamin won the election. Caperton (P) moved to disqualify now-Justice Benjamin under the Due Process Clause and the West Virginia Code of Judicial Conduct, based on the conflict caused by Blankenship's campaign involvement. Justice Benjamin denied the motion. Massey (D) then filed its petition for appeal to challenge the jury verdict. The court of appeals granted review and reversed the $50 million verdict against Massey (D). Justice Benjamin joined the majority opinion. Caperton (P) sought rehearing, and the parties moved for disqualification of three of the five justices who decided the appeal. Justice Benjamin again denied Caperton's (P) recusal motion. The court granted rehearing. Caperton (P) moved a third time for disqualification. Justice Benjamin again refused. A divided court again reversed the jury verdict.

ISSUE: Is it unconstitutional for a state court judge to hear a case involving the financial interests of a major backer of the judge's election campaign?

HOLDING AND DECISION: (Kennedy, J.) Yes. It is unconstitutional for a state court judge to hear a case involving the financial interests of a major backer of the judge's election campaign. The Due Process Clause requires a fair and impartial trial. The leading case on the subject is *Tumey v. Ohio*, 273 U.S. 510 (1927), where it was concluded that the Due Process Clause incorporated the common-law rule that a judge must recuse him- or herself when he or she has "a direct, personal, substantial, pecuniary interest" in a case. Under this rule, personal bias or prejudice "alone" would not be sufficient basis for imposing a constitutional requirement under the Due Process Clause. Over time, the Court has identified additional instances that, as an objective matter, require recusal. These are cases in which the probability of actual bias on the part of the judge is too high to be constitutionally tolerable. For example, where a judge has a financial interest in the outcome of a case, although the interest was less than what would have been considered personal or direct at common law, recusal is required. Similarly, in the criminal contempt context, where a judge had no pecuniary interest in the case but was challenged because of a conflict arising from his or her participation in an earlier proceeding, recusal was required. The problem in this case arises in the context of judicial elections, a framework not presented in the precedents. Not every campaign contribution by a litigant or attorney creates a probability of bias that requires a judge's recusal, but this is an exceptional case. Here, there is a serious risk of actual bias because a person with a personal stake in the case had a significant and disproportionate influence in placing the judge on the case by raising funds or directing the judge's election campaign when the case was pending or imminent. The inquiry centers on the contribution's relative size in comparison to the total amount of money contributed to the campaign, the total amount spent in the election, and the apparent effect such contribution had on the outcome of the election. Proving what ultimately drives the electorate to choose a particular candidate is a difficult endeavor, but Blankenship's campaign efforts had a significant and disproportionate influence in placing Justice Benjamin on the case. Blankenship contributed some $3 million to unseat the incumbent and

Continued on next page.

replace him with Benjamin. His contributions eclipsed the total amount spent by all other Benjamin supporters and exceeded by 300 percent the amount spent by Benjamin's campaign committee. In the end the people of West Virginia elected him, and they may have done so based on many reasons other than Blankenship's efforts, but whether Blankenship's campaign contributions were a necessary and sufficient cause of Benjamin's victory is not the proper inquiry. The risk that Blankenship's influence engendered actual bias is sufficiently substantial that it "must be forbidden if the guarantee of due process is to be adequately implemented." The temporal relationship between the campaign contributions, the justice's election, and the pendency of the case is also critical. It was reasonably foreseeable, when the campaign contributions were made, that the pending case would be before the newly elected justice. The $50 million adverse jury verdict had been entered before the election, and the Supreme Court of Appeals was the next step once the state trial court dealt with post-trial motions. So it became at once apparent that, absent recusal, Justice Benjamin would review a judgment that cost his biggest donor's company $50 million. Although there is no allegation of a quid pro quo agreement, the fact remains that Blankenship's extraordinary contributions were made at a time when he had a vested stake in the outcome. Just as no person is allowed to be a judge in his or her own cause, similar fears of bias may arise when—without the consent of the other parties—a person chooses the judge in his or her own cause. And applying this principle to the judicial election process, there was here a serious, objective risk of actual bias that required Justice Benjamin's recusal. Justice Benjamin did undertake an extensive search for actual bias. But that is just one step in the judicial process. Objective standards may also require recusal whether or not actual bias exists or can be proved. Blankenship's significant and disproportionate influence—coupled with the temporal relationship between the election and the pending case—"offer a possible temptation to the average . . . judge to . . . lead him not to hold the balance nice, clear and true." *Tumey v. Ohio*, 273 U.S. 510, 532 (1927). On these extreme facts the probability of actual bias rises to an unconstitutional level. Reversed and remanded.

DISSENT: (Roberts, C.J.) The majority imprudently expanded the standard for which a judge need recuse him- or herself by merely showing a "probability of bias." The "probability of bias" standard formulated by the majority was excessively vague and discretionary. It fails to provide clear, workable guidance for future cases. At the most basic level, it is unclear whether the new probability of bias standard is somehow limited to financial support in judicial elections or applies to judicial recusal questions more generally. Forty questions are unanswered by the majority opinion [the casebook excerpt does not list all 40], but these are only a few uncertainties that quickly come to mind.

DISSENT: (Scalia, J.) The majority performed its duties poorly as a clarifying body by making an area of the law vastly more uncertain. That area of law can be raised in all litigated cases in (at least) those 39 states that elect their judges. This course was urged upon us on grounds that it would preserve the public's confidence in the judicial system, but the decision will have the opposite effect. What above all else is eroding public confidence in the judicial system is the perception that litigation is just a game, that the party with the most resourceful lawyer can play it to win, and that our legal proceedings are self-perpetuating but incapable of delivering real-world justice. The majority opinion will reinforce that perception.

ANALYSIS

This case is important for the fact that through it, the Supreme Court set a new standard for judges to recuse themselves from cases, ruling a state supreme court justice who benefited from $3 million in campaign contributions from a coal executive should have stayed out of a lawsuit involving the executive's company. In light of the fact that many states–39 by last count–currently elect judges to courts, the case will have wide-reaching consequences.

Quicknotes

DUE PROCESS CLAUSE Language in the Fifth and Fourteenth Amendments to the United States Constitution providing that no person shall be deprived of "life, liberty, or property without due process of law."

QUID PRO QUO What for what; in contract law, the consideration, something of value, passed between the parties to render the contract binding.

RECUSAL Procedure whereby a judge is disqualified from hearing a case either on his or her own behalf, or on the objection of a party, due to some bias or interest on the part of the judge in the subject matter of the suit.

Monfore v. Phillips

Spouse of deceased patient (P) v. Physician (D)

778 F.3d 849 (10th Cir. 2015)

NATURE OF CASE: Appeal from denial of motion to amend a final pretrial order in action for negligence.

FACT SUMMARY: Phillips (D), a physician accused of negligence, contended that his motion to amend a final pretrial order days before jury selection was to commence—so he could completely change his litigation strategy after 20 months of discovery and motions practice—should have been granted, and that the denial of such motion was reversible error.

RULE OF LAW

It is not reversible error for a district court to deny a motion to amend a final pretrial order days before jury selection is to start, and 20 months after motions practice and discovery, so that the movant may introduce new jury instructions, exhibits, and witnesses aimed at advancing an entirely new defense.

FACTS: Tests showed Shatwell had throat cancer, but through a series of blunders, he never received the news, and as a result he died. His widowed wife (P) brought suit against the hospital and physicians, asserting claims of negligence. For 20 months, through motions practice and discovery, the defendants denied any responsibility. Then, two weeks prior to trial, some of the defendants settled. Phillips (D), one of the physicians, was not among the settling defendants. Instead, just days before jury selection was to start, Phillips (D) moved to amend the final pretrial order so he could completely change his defense strategy by blaming some of the defendants who had settled. His motion sought permission to introduce new jury instructions, exhibits, and witnesses aimed at advancing his new defense. However, the district court denied the motion, and at the trial's end, the jury found him liable for damages of a little over $1 million. Phillips (D) appealed, contending that the district court's refusal to amend the final pretrial order and allow his new defense amounted to reversible error. The U.S. Court of Appeals for the Tenth Circuit granted review.

ISSUE: Is it reversible error for a district court to deny a motion to amend a final pretrial order days before jury selection is to start, and 20 months after motions practice and discovery, so that the movant may introduce new jury instructions, exhibits, and witnesses aimed at advancing an entirely new defense?

HOLDING AND DECISION: (Gorsuch, J.) No. It is not reversible error for a district court to deny a motion to amend a final pretrial order days before jury selection is to start, and 20 months after motions practice and discovery, so that the movant may introduce new jury instructions, exhibits, and witnesses aimed at advancing an entirely new defense. Final pretrial orders are intended to formulate a trial plan and to focus the parties on trial. Given the Federal Rules' liberal approach to discovery and pretrial practices, such orders are intended to separate the wheat from the chaff, as it were, and have the parties disclose something approximating their real trial intentions to opposing counsel and the court. Toward those ends, the parties are often asked—as they were in this case—to specify the witnesses and exhibits, supply the proposed jury instructions, and identify the claims and defenses they actually intend to introduce at trial. Under Fed. R. Civ. P. 16(e), a final pretrial order focused on formulating a plan for an impending trial may be amended "only to prevent manifest injustice." This standard is as high as it is to ensure everyone involved has sufficient incentive to fulfill the order's dual purposes of encouraging self-editing and providing reasonably fair disclosure to the court and opposing parties alike of their real trial intentions. Despite his protestations that he was surprised by his co-defendants' change of heart, Phillips (D) could not have been surprised that they did so. What happened was hardly unforeseeable, given that virtually all cases settle in part or in whole, many on the eve of trial, especially in multiparty litigation, where an incentive exists to break ranks, settle relatively cheaply, and leave others on the hook before the jury. Multiparty litigation presents a variety of collective action problems and other strategic pitfalls, and those Phillips (D) encountered here are well known, not the stuff of surprise. The prejudice to the other side also cannot be ignored. Phillips (D) essentially sought to force the plaintiff to prepare for an entirely different trial on a few days' notice. The defendants adduced hardly any evidence or experts relating to contributory negligence. Thus, the plaintiff and her lawyers had some reasonable expectations about what trial would look like and the sort of evidence they would—and would not—need. They knew they'd need to prove negligence by the defendants who chose to go to trial but they wouldn't have to worry about finger pointing between defendants. Under such circumstances, a district court does not abuse its discretion in holding a party to a long-scheduled trial and to the strategy he or she articulated though pleading and discovery and in the face of such obvious risks,

Continued on next page.

especially when indulging an eleventh-hour strategic shift would mean either imposing prejudice on the other side or inviting more delay. Affirmed.

ANALYSIS

There are four primary factors that typically are considered in determining whether a district court has abused its discretion in denying a motion to amend the pretrial order: (1) prejudice or surprise to opposing party; (2) ability of the opposing party to cure the prejudice; (3) potential disruption of trial; and (4) any bad faith of moving party. Here, the court of appeals, without considering these separate factors, concluded that the district court properly exercised its discretion in refusing to permit Phillips (D) to amend the pretrial order. Judge Moritz, concurring in the opinion, argues that consideration of the relevant factors would have demonstrated that the district court could just as easily have exercised its discretion to permit Phillips (D) to amend the pretrial order, and that, contrary to the majority opinion, denying Phillips's (D) motion may not have been the only reasonable course of action.

Quicknotes

DISCRETION The authority conferred upon a public official to act reasonably in accordance with his or her own judgment under certain circumstances.

REVERSIBLE ERROR A substantial error that might reasonably have prejudiced the party complaining.

Conte v. Emmons

Founder of television magazine company (P) v. Prosecutor (D)

895 F.3d 168 (2d Cir. 2018)

NATURE OF CASE: Appeal from denial of judgment as a matter of law in action for tortious interference with contract.

FACT SUMMARY: Prosecutors (D) and law enforcement investigators (D) claimed that they were entitled to post-verdict judgment as a matter of law after Conte (P) won his action for tortious interference with contract against them, contending that the evidence, even when viewed most favorably to Conte (P), was insufficient to permit a reasonable juror to have found in Conte's (P) favor.

RULE OF LAW

To obtain a post-verdict judgment as a matter of law, a movant must show that the evidence at trial, when viewed most favorably to the nonmovant, was insufficient to permit a reasonable juror to have found in the nonmovant's favor other than as a matter of sheer surmise and conjecture.

FACTS: Antony Conte (Conte) (P) founded I Media, a company created to produce and distribute *TV Time*, a television magazine. "Route distributors," who were individuals who paid I Media upfront for the exclusive right to distribute *TV Time* in a given area and were to receive in return a sum for each magazine they delivered, became suspicious when they did not receive any magazines to distribute. Close to 50 route distributors reported their suspicions to the Nassau County, New York, District Attorney's Office. Robert Emmons (D) and William Wallace (D), prosecutors in that office, and Michael Falzarno (D), an investigator in the office, investigated the complaints, issued grand jury document subpoenas, and made significant inquiries of a number of individuals and companies. However, no charges were ultimately filed, and when I Media subsequently failed, Conte (P) sued Emmons (D), Wallace (D), Falzarno (D) (collectively, "the appellants (D)") and others in federal district court, pro se, for tortious interference with contract. The jury returned a verdict for Conte (P) and awarded him $1,381,500, including punitive damages. The appellants (D) moved for judgment as a matter of law. The district court denied the motion, and the Second Circuit Court of Appeals granted review.

ISSUE: To obtain a post-verdict judgment as a matter of law, must a movant show that the evidence at trial, when viewed most favorably to the nonmovant, was insufficient to permit a reasonable juror to have found in the nonmovant's favor other than as a matter of sheer surmise and conjecture?

HOLDING AND DECISION: (Walker, Jr., J.) Yes. To obtain a post-verdict judgment as a matter of law, a movant must show that the evidence at trial, when viewed most favorably to the nonmovant, was insufficient to permit a reasonable juror to have found in the nonmovant's favor other than as a matter of sheer surmise and conjecture. The standard is a high one, met only in rare occasions. The movant, generally, must be able to show a complete absence of evidence supporting the verdict such that the jury's findings could have been the result only of sheer surmise and conjecture. A review of the trial record here shows that no reasonable juror in this case could have properly inferred from the evidence that the intent and causation elements of a tortious interference with contract claim were satisfied. The jury instruction correctly listed the elements of such a claim, and the jury was properly instructed that the appellants (D) could be liable for tortious interference with contract only if they acted with the "purpose of inducing [a] breach of contract" of an existing contract. However, there was no record evidence that the appellants (D) had any personal interest in the breach of any contracts that Conte (P) may have had with route distributors, printers, or advertisers. Conte's (P) strongest evidence on intent (viewed in his favor) was that Falzarno (D) had a personal animus towards Conte (P), saying that Conte (P) was a "fraud" and a "scam artist," and had vowed to "get" Conte (P). Conte (P) also presented evidence that Wallace (D) contacted certain of Conte's (P) counterparties informing them that Conte (P) was under investigation for fraud, and that the term "Ponzi scheme" may have come up in a conversation Wallace (D) had with an attorney. For the jury to have inferred that this investigative conduct evinced an ulterior purpose outside of the appellants' (D) law enforcement goals could only have been sheer surmise and conjecture. Without evidence to the contrary, these actions cannot reasonably be interpreted as anything but those of public servants pursuing aggressively, and perhaps overly so, their law enforcement mandate. In other words, there was no evidence that their intent exceeded their lawful mandate. Instead, any effect the investigation had on the destruction of Conte's (P) contracts was simply incidental to Emmons, Wallace, and Falzarno's (collectively, "the appellants") (D) intent to get to the bottom of widely reported allegations of fraudulent conduct and, moreover, that appellants (D) never targeted particular contracts. Therefore, the jury's intent finding that the appellants (D) purposefully targeted particular contracts

Continued on next page.

is wholly without support. Moreover, it would be detrimental to law enforcement efforts to accept the jury's inferential finding of a purposeful intent on such a bare record, since doing so would invite suits against prosecutors and their staff any time a plausible allegation that the subject of an investigation lost business as the result of a reasonably triggered investigation is coupled with some indication that the investigators were somewhat overzealous in going after the subject. Reversed and remanded, with directions to enter judgment for appellants (D).

DISSENT: (Pooler, J.) Remarkably, Conte (P) obtained a verdict against members of a district attorney's office while representing himself pro se. The appellants (D) now attempt to undo that remarkable result by alleging deficiencies in Conte's (P) proof that they failed to point to when Conte (P) still had the opportunity to present more evidence. The district court, having experienced the trial firsthand, concluded that the shortcomings in Conte's (P) proof were not egregious enough to merit overturning a jury verdict. The majority unwisely second guesses the district court's evaluation, declining even to grant Conte (P) a chance to amend his evidence at a new trial. Because the jury's verdict had sufficient grounding in the evidence, it was inappropriate for the majority to overturn it and to replace the jury's conclusions with its own. At the very least, Conte (P) deserves a new trial to correct any evidentiary deficiencies there might have been; the appellants (D) should not be able to "get away with failing to properly defend a case just because they underestimated the pro se plaintiff who sued them."

ANALYSIS

As the court in this case notes, overturning a jury verdict for insufficient evidence should occur only on the rarest of occasions, in which there is a "complete absence of evidence." Thus, the case at bar can be said to be "extraordinary." Arguably, a court should exercise its discretion to overturn a jury verdict even more cautiously if it does so on grounds not raised when the verdict winner still had an opportunity to supplement the record, as was the situation here. Such extreme caution arguably is especially important when the verdict winner is a pro se litigant like Antony Conte (P) because individuals unfamiliar with the intricacies of the legal system stand to benefit the most from being put on notice as to any deficiencies of proof. Moreover, because a directed verdict based on grounds not raised in a pre-verdict motion deprives the nonmovant of the opportunity to cure the defects in the nonmovant's case before it goes to the jury, if the party moving has not moved for a directed verdict and if the court is nevertheless satisfied that justice requires that the judgment be vacated for insufficiency of the evidence, the court should normally grant a new trial. Overturning a jury verdict without granting a new trial is all the more extraordinary when most of the relevant evidence is from live testimony, and the overturning court has only a paper record in front of it, rather than having observed the parties and witnesses in person, as the jury would have done in evaluating the credibility of witnesses and in coloring their understanding of the words uttered by those witnesses. Arguably, an appellate court should be even more hesitant to overturn a jury's verdict when the judge who presided over the trial and had the opportunity to observe the witnesses in person upholds the verdict.

Quicknotes

BREACH OF CONTRACT Unlawful failure by a party to perform its obligations pursuant to contract.

CAUSATION The aggregate effect of preceding events that bring about a tortious result; the causal connection between the actions of a tortfeasor and the injury that follows.

CONJECTURE A guess; supposition.

DIRECTED VERDICT A verdict ordered by the court in a jury trial.

INTENT The state of mind that exists when one's purpose is to commit a criminal act.

PRO SE An individual appearing on his or her own behalf.

SURMISE A supposition based on weak evidence.

TORTIOUS INTERFERENCE WITH CONTRACTUAL RELATIONSHIP An intentional tort whereby a defendant intentionally elicits the breach of a valid contract resulting in damages.

Unitherm Food Systems, Inc. v. Swift-Eckrich, Inc.

Corporation (P) v. Corporation (D)

546 U.S. 394 (2006)

NATURE OF CASE: Appeal from intermediate court's decision to overturn a jury verdict in favor of the plaintiff.

FACT SUMMARY: ConAgra (D), owned by Swift-Eckrich, Inc. (D), attempted to enforce a patent for a product and method to brown precooked meats. Unitherm Food Systems, Inc. (P) invented a similar process six years earlier than ConAgra (D).

RULE OF LAW

In the absence of a Fed. R. Civ. P. 50(b) post-verdict motion to set aside an adverse jury verdict on the grounds the evidence was legally insufficient, an appellate court may not set aside a jury verdict that a district court has allowed to stand.

FACTS: ConAgra (D), owned by Swift-Eckrich, Inc. (D), attempted to enforce a patent for a product and method to brown precooked meats. Unitherm Food Systems, Inc. (Unitherm) (P) invented a similar process six years earlier than ConAgra (D). Unitherm (P) brought a lawsuit against ConAgra (D) on the grounds its patent was invalid and that ConAgra (D) violated the Sherman Act by attempting to enforce a patent that was obtained by committing a fraud on the Patent and Trademark Office. After the close of evidence at trial, ConAgra (D) filed a Rule 50(a) motion requesting that the court find the evidence presented was legally insufficient to support an adverse jury verdict against it. The district court denied the motion and the jury returned a verdict for Unitherm (P). ConAgra (D) did not file a Fed. R. Civ. P. 50(b) motion after the verdict to request that the court set aside the jury verdict based upon the insufficiency of the evidence. The Federal Circuit Court of Appeals reversed, finding that (1) it had the authority to vacate the jury's verdict even though ConAgra (D) failed to file a Rule 50(b) motion; and (2) the evidence was insufficient to support a verdict in favor of Unitherm (P) on the Sherman Act claim.

ISSUE: In the absence of a Fed. R. Civ. P. 50(b) post-verdict motion to set aside an adverse jury verdict on the grounds the evidence was legally insufficient, may an appellate court set aside a jury verdict that a district court has allowed to stand?

HOLDING AND DECISION: (Thomas, J.) No. In the absence of a Fed. R. Civ. P. 50(b) post-verdict motion to set aside an adverse jury verdict on the grounds the evidence was legally insufficient, an appellate court may not set aside a jury verdict that a district court has allowed to stand. A post-verdict motion is required because it allows the judge who heard the case and listened to the witnesses to make the first determination whether a jury verdict may be set aside. This holding applies to both Fed. R. Civ. P. 50(b) motions and motions for a new trial. A Rule 50(a) motion is at the discretion of the trial court. A denial of that motion, prior to the jury's consideration of the case, cannot serve as the basis of an appeal because the court is not required to grant the motion, even if it feels the evidence is insufficient. The accepted practice in civil litigation is, except in limited circumstances, to allow cases to proceed to a jury verdict and then rule upon the sufficiency of the evidence after the verdict. The only error in this matter was counsel's failure to file the post-verdict motion. Federal Circuit's decision is reversed and the jury's verdict is reinstated. Reversed.

DISSENT: (Stevens, J.) 28 U.S.C. 2106 allows the Supreme Court or any appellate court to affirm, modify, or vacate a judgment of a lower court. Nothing in the text of Rule 50(b) limits the grant of this authority to the appellate courts. A party's failure to file a Rule 50(b) motion precludes only the district court from issuing a directed verdict.

ANALYSIS

It is a primary rule of litigation to ensure that all appellate avenues are preserved during the course of trial. Well before trial, competent counsel will have prepared all motions in limine, a motion for a directed verdict at the close of all evidence, and a motion for a directed verdict or a new trial after a jury's verdict is issued.

Quicknotes

DIRECTED VERDICT A verdict ordered by the court in a jury trial.

MOTION IN LIMINE Motion by one party brought prior to trial to exclude the potential introduction of prejudicial evidence.

Lind v. Schenley Industries

Sales negotiator (P) v. Employer company (D)

278 F.2d 79 (3d Cir. 1960)

NATURE OF CASE: Appeal from granting of judgment notwithstanding the verdict and, in the alternative, a new trial.

FACT SUMMARY: Although a jury awarded Lind (P) damages in his breach of contract suit against his employer, Schenley Industries, Inc. (D), the trial judge set aside the award as being against the weight of the evidence.

RULE OF LAW

Where nothing indicates that the jury was not properly presented with correct evidence, the judge may not nullify the jury verdict by granting a new trial so long as the evidence admits of the conclusion made by the jury.

FACTS: Lind (P) sued his employer Schenley Industries, Inc. (Schenley) (D), alleging that Schenley (D) had breached its oral promise to give him an increase in pay and a share of commissions. Lind (P) and his secretary testified to such promises. Schenley's (D) agents denied making the promises. The jury found that a contract was created and awarded damages to Lind (P). The trial judge granted Schenley's (D) motion for judgment notwithstanding the verdict and, alternatively, for a new trial. Lind (P) appealed.

ISSUE: Where nothing indicates that the jury was not properly presented with correct evidence, may the judge nullify the jury verdict by granting a new trial so long as the evidence admits of the conclusion made by the jury?

HOLDING AND DECISION: (Biggs, J.) No. Where nothing indicates that the jury was not properly presented with correct evidence, the judge may not nullify the jury verdict by granting a new trial so long as the evidence admits of the conclusion made by the jury. The jury found the testimony of the plaintiff and his secretary credible. The judge disagreed. The evidence given as to what Lind (P) had received as a result of his negotiations demonstrates that the jury's finding was not against the weight of the evidence, however. Furthermore, there was evidence enough to sustain the finding that the contract was not too indefinite to be sustainable. Reversed and remanded.

DISSENT: (Hastie, J.) A judge may not substitute his or her own verdict for that of the jury. But a judge may avoid what in his or her professionally trained and experienced judgment is an unjust verdict by vacating it and causing the matter to be tried again. Here, there was a sharp conflict of testimony as to the offers and promises. It was not an abuse of discretion to grant the new trial.

ANALYSIS

A reversal of an order granting a new trial requires an abuse of discretion by the granting judge. Showing an abuse of discretion is not an easy proposition, but it is possible. Where the new trial is granted despite a logically defensible jury verdict based on properly admitted correct evidence, such an abuse is shown.

Quicknotes

ABUSE OF DISCRETION A determination by an appellate court that a lower court's decision was based on an error of law.

DIRECTED VERDICT A verdict ordered by the court in a jury trial.

Peterson v. Wilson

Employee (P) v. Employer (D)

141 F.3d 573 (5th Cir. 1998)

NATURE OF CASE: Appeal from judgment in a retrial of wrongful-termination action.

FACT SUMMARY: The trial court ordered a new trial on its own motion after meeting with a jury after their verdict.

RULE OF LAW

The admission of juror testimony to impeach a jury verdict is prohibited.

FACTS: Peterson (P) filed suit in district court after he was fired as grant director at Texas Southern University (D). After a trial, a jury awarded Peterson (P) $187,000. The defendants moved for a new trial. Four months later, the district court granted the new trial, but its order revealed that it did so because comments made by the jurors after the verdict indicated that they had disregarded the court's instructions. The case was re-tried and Peterson's (P) claims were rejected by the second jury. Peterson (P) appealed the grant of a new trial.

ISSUE: Is the admission of juror testimony to impeach a jury verdict prohibited?

HOLDING AND DECISION: (Wiener, J.) Yes. The admission of juror testimony to impeach a jury verdict is prohibited. A jury's verdict can be disregarded if it is against the great weight of the evidence. However, in the present case, the district court clearly granted the new trial due to its meeting with jurors following the verdict and the comments made at that time. This post-verdict, ex parte meeting was impermissible. Rule 606(b) of the Fed. R. Evid. provides jurors may not testify as to statements made in deliberations or concerning the mental process of decision making. The only exception is for extraneous and outside influences on the jury. This reflects a conscious decision to disallow juror testimony as to their fidelity to the court's instructions. Given this rule, the court's granting of a new trial in the present case was clearly erroneous. The only reason given for granting the new trial was the comments made by the jurors after the verdict. Therefore, the judgment in the second trial must be vacated and the results of the first trial reinstated. Grant of a new trial reversed, second trial judgment vacated, first trial reinstated, and case remanded.

ANALYSIS

The court also awarded Peterson (P) his costs and attorney's fees incurred in both trials and on appeal. The decision also found that the original verdict was not against the weight of the evidence, even if the district court had used this legal reason for granting the new trial. The exception to the rule in this case is a situation where the jurors are influenced by evidence that is brought illegally into the jury room.

Quicknotes

EX PARTE A proceeding commenced by one party without providing any opposing parties with notice or that is uncontested by an adverse party.

WRONGFUL TERMINATION Unlawful termination of an individual's employment.

CHAPTER 10

Appeal

Quick Reference Rules of Law

Liberty Mutual Insurance Co. v. Wetzel

Insurer (D) v. Employer insured (P)

424 U.S. 737 (1976)

NATURE OF CASE: Appeal from finding of liability for violation of Title VII of the Civil Rights Act of 1964.

FACT SUMMARY: Wetzel (P) alleged that Liberty Mutual Insurance Company's (D) employee insurance benefits and maternity leave regulations discriminated against women in violation of Title VII of the Civil Rights Act of 1964.

RULE OF LAW

An interlocutory appeal under Fed. R. Civ. P. 54(b) is limited expressly to multiple-claims actions.

FACTS: Wetzel (P) filed a complaint that asserted that Liberty Mutual Insurance Company's (Liberty Mutual) (D) employee insurance benefits and maternity leave regulations discriminated against women in violation of Title VII of the Civil Rights Act of 1964. Wetzel's (P) complaint sought several forms of relief, including monetary damages, attorney's fees, and injunctive relief. On January 9, 1974, after finding no issues of material fact in dispute, the district court granted partial summary judgment for Wetzel (P) on the issue of liability only. On February 20, 1974, the district court issued an order of final judgment as to Liberty Mutual's (D) liability but granted none of the relief requested in Wetzel's (P) complaint. The U.S. Court of Appeals for the Third Circuit held that it had jurisdiction over Liberty Mutual's (D) appeal under 28 U.S.C. § 1291 and affirmed the judgment of the district court.

ISSUE: Is an interlocutory appeal under Fed. R. Civ. P. 54(b) limited expressly to multiple-claims actions?

HOLDING AND DECISION: (Rehnquist, J.) Yes. An interlocutory appeal under Fed. R. Civ. P. 54(b) is limited expressly to multiple-claims actions in which one or more, but less than all, of the multiple claims have been finally decided and are found otherwise to be ready for appeal. Here, Wetzel's (P) complaint set forth a single claim, which advanced a single legal theory that was applied to only one set of facts. Even if the district court's order was a declaratory judgment on the issue of liability, it still left unresolved Wetzel's (P) requests for an injunction, for compensatory and exemplary damages, and for attorney's fees. Although it might be argued that the order of the district court, insofar as it failed to include the injunctive relief requested, was an interlocutory order refusing an injunction within the meaning of 28 U.S.C. § 1292(a)(1), even if this would have allowed the obtaining of a review in the court of appeals, there was no denial of any injunction sought. Nor was the order appealable under § 1292(b). There can be no assurance that had the requirements of § 1292(b) been complied with, the court of appeals would have exercised its discretion to entertain the interlocutory appeal. The district court's order is therefore not appealable pursuant to 28 U.S.C. § 1291. Vacated and remanded.

ANALYSIS

The basic rationale for the policy in federal courts of requiring final judgments is one based upon a cost-benefit analysis. If the trial judge turns out to have been correct, the cost of allowing an interlocutory appeal is the cost of an unnecessary extra appeal. Conversely, if the trial judge turns out to have been wrong in his or her judgment, the cost of not allowing an interlocutory appeal is the sum expended for an unnecessary or an unnecessarily long trial. However, because trial judges are affirmed far more often than they are reversed, the federal policy seems to be logical.

Quicknotes

INTERLOCUTORY APPEAL The appeal of an issue that does not resolve the disposition of the case but is essential to a determination of the parties' legal rights.

Lauro Lines, s.r.l. v. Chasser

Ship company (D) v. Passenger (P)

490 U.S. 495 (1989)

NATURE OF CASE: Interlocutory appeal of a denial of a motion to dismiss action for damages for personal injuries.

FACT SUMMARY: After the district court denied Lauro Line's (Lauro's) (D) motion for dismissal based on a forum-selection clause that purportedly limited Chasser (P) to suing in Naples, Italy, Lauro (D) sought to overturn the denial on interlocutory appeal.

RULE OF LAW

Under the collateral-order doctrine, a prejudgment order may be appealed only when it conclusively determines the disputed question, resolves an important issue completely separable from the merits of the action, and is effectively unreviewable on appeal from a final judgment.

FACTS: Chasser (P) and the other plaintiffs were passengers aboard Lauro Line's (Lauro's) (D) ship, the Achille Lauro, when it was hijacked in the Mediterranean Sea by terrorists. Lauro (D) moved to dismiss Chasser's (P) personal-injury suit on the grounds that a forum-selection clause printed on the passenger tickets limited any passenger to suing in Naples, Italy. The district court denied the motion, holding that the ticket did not give passengers reasonable notice that they were giving up the right to sue in the United States. The U.S. Court of Appeals for the Second Circuit dismissed Lauro's (D) appeal, finding that the district court's order was interlocutory and not appealable. Lauro (D) appealed to the United States Supreme Court.

ISSUE: Under the collateral-order doctrine, may a prejudgment order be appealed only when it conclusively determines the disputed question, resolves an important issue completely separable from the merits of the action, and is effectively unreviewable on appeal from a final judgment?

HOLDING AND DECISION: (Brennan, J.) Yes. Under the collateral-order doctrine, a prejudgment order may be appealed only when it conclusively determines the disputed question, resolves an important issue completely separable from the merits of the action, and is effectively unreviewable on appeal from a final judgment. An order is "effectively" unreviewable on final judgment when the order involves an asserted right, the practical value of which would be destroyed if it were not vindicated before trial. Thus, interlocutory appeal is allowed when the defendant asserts a right that is not an ultimate right upon which the suit is brought. Here, Lauro (D) asserted only a right not to be sued in a particular forum. This right was not lost. Lauro (D) could assert the forum-selection clause in appealing any unfavorable final judgment. If an appeals court agreed with Lauro's (D) position, it could vacate trial judgment and limit the refiling of the case in Naples. Affirmed.

CONCURRENCE: (Scalia, J.) Implicit in the Court's ruling is that Lauro's (D) right of forum selection is not important enough to require vindication on interlocutory appeal.

ANALYSIS

Where a criminal defendant asserts a right not to be tried, an order denying that right is reviewable on interlocutory appeal. In civil cases, a partial list of orders reviewable on interlocutory appeal includes denial of a motion to dismiss based on a claim of absolute or qualified official immunity, an order denying a party leave to proceed in forma pauperis, an order requiring class action defendants to bear the cost of notifying members of the plaintiff class, and an order vacating attachment of a vessel.

Quicknotes

COLLATERAL ORDER Doctrine pursuant to which an appeal from an interlocutory order may be brought in order to hear and determine claims that are collateral to the merits of the case and that could not be granted adequate review on appeal.

IN FORMA PAUPERIS Permission to proceed with litigation without incurring fees or costs.

INTERLOCUTORY APPEAL The appeal of an issue that does not resolve the disposition of the case but is essential to a determination of the parties' legal rights.

JUDGMENT ON THE MERITS A determination of the rights of the parties to litigation based on the presentation evidence, barring the party from initiating the same suit again.

Anderson v. Bessemer City

Sex discrimination claimant (P) v. Municipality (D)

470 U.S. 564 (1985)

NATURE OF CASE: Appeal of finding of discriminatory intent in action brought under Title VII of the Civil Rights Act of 1964.

FACT SUMMARY: In Anderson's (P) action against Bessemer City (D) for discrimination in an action brought under Title VII of the Civil Rights Act of 1964, Anderson (P), a woman applying for a job as a Recreation Director for Bessemer City (D), alleged that she had been denied the position because of her sex, and that the district court's finding of discriminatory intent in Anderson's (P) action was a factual finding that could be overturned on appeal only if it was clearly erroneous.

RULE OF LAW

Under Fed. R. Civ. P. 52(a), a finding is clearly erroneous only when, although there is evidence to support it, the reviewing court, on the entire evidence, is left with the definite and firm conviction that a mistake has been made.

FACTS: In Anderson's (P) action against Bessemer City (the City) (D) for discrimination in an action brought under Title VII of the Civil Rights Act of 1964, Anderson (P), a woman, alleged that she had been denied a position as Recreation Director in a city athletic program because of her sex. After a two-day trial, the court issued a memorandum of decision setting forth its finding that Anderson (P) had been denied the position because of her sex and that male members of the City's (D) hiring commission for the position had been biased against Anderson (P) because she was a woman. The City (D) appealed and the U.S. Court of Appeals for the Fourth Circuit reversed, holding that the lower court's findings were clearly erroneous. Anderson (P) appealed.

ISSUE: Under Fed. R. Civ. P. 52(a), is a finding clearly erroneous only when, although there is evidence to support it, the reviewing court, on the entire evidence, is left with the definite and firm conviction that a mistake has been made?

HOLDING AND DECISION: (White, J.) Yes. Under Fed. R. Civ. P. 52(a), a finding is clearly erroneous only when, although there is evidence to support it, the reviewing court, on the entire evidence, is left with the definite and firm conviction that a mistake has been made. Application of the foregoing principles to the facts of this case lays bare the errors committed. The Fourth Circuit improperly conducted what amounted to a de novo weighing of the evidence in the record. The district court's findings were based on essentially undisputed evidence and from the evidence, the court determined that Anderson's (P) more varied educational and employment background and her extensive experience in variety of civil activities left her better qualified to implement such a rounded program than the other job applicants. Our determination that the findings of the district court regarding Anderson's (P) qualifications, the conduct of her interview, and the bias of the male committee members were not clearly erroneous leads this Court to conclude that the court's finding that Anderson (P) was discriminated against on account of her sex was also not clearly erroneous. Reversed.

ANALYSIS

Anderson v. Bessemer City grows out of a practice that has its roots in the distinction between law and equity. Because cases in equity were considered only on a written record and the appellate court was able to read the record as the trial court, the rule evolved in equity that the appellate court reviewed equity decisions de novo. That standard came to dominate appellate review not just of decisions in equity, but of all decisions by a judge sitting without a jury.

Quicknotes

DE NOVO The review of a lower court decision by an appellate court, which is hearing the case as if it had not been previously heard and as if no judgment had been rendered.

FED. R. CIV. P. 52(A)(6) Requires that findings of fact not be set aside unless clearly erroneous.

Van Zee v. Hanson

Individual (P) v. Individual (D)

630 F.3d 1126 (8th Cir. 2011)

NATURE OF CASE: Appeal from district court's dismissal of the complaint.

FACT SUMMARY: The United States Army cancelled Van Zee's (P) enlistment when it learned from Hanson (D), a court clerk, that Van Zee (P) had a juvenile court record.

RULE OF LAW

Consideration of matters or evidence outside of the pleadings at the motion to dismiss stage is harmless if the reviewing court gives the nonmoving party notice and the opportunity to respond.

FACTS: While Van Zee (P) was applying for enlistment into the United States Army, he completed a release form for his court records, allowing Hanson (D), the Clerk of Courts for the Sixth Judicial District of South Dakota, to release his records to the Army recruiter. When Hanson (D) did so, the Army rescinded Van Zee's (P) enlistment. Van Zee (P) brought suit against Hanson (D) in federal court for allegedly violating his right to privacy under the Fourteenth Amendment. Hanson (D) filed a motion to dismiss. In a written order, the district court required Van Zee (P) to produce the release form that granted Hanson (D) the legal ability to produce the court records. The district court then granted Hanson's (D) motion to dismiss. Van Zee (P) appealed.

ISSUE: Is consideration of matters or evidence outside of the pleadings at the motion to dismiss stage harmless if the reviewing court gives the nonmoving party notice and the opportunity to respond?

HOLDING AND DECISION: (Benton, J.) Yes. Consideration of matters or evidence outside of the pleadings at the motion to dismiss stage is harmless if the reviewing court gives the nonmoving party notice and the opportunity to respond. First, to violate the right to privacy, the information disclosed must be a shocking degradation, an egregious humiliation, or a breach of a pledge of confidentiality. Here, the district court correctly found that Van Zee (P) lacked an expectation of privacy when he had specifically signed a valid form allowing for the release of the court records. Van Zee (P) argues on appeal that the district court's reliance on the release form converted Hanson's (D) motion to dismiss into a motion for summary judgment, without giving Van Zee (P) an opportunity to respond. Typically, if a court reviews matters beyond the plaintiff's complaint, it should convert the motion to dismiss to a summary judgment motion and provide each party with an opportunity to adequately brief the issues. However, constructive notice that a court intends to consider evidence beyond the complaint satisfies this standard. Van Zee (P) had constructive notice that the district court was going to rely upon the release form when the court issued a written order requesting the submission of the form to the court in August 2009. The court dismissed the case in February 2010. Van Zee (P) had adequate notice and the opportunity to respond to the motion and the court's consideration of the release form. Affirmed.

ANALYSIS

Because the appellate court was convinced that Van Zee (P) was going to be unable to prove his claim, it was able to find that the district court's consideration of matters outside of the pleadings was harmless error. Typically, trial courts at the state and federal level will be more explicit in converting motions to dismiss to motions for summary judgment. This will better insulate the trial court's handling of the case at the appellate stage.

Quicknotes

HARMLESS ERROR An error taking place during trial that does not require the reviewing court to overturn or modify the trial court's judgment in that it did not affect the appellant's substantial rights or the disposition of the action.

MOTION TO DISMISS Motion to terminate an action based on the adequacy of the pleadings, improper service or venue, etc.

CHAPTER 11

Respect for Judgments

Quick Reference Rules of Law

	PAGE
1. *Frier v. City of Vandalia.* Claim preclusion bars a second suit where the first suit arose out of the same transaction.	*138*
2. *Semtek Intl. Inc. v. Lockheed Martin Corp.* As a matter of federal common law, a state rule of claim preclusion applies to dismissals ordered by either state or federal courts, except where state law is incompatible with federal interests.	*139*
3. *Taylor v. Sturgell.* A claim may not be precluded under a doctrine of "virtual representation" where a second claimant brings a suit identical to a first claimant and, although the claimants know each other, there is no legal relationship between them and there is no evidence that the second claimant controlled, financed, participated in, or even had notice of the earlier suit.	*141*
4. *Gargallo v. Merrill Lynch, Pierce, Fenner & Smith.* A judgment rendered by a court lacking subject matter jurisdiction does not have claim preclusive effect in subsequent proceedings.	*144*
5. *Illinois Central Gulf Railroad v. Parks.* The doctrine of estoppel by verdict allows a judgment in a prior action to operate as a complete bar to those facts or issues actually litigated and determined in the prior action.	*145*
6. *Parklane Hosiery Co. v. Shore.* A trial judge has broad discretion to permit the offensive use of collateral estoppel to establish an element of a plaintiff's case where it is not unfair to the defendant.	*146*
7. *V.L. v. E.L.* The Full Faith and Credit Clause of the United States Constitution requires that each state recognize and give effect to valid judgments issued by the courts of all other states.	*147*
8. *United States v. Beggerly.* Independent actions pursuant to Fed. R. Civ. P. 60(b) are reserved for cases of injustice sufficiently gross to demand departure from adherence to the doctrine of res judicata.	*148*

Frier v. City of Vandalia

Owner of towed car (P) v. Municipality (D)

770 F.2d 699 (7th Cir. 1985)

NATURE OF CASE: Appeal of dismissal of action for deprivation of property without due process under color of law.

FACT SUMMARY: After Charles Frier (P) lost his state court suit against the City of Vandalia (D) for replevin of his car, he then sued Vandalia (D) in federal court under 42 U.S.C. § 1983 for depriving him of his car without due process under color of law.

RULE OF LAW

Claim preclusion bars a second suit where the first suit arose out of the same transaction.

FACTS: City of Vandalia (Vandalia) (D) police had a garage tow Charles Frier's (P) car because it was parked in traffic. Frier (P) did not receive a citation or a hearing either before the car was towed or after he refused to pay to retrieve it. Frier (P) sued Vandalia (D) and the garage in state court for replevin of his car. After a trial, the court decided that Vandalia (D) had the right to tow Frier's (P) car because it was obstructing traffic. Therefore, the court did not issue the writ of replevin. Frier (P) then filed a 42 U.S.C. § 1983 suit in federal court, seeking equitable relief and compensatory and punitive damages from Vandalia (D) for depriving him of his car without due process under color of law. The district court dismissed Frier's (P) suit for failure to state a claim, and Frier (P) appealed, arguing that he was not precluded from filing a federal suit under a different legal theory than the one on which he based his state court action.

ISSUE: Does claim preclusion bar a second suit where the first suit arose out of the same transaction?

HOLDING AND DECISION: (Easterbrook, J.) Yes. Claim preclusion bars a second suit where the first suit arose out of the same transaction. Claim preclusion, also called res judicata, is designed to impel parties to consolidate all closely related matters in the same suit. First, this prevents oppression of defendants through multiple cases. Second, when the facts and issues of all theories of liability are closely related, there is no good reason to incur the cost of litigation more than once. Frier (P) could have sued in his state court action for both replevin, to get his car back, and under § 1983, for damages. Both theories alleged the same conduct: that the City of Vandalia (D) towed and detained his cars without lawful process, i.e., without a determination of a parking violation. Thus, claim preclusion bars Frier's (P) federal suit. The district court, though it properly dismissed the case, should not have reached the merits. Affirmed.

CONCURRENCE: (Swygert, J.) Frier's (P) suit should properly have been dismissed on summary judgment, but not for claim preclusion. Illinois law, applicable in this case, follows the narrower, traditional rule of claim preclusion, not the broader Restatement rule applied by the majority. Under the traditional rule, one suit bars a second where the evidence necessary to sustain a second verdict would have sustained the first, i.e., where the causes of action are based on a common core of operative facts. To prevail on his replevin claim, Frier (P) would have had to prove a superior right to possession of the car, which turned on whether he had parked illegally. However, under § 1983, the legality of Frier's (P) parking was irrelevant. The issues as to § 1983 were whether Frier (P) had notice that he would be towed for parking where he did, and whether he had a fair hearing on the detaining of his car. The fact that Frier (P) could have brought the two causes of action in the same suit is irrelevant under the traditional rule of claim preclusion.

ANALYSIS

Judge Easterbrook and Judge Swygert agree that under the "same transaction" rule Frier's (P) second suit was barred by claim preclusion or res judicata. However, Judge Swygert applied the narrower, traditional, "core of operative facts" rule to reach the opposite result on the claim preclusion issue. The federal courts and most states follow the "same transaction" rule, which is codified in the Restatement (Second) of Judgments § 24 (1982).

Quicknotes

42 U.S.C. § 1983 Provides that every person who, under color of state law, subjects, or causes to be subjected, any citizen of the United States or person within its jurisdiction to be deprived of rights, privileges and immunities guaranteed by the federal Constitution and laws, is liable to the injured party at law or in equity.

CLAIM The demand for a right to payment or equitable relief; the fact or facts giving rise to such demand.

RES JUDICATA The rule of law a final judgment by a court precludes subsequent litigation between the parties regarding the same cause of action.

Semtek Intl. Inc. v. Lockheed Martin Corp.

Injured party (P) v. Alleged wrongdoer (D)

531 U.S. 497 (2001)

NATURE OF CASE: Appeal from affirmance of dismissal of state action on res judicata grounds, giving effect to dismissal by federal court sitting in diversity jurisdiction.

FACT SUMMARY: When Semtek International, Inc.'s (Semtek's) (P) breach of contract and tort claims against Lockheed Martin Corp. (D) were barred by California's two-year statute of limitations, Semtek (P) filed the same claims in state court in Maryland, which had a three-year statute of limitations.

RULE OF LAW

As a matter of federal common law, a state rule of claim preclusion applies to dismissals ordered by either state or federal courts, except where state law is incompatible with federal interests.

FACTS: Semtek International, Inc. (Semtek) (P) sued Lockheed Martin Corp. (Lockheed) (D) for breach of contract and tort claims. After removal to federal court in California, the action was dismissed because it was barred by California's two-year statute of limitations. Semtek (P) filed the same claims in state court in Maryland, which had a three-year statute of limitations. The Maryland court dismissed the case on res judicata grounds. In affirming, the Maryland Court of Special Appeals held that, regardless of whether California state law would have accorded claim preclusive effect to a statute-of-limitations dismissal by one of its own courts, the California federal court's dismissal barred the Maryland complaint because the res judicata effect of federal diversity judgments is prescribed by federal law, under which the earlier dismissal was on the merits and claim preclusive.

ISSUE: As a matter of federal common law, does a state rule of claim preclusion apply to dismissals ordered by either state or federal courts, except where state law is incompatible with federal interests?

HOLDING AND DECISION: (Scalia, J.) Yes. As a matter of federal common law, a state rule of claim preclusion applies to dismissals ordered by either state or federal courts, except where state law is incompatible with federal interests. Semtek (P) asserts that *Dupasseur v. Rochereau*, 21 Wall. 130 (1875), which held that the res judicata effect of a federal diversity judgment "is such as would belong to judgments of the State courts rendered under similar circumstances," governs here. That case is not dispositive, however, because it was decided under the Conformity Act of 1872, which required federal courts to apply the procedural law of the forum state in nonequity cases. However, claim-preclusive effect is not, as Lockheed (D) asserts, required by Fed. R. Civ. P. § 41(b), which provides that, unless the court "otherwise specifies," an involuntary dismissal, other than a dismissal for lack of jurisdiction, improper venue, or failure to join a party under Rule 19, "operates as an adjudication upon the merits." Although the original connotation of a judgment "on the merits" was one that passes directly on the substance of a claim (which would be claim-preclusive), the meaning of the term has changed and does not necessarily designate a judgment effecting claim preclusion. There are a number of reasons that support this conclusion. First, it would be peculiar to announce a federally prescribed rule on claim preclusion in a default rule for determining a dismissal's import, or to find a rule governing the effect to be accorded federal judgments by other courts ensconced in rules governing the internal procedures of the rendering court itself. Moreover, if the rule were interpreted as Lockheed (D) suggests, it would in many cases violate the federalism principle of *Erie R. Co. v. Tompkins*, 304 U.S. 64 (1938), by engendering substantial variations in outcomes between state and federal litigation that would likely influence forum choice. Finally, the Court itself has never relied upon Rule 41(b) when recognizing the claim-preclusive effect of federal judgments in federal-question cases. Rule 41(a) makes clear "an adjudication upon the merits" in Rule 41(b) is the opposite of a dismissal without prejudice, which means that it prevents refiling of the claim in the same court. That is undoubtedly a necessary condition, but not a sufficient one, for claim-preclusive effect in other courts. Given that neither Semtek's (P) approach, nor Lockheed's (D) approach is satisfactory, what does govern the claim-preclusive effect of the California federal diversity judgment in Maryland state court? The answer is that federal common law governs the claim-preclusive effect of a dismissal by a federal court sitting in diversity, and that it is up to this Court to determine the appropriate federal rule. Since in diversity cases, state, rather than federal, substantive law is at issue, there is no need for a uniform federal rule; and nationwide uniformity is better served by having the same claim-preclusive rule (the state rule) apply whether the dismissal has been ordered by a state or a federal court. Any other rule would produce the sort of forum shopping and inequitable administration

Continued on next page.

of the laws that *Erie* seeks to avoid. While the federal reference to state law will not be workable in situations in which the state law is incompatible with federal interests, no such conflict exists here. Reversed and remanded.

ANALYSIS

An example of where federal reference to state law will not work is where state law has not given claim-preclusive effect to dismissals for willful violation of discovery orders. In such a case, the federal courts' interest in the integrity of their own processes might justify a federal rule of claim preclusion that does not reflect state law. Of course, that kind of exceptional case was not before the court.

Quicknotes

CLAIM PRECLUSION A procedural rule or order prohibiting the support or opposition to certain claims or defenses.

***ERIE* DOCTRINE** Federal courts must apply state substantive law and federal procedural law.

RES JUDICATA The rule of law that a final judgment by a court precludes subsequent litigation between the parties regarding the same cause of action.

Taylor v. Sturgell

FOIA requester (P) v. Federal official (D)

553 U.S. 880 (2008)

NATURE OF CASE: Appeal from affirmance of summary judgment for defendant in action under the Freedom of Information Act (FOIA).

FACT SUMMARY: Taylor (P) contended that his Freedom of Information Act suit seeking records from the Federal Aviation Administration (D) should not have been dismissed on grounds of claim preclusion—on the theory of "virtual representation"—merely because his friend and close associate, Herrick, had filed a similar suit seeking the same records.

RULE OF LAW

A claim may not be precluded under a doctrine of "virtual representation" where a second claimant brings a suit identical to a first claimant and, although the claimants know each other, there is no legal relationship between them and there is no evidence that the second claimant controlled, financed, participated in, or even had notice of the earlier suit.

FACTS: Herrick, an antique aircraft enthusiast sought to restore a vintage airplane manufactured by the Fairchild Engine and Airplane Corporation (FEAC). He filed a Freedom of Information Act (FOIA) request asking the Federal Aviation Administration (FAA) (D) for copies of technical documents related to the airplane. The FAA (D) denied his request based on FOIA's exemption for trade secrets. Herrick took an administrative appeal, but when Fairchild Corporation (Fairchild) (D), FEAC's successor, objected to the documents' release, the FAA (D) adhered to its original decision. Herrick then filed a FOIA lawsuit to secure the documents, which was dismissed on summary judgment by the district court and later affirmed by the court of appeals. Less than a month after that suit was resolved, Taylor (P), Herrick's friend and an antique aircraft enthusiast himself, made a FOIA request for the same documents Herrick had unsuccessfully sued to obtain. When the FAA (D) failed to respond, Taylor (P) filed suit in federal district court. Holding the suit barred by claim preclusion, the district court granted summary judgment to the FAA (D) and to Fairchild (D), as intervener in Taylor's (P) action. The court acknowledged that Taylor (P) was not a party to Herrick's suit, but held that a nonparty may be bound by a judgment if she was "virtually represented" by a party. The court of appeals affirmed, announcing a five-factor test for "virtual representation." The first two factors of that test—"identity of interests" and "adequate representation"—are necessary but not sufficient for virtual representation. In addition, at least one of three other factors must be established: "a close relationship between the present party and his putative representative," "substantial participation by the present party in the first case," or "tactical maneuvering on the part of the present party to avoid preclusion by the prior judgment." The court of appeals acknowledged the absence of any indication that Taylor (P) participated in, or even had notice of, Herrick's suit. It nonetheless found the "identity of interests," "adequate representation," and "close relationship" factors satisfied because the two men sought release of the same documents, were "close associates," had discussed working together to restore Herrick's plane, had used the same lawyer to pursue their suits, and Herrick had given Taylor (P) documents Herrick had obtained from the FAA (D) during discovery in his suit. Because these conditions sufficed to establish virtual representation, the court left open the question whether Taylor (P) had engaged in tactical maneuvering to avoid preclusion. The United States Supreme Court granted certiorari.

ISSUE: May a claim be precluded under a doctrine of "virtual representation" where a second claimant brings a suit identical to a first claimant and, although the claimants know each other, there is no legal relationship between them and there is no evidence that the second claimant controlled, financed, participated in, or even had notice of the earlier suit?

HOLDING AND DECISION: (Ginsburg, J.) No. A claim may not be precluded under a doctrine of "virtual representation" where a second claimant brings a suit identical to a first claimant and, although the claimants know each other, there is no legal relationship between them and there is no evidence that the second claimant controlled, financed, participated in, or even had notice of the earlier suit. The preclusive effect of a federal-court judgment is determined by federal common law, subject to due process limitations. Extending the preclusive effect of a judgment to a nonparty runs up against the "deep-rooted historic tradition that everyone should have his own day in court." *Richards v. Jefferson County*, 517 U.S. 793, 798 (1996). Indicating the strength of that tradition, this Court has often repeated the general rule that "one is not bound by a judgment in personam in a litigation in which he is not designated a party or to which he has not been made a party by service of process." *Hansberry v. Lee*, 311 U.S. 32, 40 (1940); *Martin v. Wilks*, 490 U.S. 755, 761 (1989) The rule against nonparty preclusion is subject to

Continued on next page.

exceptions, currently grouped into six categories. First, "[a] person who agrees to be bound by the determination of issues in an action between others is bound in accordance with the [agreement's] terms." Restatement (Second) of Judgments § 40. Second, nonparty preclusion may be based on a pre-existing substantive legal relationship between the person to be bound and a party to the judgment, e.g., assignee and assignor. Third, "in certain limited circumstances," a nonparty may be bound by a judgment because she was "adequately represented by someone with the same interests who [wa]s a party" to the suit. *Richards*, 517 U.S., at 798. Fourth, a nonparty is bound by a judgment if she "assume[d] control" over the litigation in which that judgment was rendered. *Montana v. United States*, 440 U.S. 147, 154 (1979). Fifth, a party bound by a judgment may not avoid its preclusive force by relitigating through a proxy. Preclusion is thus in order when a person who did not participate in litigation later brings suit as the designated representative or agent of a person who was a party to the prior adjudication. Sixth, a special statutory scheme otherwise consistent with due process, e.g., bankruptcy proceedings, may "expressly foreclos[e] successive litigation by nonlitigants." *Martin*, 490 U.S., at 762, n.2. Reaching beyond these six categories, the court of appeals recognized a broad "virtual representation" exception to the rule against nonparty preclusion. None of the arguments advanced by that court, the FAA (D), or Fairchild (D) justify such an expansive doctrine. The court of appeals purported to ground its doctrine in this Court's statements that, in some circumstances, a person may be bound by a judgment if she was adequately represented by a party to the proceeding yielding that judgment. But the court of appeals' definition of "adequate representation" strayed from the meaning this Court has attributed to that term. In one case, *Richards v. Jefferson County*, 517 U.S. 793 (1996), the Alabama Supreme Court had held a tax challenge barred by a judgment upholding the same tax in a suit by different taxpayers. This Court reversed, holding that nonparty preclusion was inconsistent with due process where there was no showing (1) that the court in the first suit "took care to protect the interests" of absent parties, or (2) that the parties to the first litigation "understood their suit to be on behalf of absent [parties]." In holding that representation can be "adequate" for purposes of nonparty preclusion even where these two factors are absent, the court of appeals misapplied *Richards*. Fairchild (D) and the FAA (D) ask the Court to abandon altogether the attempt to delineate discrete grounds and clear rules for nonparty preclusion. Instead, they contend, only an equitable and heavily fact-driven inquiry can account for all the situations in which nonparty preclusion is appropriate. This argument is rejected. First, the balancing test they propose is at odds with the constrained approach advanced by this Court's decisions, which have endeavored to delineate discrete, limited exceptions to the fundamental rule that a litigant is not bound by a judgment to which she was not a party. Second, a party's representation of a nonparty is "adequate" for preclusion purposes only if, at a minimum, (1) the interests of the nonparty and her representative are aligned, and (2) either the party understood herself to be acting in a representative capacity or the original court took care to protect the nonparty's interests. Adequate representation may also require (3) notice of the original suit to the persons alleged to have been represented. In the class-action context, these limitations are implemented by Fed. R. Civ. P. 23's procedural safeguards. But an expansive virtual representation doctrine would recognize a common-law kind of class action that would lack these protections. Third, a diffuse balancing approach to non-party preclusion would likely complicate the task of district courts faced in the first instance with preclusion questions. Finally, the FAA (D) maintains that nonparty preclusion should apply more broadly in "public-law" litigation than in "private-law" controversies. First, the FAA (D) points to *Richards's* acknowledgment that when a taxpayer challenges "an alleged misuse of public funds" or "other public action," the suit "has only an indirect impact on [the plaintiff's] interests," and "the States have wide latitude to establish procedures [limiting] the number of judicial proceedings that may be entertained." In contrast to the public-law litigation contemplated in *Richards*, however, a successful FOIA action results in a grant of relief to the individual plaintiff, not a decree benefiting the public at large. Furthermore, *Richards* said only that, for the type of public-law claims there envisioned, states were free to adopt procedures limiting repetitive litigation. While it appears equally evident that Congress can adopt such procedures, it hardly follows that this Court should proscribe or confine successive FOIA suits by different requesters. Second, the FAA (D) argues that, because the number of plaintiffs in public-law cases is potentially limitless, it is theoretically possible for several persons to coordinate a series of vexatious repetitive lawsuits. But this risk does not justify departing from the usual nonparty preclusion rules. Stare decisis will allow courts to dispose of repetitive suits in the same circuit, and even when stare decisis is not dispositive, the human inclination not to waste money should discourage suits based on claims or issues already decided. The remaining question is whether the result reached by the courts below can be justified based on one of the six established grounds for nonparty preclusion. With one exception, those grounds plainly have no application here. The FAA (D) and Fairchild (D) argue that Taylor's (P) suit is a collusive attempt to relitigate Herrick's claim. That argument justifies a remand to allow the courts below the opportunity to determine whether the

Continued on next page.

fifth ground for nonparty preclusion—preclusion because a nonparty to earlier litigation has brought suit as an agent of a party bound by the prior adjudication—applies to Taylor's (P) suit. However, courts should be cautious about finding preclusion on the basis of agency. A mere whiff of "tactical maneuvering" will not suffice; instead, principles of agency law indicate that preclusion is appropriate only if the putative agent's conduct of the suit is subject to the control of the party who is bound by the prior adjudication. Finally, the Court rejects Fairchild's (D) suggestion that Taylor (P) must bear the burden of proving he is not acting as Herrick's agent. Claim preclusion is an affirmative defense for the defendant to plead and prove. Vacated and remanded.

ANALYSIS

This case presented an issue of first impression in the sense that the Supreme Court had never before addressed the doctrine of "virtual representation" adopted (in varying forms) by several circuits and relied upon by the district court and court of appeals below. For example, the Eighth Circuit had developed a seven-factor test for virtual representation, which was adopted by the district court in this case. The Eighth Circuit test requires an "identity of interests" between the person to be bound and a party to the judgment. Six additional factors counsel in favor of virtual representation under the Eighth Circuit's test, but are not prerequisites: (1) a "close relationship" between the present party and a party to the judgment alleged to be preclusive; (2) "participation in the prior litigation" by the present party; (3) the present party's "apparent acquiescence" to the preclusive effect of the judgment; (4) "deliberat[e] maneuver[ing]" to avoid the effect of the judgment; (5) adequate representation of the present party by a party to the prior adjudication; and (6) a suit raising a "public law" rather than a "private law" issue. These factors, the court of appeals (D.C. Circuit) in this case observed, "constitute a fluid test with imprecise boundaries" and call for "a broad, case-by-case inquiry." The D.C. Circuit adopted a five-factor test. The Supreme Court resolved these different approaches by rejecting the doctrine of virtual representation altogether, instead relying on well-established principles of due process and claim preclusion.

Quicknotes

CLAIM PRECLUSION A procedural rule or order prohibiting the support or opposition to certain claims or defenses.

DUE PROCESS The constitutional mandate requiring the courts to protect and enforce individuals' rights and liberties consistent with prevailing principles of fairness and justice and prohibiting the federal and state governments from such activities that deprive its citizens of life, liberty, or property interest.

INTERVENOR A party, not an initial party to the action, who is admitted to the action in order to assert an interest in the subject matter of a lawsuit.

PARTY Person designated as either the defendant or plaintiff in a lawsuit.

Gargallo v. Merrill Lynch, Pierce, Fenner & Smith

Client (P) v. Broker (D)

918 F.2d 658 (6th Cir. 1990)

NATURE OF CASE: Appeal from dismissal of action for securities violations.

FACT SUMMARY: Gargallo's (P) federal court action was dismissed because in a previous state court case, his counterclaim involving the same issues was rejected.

RULE OF LAW

A judgment rendered by a court lacking subject matter jurisdiction does not have claim preclusive effect in subsequent proceedings.

FACTS: Gargallo (P) had a brokerage account with Merrill Lynch, Pierce, Fenner & Smith (Merrill Lynch) (D). When the investments went poorly, Gargallo (P) ended up owing Merrill Lynch (D) $17,000. The broker (D) brought suit in Ohio state court for collection of the debt, and Gargallo (P) filed a counterclaim alleging that the losses were caused by violation of federal securities law. The Ohio court dismissed the counterclaim with prejudice for Gargallo's (P) failure to comply with discovery requests and orders. Gargallo (P) then filed a complaint in U.S. District Court. The court dismissed the action on res judicata grounds, finding that the claims were the same as those dismissed by the Ohio court. Gargallo (P) appealed.

ISSUE: Does a judgment rendered by a court lacking subject matter jurisdiction have claim preclusive effect in subsequent proceedings?

HOLDING AND DECISION: (Ryan, J.) No. A judgment rendered by a court lacking subject matter jurisdiction does not have claim preclusive effect in subsequent proceedings. The doctrine of res judicata provides that a final judgment by a court is conclusive of the rights, questions and facts at issue with respect to the parties in all other actions. In the present case, it is clear Gargallo's (P) federal court complaint alleges the same violations that were alleged in the state court counterclaim. Ordinarily, federal courts are required to give state court judgments the same preclusive effect such judgment would have in a state court. Ohio subscribes to the position that res judicata does not apply where the original court did not have subject matter jurisdiction over the issue. In the present case, Ohio did not have jurisdiction over Gargallo's (P) allegations of securities violations by Merrill Lynch (D). Thus, the dismissal should not have been given preclusive effect in federal district court. Reversed and remanded.

ANALYSIS

The decision did not directly address the issue that Gargallo's (P) state court counterclaim was not really decided on the merits. It was dismissed because of failure to abide by discovery requirements. However, it would still have been subject to res judicata if the state court had had subject matter jurisdiction.

Quicknotes

JUDGMENT ON THE MERITS A determination of the rights of the parties to litigation based on the presentation evidence, barring the party from initiating the same suit again.

RES JUDICATA The rule of law a final judgment by a court precludes subsequent litigation between the parties regarding the same cause of action.

SUBJECT MATTER JURISDICTION The authority of the court to hear and decide actions involving a particular type of issue or subject.

Illinois Central Gulf Railroad v. Parks

Railroad company (D) v. Injured car occupants (P)

Ind. Ct. App., 181 Ind. App. 141, 390 N.E.2d 1078 (1979)

NATURE OF CASE: Interlocutory appeal from denial of motion for summary judgment.

FACT SUMMARY: Parks (P) was injured when his car collided with an Illinois Central Gulf Railroad (D) train.

RULE OF LAW

The doctrine of estoppel by verdict allows a judgment in a prior action to operate as a complete bar to those facts or issues actually litigated and determined in the prior action.

FACTS: Parks (P) and his wife were injured when their car collided with an Illinois Central Gulf Railroad (Illinois Central) (D) train. Parks's (P) wife recovered $30,000 on her claim for damages for personal injuries, but judgment was rendered for Illinois Central (D) on Parks's (P) own claim for damages for loss of services and loss of consortium. Parks (P) then sued Illinois Central (D) to recover damages for his own injuries. On Illinois Central's (D) motion for summary judgment, the trial court held that Parks's (P) claim was not barred by res judicata, and that the prior action did not collaterally estop Parks (P) on the issue of contributory negligence.

ISSUE: Does the doctrine of estoppel by verdict allow a judgment in a prior action to operate as a complete bar to those facts or issues actually litigated and determined in the prior action?

HOLDING AND DECISION: (Lybrook, J.) Yes. The doctrine of estoppel by verdict allows the judgment in a prior action to operate as an estoppel as to those facts or questions actually litigated and determined in the prior action. Where a prior judgment may have been based upon either or any of two or more distinct facts, a party desiring to plead the judgment as an estoppel by verdict must show the actual basis for the prior judgment. Here, the basis for the prior judgment against Parks (P) could have been predicated on a finding by the jury that either Parks (P) had sustained no damages, or that his own negligence was a proximate cause of his damages. Illinois Central (D) failed to show that the judgment against Parks (P) in the prior action was based upon a finding that Parks (P) was contributorily negligent in the accident. Affirmed.

ANALYSIS

The doctrine of collateral estoppel is reflective of the policy that the needs of judicial finality and efficiency outweigh the possible gains of fairness or accuracy that would result from the continued litigation of an issue that had been decided in prior judicial proceedings. There is a strong policy favoring consistency of judicial rulings in both state and federal courts.

Quicknotes

COLLATERAL ESTOPPEL A doctrine whereby issues litigated and determined in a prior proceeding are binding upon all subsequent litigation between the parties regarding that issue.

Parklane Hosiery Co. v. Shore

Hosiery company (D) v. Shareholder (P)

439 U.S. 322 (1979)

NATURE OF CASE: Review of denial of relitigation of issue determined in a separate case.

FACT SUMMARY: Shore (P) sought rescission of a merger on the grounds that Parklane Hosiery Co. (Parklane) (D), a party to the merger, had issued a false and misleading proxy statement, and in a separate action filed by the Securities Exchange Commission, the district court found the proxy statement to be false, so Shore (P) moved for partial summary judgment in this action on that issue, alleging that Parklane (D) was collaterally estopped from relitigating the issue.

RULE OF LAW

A trial judge has broad discretion to permit the offensive use of collateral estoppel to establish an element of a plaintiff's case where it is not unfair to the defendant.

FACTS: Shore (P) brought a shareholder's class action against Parklane Hosiery Co. (Parklane) (D) alleging that Parklane (D) had issued a materially false and misleading proxy statement in violation of §§ 14(a), 10(b), and 20(a) of the Securities Exchange Act. Shore (P) sought rescission of merger to which Parklane (D) was a party because of the proxy statement, which related to the merger. Before trial, however, the Securities Exchange Commission (SEC) filed suit on the same basis seeking injunctive relief. The court in that suit found the statement false and misleading and entered a declaratory judgment to that effect. Shore (P) then moved for partial summary judgment on the issue of falsity, alleging that Parklane (D) was collaterally estopped from relitigating the issue. The district court denied the motion, but the court of appeals reversed. The United States Supreme Court granted certiorari.

ISSUE: Does a trial judge have broad discretion to permit the offensive use of collateral estoppel to establish an element of a plaintiff's case where it is not unfair to the defendant?

HOLDING AND DECISION: (Stewart, J.) Yes. A trial judge has broad discretion to permit the offensive use of collateral estoppel to establish an element of a plaintiff's case where it is not unfair to the defendant. The defensive use of collateral estoppel to prevent relitigation of issues previously litigated and lost by a plaintiff against another defendant has been upheld by this Court. But the present case involves the offensive use of collateral estoppel to prevent relitigation of issues by a defendant against whom a different plaintiff has obtained a ruling. It is argued that such offensive use will not promote judicial economy because plaintiffs can await a ruling in another matter without intervening, and then be relieved of making proofs if the issue is resolved to their satisfaction, but not be foreclosed from raising it again if it is not. Here, however, it is doubtful that Shore (P) could have joined in the SEC injunction suit, so that this argument is inapplicable. Another argument is that a defendant may have little incentive to defend in an action for small or nominal damages and should not be subjected to unforeseeable future suits against which he or she will not be adequately able to defend. But here, Parklane (D) had a strong incentive for offensive use of collateral estoppel to establish an element of a plaintiff's case where it is not unfair to the defendant. Under these circumstances, it is not unfair to use collateral estoppel against Parklane (D), who had a full and fair opportunity to litigate its claims. Preclusion did not violate the Seventh Amendment.

ANALYSIS

In a separate part of the opinion, the Court found that the offensive use of collateral estoppel in this case would violate Parklane Hosiery Co.'s (D) right to a jury trial in the legal action as opposed to the Security Exchange Commission's equitable suit. This Seventh Amendment right did not, however, affect the propriety of use of collateral estoppel offensively where not unfair to the defendant if the jury trial right was not at issue.

Quicknotes

JOINDER OF PARTIES The joining of parties in one lawsuit.

OFFENSIVE COLLATERAL ESTOPPEL A doctrine that may be invoked by a plaintiff whereby a defendant is prohibited from relitigating issues litigated and determined in a prior proceeding against another plaintiff.

V.L v. E.L.

Individual (P) v. Individual (D)

577 U.S. 404 (2016)

NATURE OF CASE: Appeal from Alabama Supreme Court's ruling in favor of the defendant.

FACT SUMMARY: V.L. (P) formally adopted E.L.'s (D) biological children in Georgia. After the couple later separated while living in Alabama, V.L. (P) sought to enforce her parental rights as granted to her by the earlier adoption proceedings in Georgia.

RULE OF LAW

The Full Faith and Credit Clause of the United States Constitution requires that each state recognize and give effect to valid judgments issued by the courts of all other states.

FACTS: V.L. (P) formally adopted E.L.'s (D) biological children in Georgia. After the couple later separated while living in Alabama, V.L. (P) sought to enforce her parental rights as granted to her by the earlier adoption proceedings in Georgia. V.L. (P) specifically sought the Alabama court to recognize her valid adoption from Georgia and to grant her some level of custody or visitation rights. The trial court agreed, but the Alabama Supreme Court reversed on the grounds that the Georgia court did not have proper jurisdiction to allow V.L. (P) to adopt the children. V.L. (P) appealed to the United States Supreme Court.

ISSUE: Does the Full Faith and Credit Clause of the United States Constitution require that each state recognize and give effect to valid judgments issued by the courts of all other states?

HOLDING AND DECISION: (Per curiam). Yes. The Full Faith and Credit Clause of the United States Constitution requires that each state recognize and give effect to valid judgments issued by the courts of all other states. The clause transformed the states of the early union from sovereign entities, each free to ignore the rulings of the others, into part of single nation. Any final judgment issued by a state court with subject matter and personal jurisdiction over the case shall be recognized as valid throughout the country. One state may not disregard the rulings of another state even if it disagrees with the ruling or the reasoning supporting the decision. Essentially, the Full Faith and Credit Clause prohibits one state court from inquiring into the merits of a valid final decision by another state court. The only caveat is that a court need not afford full faith and credit to another court's decision if that court did not have jurisdiction over the case. Here, Georgia clearly had subject matter jurisdiction over V.L.'s (P) adoption of E.L.'s (D) biological children. The Alabama Supreme Court relied upon a Georgia statue that stated that a third party—here, V.L. (P)—could adopt E.L.'s (D) children only if E.L. (D) gave up her parental rights at the time. However, that statute is not a jurisdictional one. Georgia's interpretation of its own adoption scheme is not open to inquiry as it is clear the Georgia court had subject matter jurisdiction over the adoption. Reversed and remanded.

ANALYSIS

This case is a straightforward example of the application of the Full Faith and Credit Clause. As with this case, the Clause is most often tested in the arena of family law, where individuals marry, separate, move among the states, and seek to enforce prior court orders issued by other states.

Quicknotes

FULL FAITH AND CREDIT CLAUSE As provided in the U.S. Constitution, Article IV, any state judicial proceedings shall have such faith and credit given them in every court in the United States as they would in their own state.

PER CURIAM Denotes a decision that represents the opinion of the entire court.

United States v. Beggerly

Federal government (D) v. Alleged property owner (P)

524 U.S. 38 (1998)

NATURE OF CASE: Appeal from dismissal of action to set aside settlement in prior quiet title litigation.

FACT SUMMARY: Beggerly (P) sought to set aside an earlier judgment based on a settlement.

RULE OF LAW

Independent actions pursuant to Fed. R. Civ. P. 60(b) are reserved for cases of injustice sufficiently gross to demand departure from adherence to the doctrine of res judicata.

FACTS: In 1979, the United States (D) brought a quiet title action in Mississippi against Beggerly (P) over certain real property. The issue was whether the land in question had been deeded prior to the date of the Louisiana Purchase in 1803. If not, the United States (D) would own it and not have to purchase it from Beggerly (P). During discovery, Beggerly (P) sought proof of title. A search by government officials of public records revealed nothing that proved a land grant prior to 1803. On the eve of trial, the case was settled for a modest sum and judgment entered based on the agreement. However, Beggerly (P) continued to search for information and in 1991, a specialist claimed to have found a grant in 1781. Beggerly (P) then filed a complaint seeking to set aside the settlement and award damages. The district court dismissed the case on jurisdictional grounds but the court of appeals reversed, deciding that it qualified as an independent action under Fed. R. Civ. P. 60(b).

ISSUE: Are independent actions pursuant to Fed. R. Civ. P. 60(b) reserved for cases of injustice sufficiently gross to demand departure from adherence to the doctrine of res judicata?

HOLDING AND DECISION: (Rehnquist, C.J.) Yes. Independent actions pursuant to Fed. R. Civ. P. 60(b) are reserved for cases of injustice sufficiently gross to demand departure from adherence to the doctrine of res judicata. Prior to the adoption of the Federal Rules of Civil Procedure, the availability of relief from a judgment turned on whether the court was still in the same term in which the challenged judgment was entered. The 1946 amendment to Fed. R. Civ. P. 60 made clear that all old forms of relief from a judgment were abolished except for the independent action. However, an independent action is only available to prevent a grave miscarriage of justice. In the present case, it is obvious that Beggerly's (P) allegations do not come close to meeting this standard. Beggerly (P) alleges only that the Government (D) failed to thoroughly search its record. It would surely result in no grave injustice to allow the settlement and judgment in the prior litigation to stand. Therefore, the court of appeals is reversed, and the case remanded.

ANALYSIS

The decision noted that the alleged failure to furnish relevant information could possibly fit under Fed. R. Civ. P. 60(b)(3). This subsection provides for a one-year limit on motions. Given that the time limit had long expired, the court declined to fully rule on this possibility.

Quicknotes

ACTION TO QUIET TITLE Equitable action to resolve conflicting claims to an interest in real property.

RES JUDICATA The rule of law that a final judgment by a court precludes subsequent litigation between the parties regarding the same cause of action.

CHAPTER 12

Joinder

Quick Reference Rules of Law

PAGE

1. *Cordero v. Voltaire, LLC.* Federal courts may have supplemental jurisdiction pursuant to 28 U.S.C. 1367 over state law claims if those claims are so related to the federal claim as to form part of the same case or controversy under Article III of the United States Constitution. *151*

2. *Mosley v. General Motors Corp.* Permissive joinder of parties is to be broadly granted under Fed. R. Civ. P. 20 where each party seeks relief arising out of the same transaction or series of transactions and a common question of fact or law will arise in the action. *153*

3. *Price v. CTB, Inc.* A defendant may assert a claim against anyone not a party to the original action if that third party's liability is in some way dependent upon the outcome of the original action. *154*

4. *Temple v. Synthes Corp.* Joint tortfeasors are not necessary parties under Fed. R. Civ. P. 19. *155*

5. *Marvel Characters, Inc. v. Kirby.* A person is not an "indispensable party" to an action under Fed. R. Civ. P. 19(b) where a judgment rendered in the person's absence will not prejudice that person or the parties to the action; where the judgment will be adequate in settling the parties' dispute; where any prejudice to the absent person is minimized because that person's interests are aligned in all respects with, and represented by the same counsel for, the remaining parties on one side of the action; and the plaintiff would not have an adequate remedy if the action were dismissed for nonjoinder. *156*

6. *United States v. City of Los Angeles.* (1) A third party must be permitted to intervene in an action as of right where (1) it has a significant protectable interest relating to the property or transaction that is the subject of the action; (2) the disposition of the action may, as a practical matter, impair or impede the applicant's ability to protect its interest; (3) the application is timely; and (4) the existing parties may not adequately represent the applicant's interest. (2) A third party may be granted permissive intervention for the enforcement of a proposed government consent decree where its claim or defense and the main action have a question of law or fact in common, it otherwise has satisfied the requirements of Fed. R. Civ. P. 24(b), and granting intervention will not unduly delay or prejudice the adjudication of the rights of the original parties. *158*

7. *Martin v. Wilks.* A party may not be bound by a judgment rendered in an action in which he or she was not a party, even if he or she had knowledge of the action. *161*

8. *Hansberry v. Lee.* There must be adequate representation of the members of a class action or the judgment is not binding on the parties not adequately represented. *162*

9. *Phillips Petroleum v. Shutts.* A state may exercise jurisdiction over absent plaintiffs in a classification suit even if the plaintiffs have no contacts with that state. *163*

10. *Standard Fire Ins. Co. v. Knowles.* A class action representative plaintiff's stipulation as to the amount of damages the class will seek is not binding for purposes of determining a jurisdictional amount-in-controversy. *164*

CHAPTER 12

Cordero v. Voltaire, LLC

Individuals (P) v. Corporation (D)

2013 WL 6415667 (W.D. Tex. 2013)

NATURE OF CASE: United States magistrate judge's report and recommendation to district court regarding plaintiffs' motion to dismiss defendant's counterclaims.

FACT SUMMARY: Cordero (P) and several other employees of Voltaire, LLC (D), a construction company, filed wage and hour claims against Voltaire (D) on the grounds the company failed to pay them for overtime. Voltaire (D) filed counterclaims for fraud and theft against the plaintiffs.

RULE OF LAW

Federal courts may have supplemental jurisdiction pursuant to 28 U.S.C. 1367 over state law claims if those claims are so related to the federal claim as to form part of the same case or controversy under Article III of the United States Constitution.

FACTS: Cordero (P) and several other employees of Voltaire, LLC (D), a construction company, filed wage and hour claims against Voltaire (D) on the grounds the company failed to pay them for overtime in violation of the Fair Labor Standards Act (FLSA). Voltaire (D) filed counterclaims for fraud against Cordero (P) and the other plaintiffs on the grounds they falsified their timesheets. In addition, Voltaire (D) alleges the plaintiffs stole equipment and other construction materials from Voltaire. Cordero (P) and the plaintiffs filed a motion to dismiss all of Voltaire's (D) counterclaims on the grounds the federal court did not have supplemental jurisdiction over Voltaire's (D) state law claims. The case was referred to a United States magistrate judge to consider the plaintiffs' motion to dismiss.

ISSUE: May federal courts have supplemental jurisdiction pursuant to 28 U.S.C. 1367 over state law claims if those claims are so related to the federal claim as to form part of the same case or controversy under Article III of the United States Constitution?

HOLDING AND DECISION: (Austin, J.). Yes. Federal courts may have supplemental jurisdiction pursuant to 28 U.S.C. 1367 over state law claims if those claims are so related to the federal claim as to form part of the same case or controversy under Article III of the United States Constitution. Before 1990, whether a state law claim could be heard by a federal court depended mainly upon whether the claim was compulsory or permissive. Compulsory state law counterclaims were those that arose from the same transaction or occurrence as the plaintiff's federal claim. Under Fed. R. Civ. P. 13(a), the defendant must bring the claim or waive it. A permissive state law counterclaim, arising independently from the facts supporting the plaintiff's claim, must have an independent ground for federal subject matter jurisdiction. Congress essentially did away with the distinction of compulsory versus permissive counterclaims with the enactment of 28 U.S.C 1367 in 1990. Now, permissive counterclaims need not have an independent basis for jurisdiction, but they must be so related to the federal claim as to form the same case under Article III. Here, Voltaire's (D) counterclaim for fraud against Cordero (P) for falsifying timesheets arises from the same facts supporting Cordero's (P) FLSA claim. Both claims will rely upon similar evidence: number of hours worked, Cordero's (P) timesheets, and the amounts he was actually paid. Conversely, Voltaire's (D) claims against the plaintiffs that they stole equipment and materials from the company arise from a different set of facts. An entirely different body of evidence will be required to prove those particular claims. Those claims do not satisfy the standard of supplemental jurisdiction. Accordingly, it is recommended that the district court deny Cordero's (P) motion to dismiss Voltaire's (D) counterclaim for fraud but grant Cordero's (P) motion to dismiss Voltaire's (D) counterclaim for theft.

ANALYSIS

The *Cordero v. Voltaire, LLC* decision also notes the accepted guidance that federal courts should be hesitant to allow employers to clutter up a plaintiff's wage and hour claim with counterclaims that are independent of the plaintiff's claims. The main function of federal courts when faced with a Fair Labor Standards Act claim is to determine whether a company paid its employees the proper wages.

Quicknotes

COMPULSORY COUNTERCLAIM An independent cause of action brought by a defendant to a lawsuit that arises out of the same transaction or occurrence that is the subject matter of the plaintiff's claim.

FAIR LABOR STANDARDS ACT (FLSA) Enacted in 1938, the statute establishes a minimum wage applicable to all employees of covered employers and provides for mandatory overtime payment for covered employees who

Continued on next page.

work more than 40 hours a week. Executive, administrative and professional employees paid on a salary basis are exempt from the statute.

PERMISSIVE COUNTERCLAIM An independent cause of action brought by a defendant to a lawsuit in order to oppose or deduct from the plaintiff's claim that does not arise out of the transaction or occurrence that is the subject matter of the plaintiff's claim.

Mosley v. General Motors Corp.

Class-action plaintiffs (P) v. Car company (D)

497 F.2d 1330 (8th Cir. 1974)

NATURE OF CASE: Appeal from order requiring severance of joint action.

FACT SUMMARY: Mosley (P) and nine other plaintiffs brought this class action against General Motors Corp. (D) for various acts of race and sex discrimination, and the district court ordered the ten plaintiffs to bring ten separate actions due to the wide variety of the claims and the unmanageability of the joint proceeding.

RULE OF LAW

Permissive joinder of parties is to be broadly granted under Fed. R. Civ. P. 20 where each party seeks relief arising out of the same transaction or series of transactions and a common question of fact or law will arise in the action.

FACTS: Mosley (P) and nine other plaintiffs brought this class action against General Motors Corp. (GM) (D) alleging various different acts that in some cases they contended constituted racial discrimination and in others sex discrimination. They filed complaints individually with the Equal Employment Opportunity Commission (EEOC), and the EEOC notified each of their right to bring a civil action in federal court. At that point the plaintiffs joined in bringing the class action. The district court ordered that each plaintiff bring a separate action, separately filed, due to the differing types of claims alleged and the unmanageability of the joint proceeding. The judge found that there was no right to relief arising out of the same transaction or series of transactions or a common question of fact or law as required by Fed. R. Civ. P. 20. Mosley (P) appealed.

ISSUE: Is permissive joinder of parties to be broadly granted under Fed. R. Civ. P. 20 where each party seeks relief arising out of the same transaction or series of transactions and a common question of fact or law will arise in the action?

HOLDING AND DECISION: (Ross, J.) Yes. Permissive joinder of parties is to be broadly granted under Fed. R. Civ. P. 20 where each party seeks relief arising out of the same transaction or series of transactions and a common question of fact or law will arise in the action. The purpose of Fed. R. Civ. P. 20 is to promote trial convenience and expedite the final determination of disputes. The rules permit the trial judge, however, to order separate trials within his discretion if such an order will prevent delay or prejudice. Reversal of such an order depends upon an abuse of that discretion. In this case, a series of "logically related" events occurred, which has been held to constitute a single series of transactions as required. Furthermore, the rights asserted depend on a common question of law. The district court abused its discretion, therefore, in ordering the separate trials. Reversed and remanded.

ANALYSIS

It is not often easy to determine a single series of transactions when distinct events have taken place. However, a series of employment or advancement decisions together appearing like a policy of discrimination is the kind of matter that Fed. R. Civ. P. 20 seeks to have determined in one action. It is when the rights of the parties suffer at the expense of judicial economy that Fed. R. Civ. P. 20(b) can be involved to require separate trials, rather than when the judge finds the case "unmanageable."

Quicknotes

FED. R. CIV. P. 20 Provides that parties requesting relief for injuries arising from the same transaction or common question of law or fact be permitted to consolidate their actions into a single action.

PERMISSIVE JOINDER The joining of parties or claims in a single suit if the claims against the parties arise from the same transaction or occurrence or involve common issues of law or fact; such joinder is not mandatory.

Price v. CTB, Inc.

Chicken farmer (P) v. Construction contractor (D)

168 F. Supp. 2d 1299 (M.D. Ala. 2001)

NATURE OF CASE: Motion to dismiss an impleaded party.

FACT SUMMARY: When Price (P) sued Latco (D) for faulty construction of a chicken house, Latco (D), in turn, impleaded ITW (D), the manufacturer of the nails, on theories of statutory and common-law indemnity.

RULE OF LAW

A defendant may assert a claim against anyone not a party to the original action if that third party's liability is in some way dependent upon the outcome of the original action.

FACTS: Price (P), a chicken farmer, hired Latco (D) to build a chicken house. Alleging defective construction, Price (P) sued CTB (D), which equips poultry houses, and Latco (D), who was the original defendant in the underlying suit concerning the quality of construction workmanship. Latco (D), in turn, moved to implead ITW (D), alleging that ITW (D), a nail manufacturer, defectively designed the nails used in the construction. The specific causes of action against ITW (D) included (1) breach of warranty, (2) Alabama's extended manufacturer's liability doctrine, and (3) common-law indemnity. ITW (D) moved that it be dismissed from the suit on the grounds that it had been improperly impleaded under Fed. R. Civ. P. Rule 14.

ISSUE: May a defendant assert a claim against anyone not a party to the original action if that third party's liability is in some way dependent upon the outcome of the original action?

HOLDING AND DECISION: (De Ment, J.) Yes. A defendant may assert a claim against anyone not a party to the original action if that third party's liability is in some way dependent upon the outcome of the original action. Under the doctrine of implied contractual indemnity, Alabama courts recognize that a manufacturer of a product has impliedly agreed to indemnify the seller when (1) the seller is without fault, (2) the manufacturer is responsible, and (3) the seller has been required to pay a monetary judgment. Here, under Latco's (D) theory, should it be found liable for its construction of the chicken houses, it can demonstrate that the true fault lies with the nail guns and the nails manufactured by ITW (D). Accordingly, Alabama law provides Latco (D) a cause of action under common-law indemnity against ITW (D). Although the doctrine permits recovery only when the party to be indemnified is without fault, whether such a factual scenario will be proven at trial is irrelevant for present purposes. The only issue presently is whether there is a legal basis to implead ITW (D), not whether ITW (D) is, in fact, liable to Latco (D). Since Fed. R. Civ. P. 14 permits Latco (D) to implead any party who "may be liable," it follows that the court must permit development of the factual-record so the extent of that liability may be determined. Furthermore, it is well established that a properly impleaded claim may serve as an anchor for separate and independent claims under Rule 18(a). In short, Latco (D) has properly impleaded ITW (D) under Rule 14(a). ITW's (D) motion to dismiss is denied.

ANALYSIS

In *Price*, the court noted that there is a limitation on the general rule of permitting a defendant to assert a claim against anyone not a party to the original action if that third party's liability is in some way dependent upon the outcome of the original action. Even though it may arise out of the same general set of facts as the main claim, a third-party claim will not be permitted when it is based upon a separate and independent claim. Rather, the third-party liability must in some way be derivative of the original claim; a third party may be impleaded only when the original defendant is trying to pass all or part of the liability onto that third party.

Quicknotes

FED. R. CIV. P. 14 Permits the impleader of a party who is or may be liable in order to determine the rights of all parties in one proceeding.

IMPLEADER Procedure by which a third party, who may be liable for all or part of liability, is joined to an action so that all issues may be resolved in a single suit.

INDEMNITY The duty of a party to compensate another for damages sustained.

Temple v. Synthes Corp.

Medical implant user (P) v. Implant manufacturer (D)

498 U.S. 5, *reh'g. denied*, 498 U.S. 1092 (1990)

NATURE OF CASE: Appeal of dismissal with prejudice of action for damages for products liability, medical malpractice, and negligence.

FACT SUMMARY: Temple's (P) federal suit against Synthes Corp. (D), the manufacturer of a plate implanted in Temple's (P) back, was dismissed when Temple (P) failed to join the doctor and the hospital responsible for installing the plate.

RULE OF LAW

Joint tortfeasors are not necessary parties under Fed. R. Civ. P. 19.

FACTS: A plate and screw device implanted in Temple's (P) back malfunctioned. Temple (P) filed a federal court products liability action against Synthes Corp. (D), the manufacturer of the device. Temple (P) also filed a state-court medical-malpractice and negligence action against the doctor who implanted the device and the hospital where the operation was performed. Synthes (D) filed a motion to dismiss the federal lawsuit under Fed. R. Civ. P. 19 for Temple's (P) failure to join necessary parties. The district court agreed that the doctor and the hospital were necessary parties and gave Temple (P) 20 days to join them. When Temple (P) did not, the court dismissed the suit with prejudice. The court of appeals affirmed, finding that Rule 19 allowed the district court to order joinder in the interest of complete, consistent, and efficient settlement of controversies. It further found that overlapping, separate lawsuits would have prejudiced Synthes (D) because Synthes (D) might claim the device was not defective but that the doctor and the hospital were negligent, and the doctor and the hospital might claim the opposite. Temple (P) appealed, arguing that joint tortfeasors are not necessary parties under Fed. R. Civ. P. 19.

ISSUE: Are joint tortfeasors necessary parties under Fed. R. Civ. P. 19?

HOLDING AND DECISION: (Per curiam) No. Joint tortfeasors are not necessary parties under Fed. R. Civ. P. 19. It has long been the rule that joint tortfeasors need not be named as defendants in a single lawsuit. Fed. R. Civ. P. 19 does not change that principle. The Advisory Committee Notes to Fed. R. Civ. P. 19(a) state that a tortfeasor with the usual joint and several liability is merely a permissive party. There is a public interest in avoiding multiple lawsuits. However, since the requirements of Fed. R. Civ. P. 19(a) have not been met, the district court had no authority to order dismissal. Reversed and remanded.

ANALYSIS

The function of compulsory joinder codified in Fed. R. Civ. P. 19 is to bring all affected parties into the same lawsuit. Joinder is often required where the suit involves jointly held rights or liabilities, where more than one party claims the same property, or where granting relief necessarily would affect the rights of parties not in the lawsuit. Though there is a strong interest in "complete, consistent, and efficient settlement of controversies," compulsory joinder is limited. There is a strong tradition of allowing the parties themselves to determine who shall be a party, what claims shall be litigated, and what litigation strategies shall be followed.

Quicknotes

COMPULSORY JOINDER The joining of a party to a lawsuit that is mandatory if complete relief cannot be afforded to the parties in his or her absence or if his or her absence will result in injustice.

FED. R. CIV. P. 19 Sets forth the rules governing required joinder of parties.

JOINDER The joining of claims or parties in one lawsuit.

JOINT TORTFEASORS Two or more parties who either act in concert, or whose individual acts combine to cause a single injury, rendering them jointly and severally liable for any damages incurred.

NECESSARY PARTIES Parties whose joining in a lawsuit is essential to the disposition of the action.

Marvel Characters, Inc. v. Kirby

Comic books publisher (P) v. Comic book artist's child and heir (D)

726 F.3d 119 (2d Cir. 2013)

NATURE OF CASE: Appeal by defendants from grant of summary judgment to plaintiff in action for declaratory judgment as to the copyright owner of comics drawn by defendants' father.

FACT SUMMARY: After Marvel Characters, Inc. (Marvel) (P) was granted summary judgment against Lisa (D), Neal (D), Susan (D), and Barbara (D) Kirby (collectively, the "Kirbys" (D)) in a declaratory judgment action Marvel (P) brought in New York federal district court to establish that it owned the copyright in comic books drawn by Jack Kirby, the Kirbys (D) contended that because the district court lacked jurisdiction over Lisa (D) and Neal (D), who resided in California and as to whom judgment had been vacated, the judgment as against Barbara (D) and Susan (D) likewise had to be vacated on the grounds that Lisa (D) and Neal (D) were "indispensable" parties under Fed. R. Civ. P. 19.

RULE OF LAW

A person is not an "indispensable party" to an action under Fed. R. Civ. P. 19(b) where a judgment rendered in the person's absence will not prejudice that person or the parties to the action; where the judgment will be adequate in settling the parties' dispute; where any prejudice to the absent person is minimized because that person's interests are aligned in all respects with, and represented by the same counsel for, the remaining parties on one side of the action; and the plaintiff would not have an adequate remedy if the action were dismissed for nonjoinder.

FACTS: Jack Kirby (Kirby) drew comic books for over 50 years. Marvel Characters, Inc. (Marvel (P)) claimed that Kirby had drawn the comic books as "works made for hire," and that, therefore, it owned the copyright in the comic books. Kirby's children and heirs, Lisa (D), Neal (D), Susan (D), and Barbara (D) Kirby (collectively, the "Kirbys" (D)) contended that Kirby had owned the copyrights to the works, such that "termination rights"—i.e., the right to revoke any property interest that Kirby had granted to Marvel (P) with respect to the works—passed to them upon his death. Marvel (P) filed suit in federal district court in New York, seeking a declaratory judgment against the Kirbys (D) that it was the rightful copyright owner. The Kirbys, who were all represented by the same counsel, (D) moved for dismissal, and Lisa (D) and Neal (D), who were California residents, asserted that there was no personal jurisdiction over them. The Kirbys also argued that Lisa (D) and Neal (D) were indispensable to the action under Fed. R. Civ. P. 19, and that Marvel's (P) entire suit, therefore, had to be dismissed as against all parties. It was in the Kirbys'(P) interest to have the entire suit dismissed, because to effect their termination rights, they needed three of the four siblings ("more than one-half" under the relevant copyright statute). If Barbara (D) and Susan (D) were disabled by an adverse judgment in this suit from effecting termination, all four Kirbys (D) would lose. The district court denied the Kirbys' (D) motion, finding there was personal jurisdiction over Lisa (D) and Neal (D) under New York's long-arm statute, and that the court could constitutionally exercise such jurisdiction. After discovery, the parties filed cross-motions for summary judgment. The district court sided with Marvel (P), concluding that Kirby's comic book drawings were works made for hire and granted its motion. The Second Circuit Court of Appeals granted review.

ISSUE: Is a person an "indispensable party" to an action under Fed. R. Civ. P. 19(b) where a judgment rendered in the person's absence will not prejudice that person or the parties to the action; where the judgment will be adequate in settling the parties' dispute; where any prejudice to the absent person is minimized because that person's interests are aligned in all respects with, and represented by the same counsel for, the remaining parties on one side of the action; and the plaintiff would not have an adequate remedy if the action were dismissed for nonjoinder?

HOLDING AND DECISION: (Sack, J.) No. A person is not an "indispensable party" to an action under Fed. R. Civ. P. 19(b) where a judgment rendered in the person's absence will not prejudice that person or the parties to the action; where the judgment will be adequate in settling the parties' dispute; where any prejudice to the absent person is minimized because that person's interests are aligned in all respects with, and represented by the same counsel for, the remaining parties on one side of the action; and the plaintiff would not have an adequate remedy if the action were dismissed for nonjoinder. It is assumed that Lisa (D) and Neal (D) are "required" parties under Rule 19(a), that is, their participation is so important or desirable that they must joined as long as certain prudential requirements are met. Rule 19(b) is triggered where a "required" person cannot be joined for some reason. That is the case here, because the court does not have jurisdiction over Lisa (D) and Neal (D), who are

Continued on next page.

unwilling to consent to suit in New York. Rule 19(b) sets forth four factors for a court to consider in determining whether the equities are such that it would be more equitable to dismiss the suit in its entirety rather than leaving the required person out of the litigation. These four considerations are (1) whether a judgment rendered in a person's absence might prejudice that person or parties to the action, (2) the extent to which any prejudice could be alleviated, (3) whether a judgment in the person's absence would be adequate, and (4) whether the plaintiff would have an adequate remedy if the court dismissed the suit. As to the first factor, Marvel (P) will not be prejudiced by Lisa (D) and Neal's (D) absence, because a judgment against Barbara (D) and Susan (D) will foreclose Lisa (D) and Neal's (D) rights too. Nor can Barbara and Susan claim prejudice, as their rights will be fully adjudicated. There is thus no prejudice to Marvel (P), Barbara (D), or Susan (D) as "existing parties." As to the second factor, there is no way to craft a judgment that would alleviate any possible prejudice to Lisa (D) and Neal (D), as it will declare only whether Barbara (D) and Susan (D) have rights of termination or not. Regarding the third factor, any judgment would be "adequate" in the sense that the dispute likely will be settled without further litigation and would promote the public interest in settling disputes by wholes. Also, although Lisa (D) and Neal's (D) legal rights will be determined in their absence, the potential prejudice to an absent party under Rule 19(b) is mitigated where a remaining party can champion the absentee's interest, and such prejudice practically vanishes when, as in this case, the remaining parties are represented by the same counsel, and when the absent and remaining parties' interests are aligned in all respects. Finally, as to the fourth factor, Marvel (P) would not have an adequate remedy if the action were dismissed for nonjoinder because, given that two of the Kirbys (D) reside in New York and two reside in California, the Kirbys (D) could well thwart a declaratory judgment action brought by Marvel (P) in either state. For these reasons, Lisa (D) and Neal (D) are not so-called "indispensable" parties, and it was appropriate for the action against Barbara (D) and Susan (D) to have proceeded on its merits. Moreover, summary judgment against them was appropriate. Accordingly, the district court's judgment against Lisa (D) and Neal (D) is vacated and remanded with instructions to dismiss the action as against them for want of personal jurisdiction, and the judgment in favor of Marvel (P) against Barbara (D) and Susan (D) is affirmed.

ANALYSIS

As this case illustrates, Fed. R. Civ. P. 19 recognizes exceptional circumstances in which the plaintiff's choice of parties or forum must give way because of an absent party's interest in the outcome of the action or involvement in the underlying dispute. The Rule's principal provisions are divided into two subsections. Subsection (a) protects certain parties by deeming them "required"; a party who is "required" according to the factors enumerated in subsection (a) is one whose participation is so desirable or important that the party must be joined so long as the person is subject to service of process and joinder will not deprive the court of subject-matter jurisdiction. Subsection (b) addresses situations in which a party otherwise "required" under subsection (a) cannot be joined for some reason, for example (as in this case), want of personal jurisdiction. In such circumstances, Rule 19(b) requires courts to consider whether, "in equity and good conscience," the party is one without whom the action between the remaining parties cannot proceed – or, in the former terminology of the subsection, whether the absent party is "indispensable." The term "indispensable" was used only in a conclusory sense, that is, a person was "regarded as indispensable" when the person could not be made a party and, upon consideration of the four factors enumerated in subsection 19(b), it was determined that in the person's absence it would be preferable to dismiss the action, rather than to retain it. Because the phrase was used only to express a conclusion reached by applying the tests already in Rule 19(b), it was discarded as redundant and no longer appears in the statute.

Quicknotes

DECLARATORY JUDGMENT A judgment of the court establishing the rights of the parties in a controversy that does not grant damages but is binding.

INDISPENSABLE PARTY A party whose joining in a lawsuit is essential for the adequate disposition of the action and without whom the action cannot proceed.

PERSONAL JURISDICTION The court's authority over a person or parties to a lawsuit.

SUMMARY JUDGMENT Judgment rendered by a court in response to a motion made by one of the parties, claiming that the lack of a question of material fact in respect to an issue warrants disposition of the issue without consideration by the jury.

United States v. City of Los Angeles

Federal government (P) v. Municipality (D)

288 F.3d 391 (9th Cir. 2002)

NATURE OF CASE: Appeal from denial of motions by various third parties to intervene as of right and permissively in action challenging as unconstitutional a municipal police force's pattern of police misconduct and corruption.

FACT SUMMARY: The United States (P) brought an action in federal district court against the City of Los Angeles (the City) (D), the City's (D) Board of Police Commissioners (D), and the Los Angeles Police Department (LAPD) (D), alleging that they engaged in pattern or practice of depriving individuals of constitutional rights through use of excessive force, false arrests, and improper searches and seizures. After the parties lodged a proposed consent decree, the Los Angeles Police Protective League (the Police League), which served as the designated bargaining unit for the City's (D) rank and file police officers, moved to intervene as of right and permissively, contending that the consent decree would violate a Memorandum of Understanding between the Police League and the City (D) pursuant to which the City (D) employed police officers. Various individuals and organizations, who were affected by the allegedly unconstitutional police misconduct at issue and who had previously sought police reform, also moved to intervene as of right and permissively, seeking to ensure that they would be able to participate in the reform process and that the reform sought by the United States (P) would be successful.

RULE OF LAW

(1) A third party must be permitted to intervene in an action as of right where (1) it has a significant protectable interest relating to the property or transaction that is the subject of the action; (2) the disposition of the action may, as a practical matter, impair or impede the applicant's ability to protect its interest; (3) the application is timely; and (4) the existing parties may not adequately represent the applicant's interest.

(2) A third party may be granted permissive intervention for the enforcement of a proposed government consent decree where its claim or defense and the main action have a question of law or fact in common, it otherwise has satisfied the requirements of Fed. R. Civ. P. 24(b), and granting intervention will not unduly delay or prejudice the adjudication of the rights of the original parties.

FACTS: The United States (P) brought an action in federal district court against the City of Los Angeles (the City) (D), the City's (D) Board of Police Commissioners (D), and the Los Angeles Police Department (LAPD) (D), alleging that they engaged in pattern or practice of depriving individuals of constitutional rights through use of excessive force, false arrests, and improper searches and seizures. After the parties lodged a proposed consent decree with the district court, the Los Angeles Police Protective League (the Police League), which served as the designated bargaining unit for the City's (D) rank and file police officers, filed a motion to intervene. The Police League and the City (D) operated pursuant to a Memorandum of Understanding (MOU) that governed the terms and conditions under which members of the Police League were employed by the City (D). The Police League claimed that the consent decree proposed to the district court is incompatible with the MOU. The district court denied the Police League's motion to intervene as a matter of right and its motion for permissive intervention. Additionally, a number of community groups and individuals (collectively, the "Community Interveners") also moved to intervene, both as of right and permissively. The individuals were people of color, many of whom lived in areas of the City (D) that had high crime rates, who submitted uncontroverted declarations stating that they have suffered from, and were likely to continue to suffer from, the unconstitutional police misconduct that formed the basis of the action. The organizations were various community action groups that have worked with such individuals and the LAPD (D) for many years, seeking police reform. The Community Interveners desired to intervene to help ensure that the reform sought would be successful and to be able to participate in that reform process. The district court denied all the Community Interveners' motions, holding that as a matter of law, intervention for enforcement of a proposed government consent decree is never permissible. The Police League and the Community Interveners appealed, and the Ninth Circuit Court of Appeals granted review.

ISSUE:

(1) Must a third party be permitted to intervene in an action as of right where (1) it has a significant protectable interest relating to the property or transaction that is the subject of the action; (2) the disposition of the action may, as a practical matter, impair or impede the applicant's ability to protect its interest; (3) the application is timely; and (4) the

Continued on next page.

existing parties may not adequately represent the applicant's interest?

(2) May a third party be granted permissive intervention for the enforcement of a proposed government consent decree where its claim or defense and the main action have a question of law or fact in common, it otherwise has satisfied the requirements of Fed. R. Civ. P. 24(b), and granting intervention will not unduly delay or prejudice the adjudication of the rights of the original parties?

HOLDING AND DECISION: (Thomas, J.)

(1) Yes. A third party must be permitted to intervene in an action as of right where (1) it has a significant protectable interest relating to the property or transaction that is the subject of the action; (2) the disposition of the action may, as a practical matter, impair or impede the applicant's ability to protect its interest; (3) the application is timely; and (4) the existing parties may not adequately represent the applicant's interest. Here, that the Police League's motion to intervene was timely is not at issue, so the third factor is satisfied. The district court determined that the Police League had no protectable interest in the merits of the action, but that it had a protectable interest in the proposed consent decree as a remedy. The district court was correct regarding the Police League's interest in the consent decree, given that the Police League has state-law rights to negotiate about the terms and conditions of its members' employment as LAPD (D) officers and to rely on the collective bargaining agreement that is a result of those negotiations. These rights give it an interest in the consent decree at issue. However, the district court erred as to the merits of the action because the complaint seeks injunctive relief against the Police League's members and raises factual allegations that its member officers committed unconstitutional acts in the line of duty. Except as part of court-ordered relief after a judicial determination of liability, an employer cannot unilaterally change a collective bargaining agreement as a means of settling a dispute over whether the employer has engaged in constitutional violations. Thus, the Police League's interest in the consent decree is twofold. To the extent that it contains or might contain provisions that contradict terms of the officers' Memorandum of Understanding (MOU), the Police League has an interest. Further, to the extent that it is disputed whether or not the consent decree conflicts with the MOU, the Police League has the right to present its views on the subject to the district court and have them fully considered in conjunction with the district court's decision to approve the consent decree. Moreover, the existing parties do not adequately represent the Police League. Normally, a presumption of adequate representation generally arises when the representative is a governmental body or officer charged by law with representing the interests of the absentee. However, this presumption arises when the government is acting on behalf of a constituency that it represents, not when the government acts as an employer, as here, where parties are antagonists in the collective bargaining process. The Police League is the designated representative of its members in that endeavor; the City (D) is not. Further, the record in the action and the past dealings of the parties indicate a marked divergence of positions concerning key elements of the decree and underlying theories of liability. Therefore, the Police League has made the minimal showing needed to establish that the City's (D) representation of member police officers "may" be inadequate. For these reasons, the district court erred in denying the Police League's motion to intervene as of right. The district court's order denying the Police League's motion for intervention as a matter of right is reversed.

The district court did not err in denying the Community Intervener's motion to intervene as of right. It is assumed that the Community Interveners timely filed their motion, and although they may have a protectable interest related to the subject matter of the litigation, it is doubtful that their interests are impaired by the litigation. The litigation does not prevent any individual from initiating suit against LAPD (D) officers who engage in unconstitutional practices or against the City (D) for engaging in unconstitutional patterns or practices. Nor does any aspect of the litigation prevent the community organizations from continuing to work on police reform. More importantly, neither the individual nor organizational community members have overcome the presumption that the United States (P), as a government litigant, is adequately protecting their interests, as both the individual and organizational community members are the constituents the United States (P) is seeking to protect in the action. The Community Interveners did not contest any portion of the consent decree. Rather, they sought to intervene merely to ensure that it is strictly enforced. Thus, they share the same objective as the United States (P), and any differences they have are differences merely in strategy, which are not enough to justify intervention as a matter of right. Therefore, the district court's denial of the Community Intervener's motion to intervene as a matter of right is affirmed.

(2) Yes. A third party may be granted permissive intervention for the enforcement of a proposed government consent decree where its claim or defense and

Continued on next page.

the main action have a question of law or fact in common, it otherwise has satisfied the requirements of Fed. R. Civ. P. 24(b), and granting intervention will not unduly delay or prejudice the adjudication of the rights of the original parties. The district court erroneously held that, as a matter of law, intervention for enforcement of a proposed government consent decree is never permissible. Instead, the determination whether permissive intervention should be granted is made on a case-by-case basis, founded on an analysis of the factors identified in Rule 24(b). Here it is assumed that jurisdictional and timeliness factors of Rule 24(b) are satisfied. If the court had allowed permissive intervention, the Community Interveners would have made proposals in connection with the proposed consent decree. The fact that the Community Interveners may be also interested in enforcement of the consent decree is not fatal to their permissive intervention request. Because the request was filed before the consent decree was approved, the request should have been analyzed on its own merits without anticipatory consideration of the effect of the proposed consent decree. Thus, this issue must be remanded so that the district court may reassess the request for permissive intervention under the criteria established by Rule 24(b). Under Rule 24(b), a court must consider whether a proposed intervention will unduly delay or prejudice the adjudication of the rights of the original parties. Here, the United States (P) and the City (D) contend that permitting intervention will slow the process. However, the district court's management of this case demonstrates that it is perfectly capable of managing this litigation in a fair, but expedient fashion. More importantly, the idea of "streamlining" the litigation should not be accomplished at the risk of marginalizing those—such as the Police League and the Community Interveners—who have some of the strongest interests in the outcome. For these reasons, the district court's denial of the Community Interveners' motion for permissive intervention is reversed, and the issues the motion poses are remanded to the district court for re-analysis under Rule 24(b). Affirmed in part; reversed in part; remanded.

ANALYSIS

After the notices of appeal were filed in this case, the district court approved and entered the consent decree. According to the court of appeals, it was proper for the district court to continue to act in the case notwithstanding the intervention appeal because no stay had been entered. Thus, although the appeal involved intervention decisions made at the onset of the case, the court of appeals' holding did not require the district court to look backward or rescind the consent decree. Thus, any intervention order that might be issued on remand would allow the affected parties to intervene as of the date of the intervention order and to be treated as intervenor parties from that date forward, but not from the date the consent order was entered or earlier.

Quicknotes

COLLECTIVE BARGAINING Negotiations between an employer and employee that are mediated by a specified third party.

CONSENT DECREE A decree issued by a court of equity ratifying an agreement between the parties to a lawsuit; an agreement by a defendant to cease illegal activity.

INJUNCTIVE RELIEF A court order issued as a remedy, requiring a person to do, or prohibiting that person from doing, a specific act.

INTERVENER A party, not an initial party to the action, who is admitted to the action in order to assert an interest in the subject matter of a lawsuit.

Martin v. Wilks

Firefighters (P) v. Court (D)

490 U.S. 755 (1989)

NATURE OF CASE: Review of reversal of dismissal of reverse-discrimination action.

FACT SUMMARY: Several White firefighters challenged affirmative action plans mandated by a consent decree that was entered in an action of which they had knowledge but had not intervened.

RULE OF LAW

A party may not be bound by a judgment rendered in an action in which he or she was not a party, even if he or she had knowledge of the action.

FACTS: As part of a discrimination action, a consent decree was rendered between the City of Birmingham, Alabama, and a class of Black firefighters. As part of the decree, the City instituted an affirmative action program. Subsequent to this, a group of White firefighters filed a reverse-discrimination action. The district court dismissed, holding that because the White firefighters had notice of the prior action but had elected not to intervene, the matter was res judicata as to them. The U.S. Court of Appeals for the Eleventh Circuit reversed, and the United States Supreme Court granted review.

ISSUE: May a party be bound by a judgment rendered in an action in which he or she was not a party, if he or she had knowledge of the action?

HOLDING AND DECISION: (Rehnquist, C.J.) No. A party may not be bound by a judgment rendered in an action in which he or she was not a party, even if he or she had knowledge of the action. It is a principle of general application that one is not bound by an in personam judgment in a litigation in which one is not designated as a party or has not been made a party by service of process. The argument asserted by those defending the consent decree is that by knowing about the underlying action and failing to intervene, the plaintiffs herein waived that objection to being bound. This is incorrect. A party seeking a judgment binding on another cannot obligate that person to intervene; he or she must be joined. This was the position taken by the Eleventh Circuit, and it was correct in so doing. Affirmed.

DISSENT: (Stevens, J.) In no sense were the White firefighters herein "bound" by the consent decree; rather it was the City of Birmingham that was so bound. The district court properly dismissed the action because the City was fulfilling its legal obligations, not because the White firefighters were somehow bound by the consent decree.

ANALYSIS

Joinder is governed by Fed. R. Civ. P. 19. The rule distinguishes between parties that should be joined and parties that must be joined. Parties may be joined either as defendants or as involuntary plaintiffs.

Quicknotes

COMPULSORY JOINDER The joining of a party to a lawsuit that is mandatory if complete relief cannot be afforded to the parties in his or her absence or if his or her absence will result in injustice.

FED. R. CIV. P. 19 Sets forth the rules governing required joinder of parties.

INTERVENTION The method by which a party, not an initial party to the action, is admitted to the action in order to assert an interest in the subject matter of a lawsuit.

PERMISSIVE JOINDER The joining of parties or claims in a single suit if the claims against the parties arise from the same transaction or occurrence or involve common issues of law or fact; such joinder is not mandatory.

RES JUDICATA The rule of law a final judgment by a court precludes subsequent litigation between the parties regarding the same cause of action.

Hansberry v. Lee

Black land purchaser (D) v. Party to covenant (P)

311 U.S. 32 (1940)

NATURE OF CASE: A class action to enforce a racially restrictive covenant.

FACT SUMMARY: Lee (P) sought to enjoin a sale of land to the Hansberrys (D) on the grounds that the sale violated a racially restrictive covenant.

RULE OF LAW

There must be adequate representation of the members of a class action or the judgment is not binding on the parties not adequately represented.

FACTS: The Hansberrys (D), a Black family, purchased land from a party who had signed a restrictive covenant forbidding the sale of the land to Black people. Lee (P), one of the parties who signed the covenant, sought to have the sale enjoined because it breached the covenant. Lee (P) contended that the validity of the covenant was established in a prior case in which one of the parties was a class of landowners involved with the covenant. To be valid, 95 percent of the landowners had to sign the covenant, and the trial court in the prior case held that 95 percent of the landowners had signed the covenant. That case was appealed, and the Illinois Supreme Court upheld the decision, even though it found that 95 percent of the landowners had not signed the covenant, but the court held that since it was a class action, all members of the class would be bound by the decision of the court. Hansberry (D) claimed that he and the party selling him the house were not bound by the res judicata effect of the prior decision, as they were not parties to the litigation. The lower court held that the decision of the Illinois Supreme Court would have to be challenged directly in order for it be set aside or reversed. Otherwise, the decision was still binding. The case was appealed to the United States Supreme Court.

ISSUE: Must there be adequate representation of the members of a class action to make the judgment binding on the parties not adequately represented?

HOLDING AND DECISION: (Stone, J.) Yes. There must be adequate representation of the members of a class action or the judgment is not binding on the parties not adequately represented. It is not necessary that all members of a class be present as parties to the litigation to be bound by the judgment if they are adequately represented by parties who are present. In regular cases, to be bound by the judgment the party must receive notice and an opportunity to be heard. If due process is not afforded the individual, then the judgment is not binding. The class action is an exception to the general rule. Because of the numbers involved in class actions, it is enough if the party is adequately represented by a member of the class with a similar interest. The Hansberrys (D) were not adequately represented by the class of landowners. Their interests were not similar enough to even be considered members of the same class. Lee (P) and the landowners were trying to restrict Black people from buying any of the land, and the Hansberrys (D) were Black people attempting to purchase land. When there is such a conflicting interest between members of a class, there is most likely not adequate representation of one of the members of the class. There must be a similarity of interest before there can even be a class. Since there was no similarity of interests between Lee (P) and the Hansberrys (D), the Hansberrys (D) could not be considered a member of the class and so the prior judgment was not binding on the Hansberrys (D). The Hansberrys (D) were not afforded due process because of the lack of adequate representation. The judgment is reversed.

ANALYSIS

Fed. R. Civ. P. 23(c)(3) requires that the court describe those whom the court finds to be members of the class. The court is to note those to whom notice was provided and also those who had not requested exclusion. These members are considered members of the class and are bound by the decision of the court whether it is in their favor or not. The Federal Rules of Civil Procedure allow a member of the class to request exclusion from the class, and that party will not be bound by the decision of the court. Since a party must receive notice of the class action before he can request exclusion from the class, the court must determine if a party received sufficient notice of the action or if sufficient effort was made to notify him of the action. The rules state if the court finds that the party did have sufficient notice and was considered a member of the class, he is bound by the decision.

Quicknotes

CLASS ACTION A suit commenced by a representative on behalf of an ascertainable group that is too large to appear in court, shares a commonality of interests, and will benefit from a successful result.

COVENANT A written promise to do, or to refrain from doing, a particular activity.

FED. R. CIV. P. 23 Sets forth the requirements in order to maintain a class-action suit.

Phillips Petroleum v. Shutts

Gas and oil company (D) v. Class of lessees (P)

472 U.S. 797 (1985)

NATURE OF CASE: Appeal of a judgment in a class-action suit.

FACT SUMMARY: Shutts (P) filed a class-action suit against Phillips Petroleum (D) for allegedly underpaying royalties on gas leases.

RULE OF LAW

A state may exercise jurisdiction over absent plaintiffs in a classification suit even if the plaintiffs have no contacts with that state.

FACTS: Phillips Petroleum (Phillips) (D) had gas and mineral leases with numerous individuals. Royalties were based on the selling price of the final product. When prices were raised, Phillips (D) would often pay royalties at a lower price. Shutts (P) filed a class-action suit on behalf of over 33,000 individuals, seeking damages. A Kansas court certified the class. Letters were sent to all members of the plaintiff class. A plaintiff had the right to opt out of the class or be bound by the judgment. About 3,000 opted out. A judgment for the plaintiffs was entered. The Kansas Supreme Court rejected an appeal by Phillips (D) claiming that Kansas could not exercise jurisdiction over plaintiffs not residents of Kansas. Phillips (D) appealed to the United States Supreme Court.

ISSUE: May a state exercise jurisdiction over absent plaintiffs in a class-action suit even if the plaintiffs have no contacts with that state?

HOLDING AND DECISION: (Rehnquist, J.) Yes. A state may exercise jurisdiction over absent plaintiffs in a class-action suit even if the plaintiffs have no contacts with that state. The "minimum contacts" rule is a matter of personal liberty, not state sovereignty. It exists to protect defendants from being hauled into a distant forum unfairly. A plaintiff in a class-action suit is in a much different position. He or she is in no danger of a loss of freedom or assets and, in fact, can sit back and let others do the work for him or her. The plaintiff's ability to opt out of the class further protects him or her, as the plaintiff is not forced to enter a class unwillingly. Affirmed in part, reversed in part, and remanded.

ANALYSIS

The Court stated in this opinion that minimum contacts is an issue of liberty, not sovereignty. This issue has been touched upon since *Pennoyer v. Neff*, 95 U.S. 714 (1877). The Court here held that the opt-out procedure was a sufficient protection of personal liberty.

Quicknotes

CLASS ACTION A suit commenced by a representative on behalf of an ascertainable group that is too large to appear in court, shares a commonality of interests, and will benefit from a successful result.

MINIMUM CONTACTS The minimum degree of contact necessary in order to sustain a cause of action within a particular forum, consistent with the requirements of due process.

Standard Fire Ins. Co. v. Knowles

Insurer (D) v. Insured class action representative (P)

568 U.S. 588 (2013)

NATURE OF CASE: Appeal from remand of a proposed class action from federal court to state court.

FACT SUMMARY: Knowles (P), an insured of Standard Fire Ins. Co. (Standard) (D), filed a proposed class action in state court against Standard (D), stipulating that the class would seek less than $5 million in damages. After removal to federal district court, the court remanded, finding that the amount in controversy fell below the $5 million jurisdictional threshold of the Class Action Fairness Act. Standard (D) contended that the jurisdictional amount had been met based on an aggregation of all potential claims.

RULE OF LAW

A class action representative plaintiff's stipulation as to the amount of damages the class will seek is not binding for purposes of determining a jurisdictional amount-in-controversy.

FACTS: Knowles (P), an insured of Standard Fire Ins. Co. (Standard) (D), filed a proposed class action in state court against Standard (D), stipulating that the class would seek less than $5 million in damages. However, Knowles (P) sought to certify a class of "hundreds, and possibly thousands" of similarly harmed state policyholders, and if all these potential claims were aggregated, the total amount of damages would exceed $5 million. After removal to federal district court, the court remanded, finding that the amount in controversy fell below the $5 million jurisdictional threshold of the Class Action Fairness Act (CAFA). CAFA provides that in determining the threshold amount, the "claims of the individual class members shall be aggregated." Standard (D) contended that the jurisdictional amount had been met based on an aggregation of all potential claims, and that the district court should not have held that Knowles's (P) stipulation was binding. Standard (D) appealed, but the court of appeals in its discretion denied review. The United States Supreme Court, however, granted certiorari.

ISSUE: Is a class action representative plaintiff's stipulation as to the amount of damages the class will seek binding for purposes of determining a jurisdictional amount-in-controversy?

HOLDING AND DECISION: (Breyer, J.) No. A class action representative plaintiff's stipulation as to the amount of damages the class will seek is not binding for purposes of determining a jurisdictional amount-in-controversy. Here, the precertification stipulation can tie Knowles's (P) hands because stipulations are binding on the party who makes them. However, the stipulation does not speak for those Knowles (P) purports to represent, because a plaintiff who files a proposed class action cannot legally bind members of the proposed class before the class is certified. Because Knowles (P) lacked authority to concede the amount in controversy for absent class members, the district court wrongly concluded that his stipulation could overcome its finding that the CAFA jurisdictional threshold had been met. Although Knowles (P) concedes that federal jurisdiction cannot be based on contingent future events, he asserts that the amount he stipulated is not contingent. Nevertheless, because a stipulation must be binding and a named plaintiff cannot bind precertification class members, the amount he stipulated is in effect contingent. CAFA does not forbid a federal court to consider the possibility that a nonbinding, amount-limiting, stipulation may not survive the class certification process. To hold otherwise would, for CAFA jurisdictional purposes, treat a nonbinding stipulation as if it were binding, exalt form over substance, and run counter to CAFA's objective of ensuring that federal courts consider interstate cases of national importance. Finally, Knowles (P) points out individual plaintiffs may avoid removal to federal court by stipulating to amounts that fall below the federal jurisdictional threshold. Although that is true in cases where the stipulations are binding, that is not the case here, since the stipulation cannot be legally binding on any class members other than Knowles (P). For these reasons, the district court erred in remanding the case to state court. Vacated and remanded.

ANALYSIS

The key to this decision is that the class had as yet not been certified. Neither a proposed class action nor a rejected class action may bind nonparties, and a non-named class member is not a party to the class-action litigation before the class is certified. Thus, for example, a damages limitation cannot have a binding effect on the merits of absent class members' claims unless and until the class is certified.

Quicknotes

AMOUNT IN CONTROVERSY The value of a claim sought by a party to a lawsuit.

JURISDICTION The authority of a court to hear and declare judgment in respect to a particular matter.

Amchem Products, Inc. v. Windsor

Asbestos producer (D) v. Class-action plaintiffs (P)

521 U.S. 591 (1997)

NATURE OF CASE: Appeal from reversal of class certification in mass tort action.

FACT SUMMARY: The district court certified a class (P) of persons exposed to asbestos products in order to affect a settlement of the case.

RULE OF LAW

Fed. R. Civ. P. 23 requirements for class certification must be met even if the certification is for settlement only.

FACTS: All the asbestos exposure cases pending in federal courts were transferred and consolidated for pretrial proceedings to a single district court. Following this consolidation, the parties began settlement negotiations. The defendants' steering committee (D) made an offer to settle all pending and future asbestos cases by providing a fund from which to pay claims. Eventually, a settlement was reached for pending cases. A second settlement for potential plaintiffs was then reached. The parties then sought certification of this class of potential plaintiffs for purposes of settlement only. Nine lead plaintiffs were named who were designed to be representative of a class of all persons and family members who had been exposed to asbestos products but had not yet filed suit. The district court approved the settlement, certified the class (P), and enjoined class members from filing additional suits. Objectors raised numerous challenges to the settlement, claiming that it unfairly disadvantaged those without current problems. The court of appeals reversed the certification on the grounds that Fed. R. Civ. P. 23 requirements were not met. The defendants appealed.

ISSUE: Must Fed. R. Civ. P. 23 requirements for class certification be met even if the certification is for settlement only?

HOLDING AND DECISION: (Ginsburg, J.) Yes. Fed. R. Civ. P. 23 requirements for class certification must be met even if the certification is for settlement only. Rule 23, authorizing class actions, has several requirements that must be satisfied. These standards are designed to protect absent class members. They may not be disregarded simply because a court believes that a settlement is fair. First, common questions of law or fact must predominate over questions affecting individual members. The district court's reliance on the claimants' interest in a compensation scheme does not meet this requirement. A compensation scheme is a matter for legislative consideration. Secondly, the named parties in a class action must fairly and adequately protect the interests of the class. The district court failed to break the class into subclasses. Thus, the named parties had diverse medical conditions and diverse interests that could cause conflicts of interest. Furthermore, there are impediments to the provision of adequate notice because there are persons in the class who may not even know of their exposure to asbestos yet. The only proper accommodation that should be made to settlement-only class certification is that the problems of trial administration should be ignored. Accordingly, in the present case, the class was improperly certified because the requirements of Rule 23 were not satisfied. Affirmed.

CONCURRENCE AND DISSENT: (Breyer, J.) The need for settlement in mass tort cases is greater than the majority suggests. Also, settlement-related issues should be given more weight for purposes of determining whether common issues predominate. Settlement is something that should help the class meet the Rule 23 requirements.

ANALYSIS

Settlement classes have become more and more common since the advent of Rule 23, which does not make provision for such classes. Many commentators have called for revision to Rule 23 to address the reality of settlement classes. However, others have objected on the basis that settlement classes invite collusion among class counsel and the defense.

Quicknotes

FED. R. CIV. P. 23 Sets forth the requirements in order to maintain a class-action suit.

SETTLEMENT An agreement entered into by the parties to a civil lawsuit agreeing upon the determination of rights and issues between them, thus disposing of the need for judicial determination.

Glossary

Common Latin Words and Phrases Encountered in the Law

A FORTIORI: Because one fact exists or has been proven, therefore a second fact that is related to the first fact must also exist.

A PRIORI: From the cause to the effect. A term of logic used to denote that when one generally accepted truth is shown to be a cause, another particular effect must necessarily follow.

AB INITIO: From the beginning; a condition that has existed throughout, as in a marriage that was void ab initio.

ACTUS REUS: The wrongful act; in criminal law, such action as is sufficient to trigger criminal liability.

AD VALOREM: According to value; an ad valorem tax is imposed upon an item located within the taxing jurisdiction calculated by the value of such item.

AMICUS CURIAE: Friend of the court. Its most common usage takes the form of an amicus curiae brief, filed by a person who is not a party to an action but is nonetheless allowed to offer an argument supporting his or her legal interests.

ARGUENDO: In arguing. A statement, possibly hypothetical, made for the purpose of argument.

BILL QUIA TIMET: A bill to quiet title (establish ownership) to real property.

BONA FIDE: True, honest, or genuine. May refer to a person's legal position based on good faith or lacking notice of fraud (such as a bona fide purchaser for value) or to the authenticity of a particular document (such as a bona fide last will and testament).

CAUSA MORTIS: With approaching death in mind. A gift causa mortis is a gift given by a party who feels certain that death is imminent.

CAVEAT EMPTOR: Let the buyer beware. This maxim is reflected in the rule of law that a buyer purchases at his or her own risk because it is the buyer's responsibility to examine, judge, test, and otherwise inspect what he or she is buying.

CERTIORARI: A writ of review. Petitions for review of a case by the United States Supreme Court are most often done by means of a writ of certiorari.

CONTRA: On the other hand. Opposite. Contrary to.

CORAM NOBIS: Before us; a writ of error directed to the court that originally rendered the judgment.

CORAM VOBIS: Before you; a writ of error directed by an appellate court to a lower court to correct a factual error.

CORPUS DELICTI: The body of the crime; the requisite elements of a crime amounting to objective proof that a crime has been committed.

CUM TESTAMENTO ANNEXO, ADMINISTRATOR (ADMINISTRATOR C.T.A.): With will annexed; an administrator c.t.a. settles an estate pursuant to a will in which he or she is not appointed.

DE BONIS NON, ADMINISTRATOR (ADMINISTRATOR D.B.N.): Of goods not administered; an administrator d.b.n. settles a partially settled estate.

DE FACTO: In fact; in reality; actually. Existing in fact but not officially approved or engendered.

DE JURE: By right; lawful. Describes a condition that is legitimate "as a matter of law," in contrast to the term "de facto," which connotes something existing in fact but not legally sanctioned or authorized. For example, de facto segregation refers to segregation brought about by housing patterns, etc., whereas de jure segregation refers to segregation created by law.

DE MINIMUS: Of minimal importance; insignificant; a trifle; not worth bothering about.

DE NOVO: Anew; a second time; afresh. A trial de novo is a new trial held at the appellate level as if the case originated there and the trial at a lower level had not taken place.

DICTA: Generally used as an abbreviated form of obiter dicta, a term describing those portions of a judicial opinion incidental or not necessary to resolution of the specific question before the court. Such nonessential statements and remarks are not considered to be binding precedent.

DUCES TECUM: Refers to a particular type of writ or subpoena requesting a party or organization to produce certain documents in their possession.

EN BANC: Full bench. Where a court sits with all justices present rather than the usual quorum.

EX PARTE: For one side or one party only. An ex parte proceeding is one undertaken for the benefit of only one party, without notice to, or an appearance by, an adverse party.

EX POST FACTO: After the fact. An ex post facto law is a law that retroactively changes the consequences of a prior act.

EX REL.: Abbreviated form of the term "ex relatione," meaning upon relation or information. When the state brings an action in which it has no interest against an individual at the instigation of one who has a private interest in the matter.

FORUM NON CONVENIENS: Inconvenient forum. Although a court may have jurisdiction over the case, the action should be tried in a more conveniently located court, one to which parties and witnesses may more easily travel, for example.

GUARDIAN AD LITEM: A guardian appointed by the court to represent a minor or incompetent person in a legal action.

HABEAS CORPUS: You have the body. The modern writ of habeas corpus is a writ directing that a person (body) being detained (such as a prisoner) be brought before the court so that the legality of his or her detention can be judicially ascertained.

IN CAMERA: In private, in chambers. When a hearing is held before a judge in his or her chambers or when all spectators are excluded from the courtroom.

IN FORMA PAUPERIS: In the manner of a pauper. A party who proceeds in forma pauperis because of his or her poverty is one who is allowed to bring suit without liability for costs.

INFRA: Below, under. A word referring the reader to a later part of a book. (The opposite of supra.)

IN LOCO PARENTIS: In the place of a parent.

IN PARI DELICTO: Equally wrong; a court of equity will not grant requested relief to an applicant who is in pari delicto, or as much at fault in the transactions giving rise to the controversy as is the opponent of the applicant.

IN PARI MATERIA: On like subject matter or upon the same matter. Statutes relating to the same person or things are said to be in pari materia. It is a general rule of statutory construction that such statutes should be construed together, i.e., looked at as if they together constituted one law.

IN PERSONAM: Against the person. Jurisdiction over the person of an individual.

IN RE: In the matter of. Used to designate a proceeding involving an estate or other property.

IN REM: Signifies an action against the res, or thing. An action in rem is basically one that is taken directly against property, as distinguished from an action in personam, i.e., against the person.

INTER ALIA: Among other things. Used to show that the whole of a statement, pleading, list, statute, etc., has not been set forth in its entirety.

INTER PARTES: Between the parties. May refer to contracts, conveyances, or other transactions having legal significance.

INTER VIVOS: Between the living. An inter vivos gift is a gift made by a living grantor, as distinguished from bequests contained in a will, which pass upon the death of the testator.

IPSO FACTO: By the mere fact itself.

JUS: Law or the entire body of law.

LEX LOCI: The law of the place; the notion that the rights of parties to a legal proceeding are governed by the law of the place where those rights arose.

MALUM IN SE: Evil or wrong in and of itself; inherently wrong. Describes an act that is wrong by its very nature, as opposed to one which would not be wrong but for the fact that there is a specific legal prohibition against it (malum prohibitum).

MALUM PROHIBITUM: Wrong because prohibited, but not inherently evil. Describes something that is wrong because it is expressly forbidden by law but that is not in and of itself evil, e.g., speeding.

MANDAMUS: We command. A writ directing an official to take a certain action.

MENS REA: A guilty mind; a criminal intent. A term used to signify the mental state that accompanies a crime or other prohibited act. Some crimes require only a general mens rea (general intent to do the prohibited act), but others, like assault with intent to murder, require the existence of a specific mens rea.

MODUS OPERANDI: Method of operating; generally refers to the manner or style of a criminal in committing crimes, admissible in appropriate cases as evidence of the identity of a defendant.

NEXUS: A connection to.

NISI PRIUS: A court of first impression. A nisi prius court is one where issues of fact are tried before a judge or jury.

N.O.V. (NON OBSTANTE VEREDICTO): Notwithstanding the verdict. A judgment n.o.v. is a judgment given in favor of one party despite the fact that a verdict was returned in favor of the other party, the justification being that the verdict either had no reasonable support in fact or was contrary to law.

NUNC PRO TUNC: Now for then. This phrase refers to actions that may be taken and will then have full retroactive effect.

PENDENTE LITE: Pending the suit; pending litigation underway.

PER CAPITA: By head; beneficiaries of an estate, if they take in equal shares, take per capita.

PER CURIAM: By the court; signifies an opinion ostensibly written "by the whole court" and with no identified author.

PER SE: By itself, in itself; inherently.

PER STIRPES: By representation. Used primarily in the law of wills to describe the method of distribution where a person, generally because of death, is unable to take that which is left to him or her by the will of another, and therefore his or her heirs divide such property between them rather than take under the will individually.

PRIMA FACIE: On its face, at first sight. A prima facie case is one that is sufficient on its face, meaning that the evidence supporting it is adequate to establish the case until contradicted or overcome by other evidence.

PRO TANTO: For so much; as far as it goes. Often used in eminent domain cases when a property owner receives partial payment for his or her land without prejudice to his or her right to bring suit for the full amount he or she claims the land to be worth.

QUANTUM MERUIT: As much as the party deserves. Refers to recovery based on the doctrine of unjust enrichment in those cases in which a party has rendered valuable services or furnished materials that were accepted and enjoyed by another under circumstances that would reasonably notify the recipient that the rendering party expected to be paid. In essence, the law implies a contract to pay the reasonable value of the services or materials furnished.

QUASI: Almost like; as if; nearly. Essentially used to signify that one subject or thing is almost analogous to another but that material differences between them do exist. For example, a quasi-criminal proceeding is one that is not strictly criminal but shares enough of the same characteristics to require some of the same safeguards (e.g., procedural due process must be followed in a parole hearing).

QUID PRO QUO: Something for something. In contract law, the consideration, something of value, passed between the parties to render the contract binding.

RES GESTAE: Things done. In evidence law, this principle justifies the admission of a statement that would otherwise be hearsay when it is made so closely to the event in question as to be said to be a part of it, or with such spontaneity as not to have the possibility of falsehood.

RES IPSA LOQUITUR: The thing speaks for itself. This doctrine gives rise to a rebuttable presumption of negligence when the instrumentality causing the injury was within the exclusive control of the defendant, and the injury was one that does not normally occur unless a person has been negligent.

RES JUDICATA: A matter adjudged. Doctrine that provides that once a court of competent jurisdiction has rendered a final judgment or decree on the merits, that judgment or decree is conclusive upon the parties to the case and prevents them from engaging in any other litigation on the points and issues determined therein.

RESPONDEAT SUPERIOR: Let the master reply. This doctrine holds the master liable for the wrongful acts of his or her servant (or the principal for his or her agent) in those cases in which the servant (or agent) was acting within the scope of his or her authority at the time of the injury.

STARE DECISIS: To stand by or adhere to that which has been decided. The common law doctrine of stare decisis attempts to give security and certainty to the law by following the policy that once a principle of law as applicable to a certain set of facts has been set forth in a decision, it forms a precedent that will subsequently be followed, even though a different decision might be made were it the first time the question had arisen. Of course, stare decisis is not an inviolable principle and is departed from in instances where there is good cause (e.g., considerations of public policy led the Supreme Court to disregard prior decisions sanctioning segregation).

SUPRA: Above. A word referring a reader to an earlier part of a book. (The opposite of infra.)

ULTRA VIRES: Beyond the power. This phrase is most commonly used to refer to actions taken by a corporation that are beyond the power or legal authority of the corporation.

Addendum of French Derivatives

CHATTEL: Tangible personal property.

CY PRES: Doctrine permitting courts to apply trust funds to purposes not expressed in the trust but necessary to carry out the settlor's intent.

IN PAIS: Not pursuant to legal proceedings.

PER AUTRE VIE: For another's life; during another's life. In property law, an estate may be granted that will terminate upon the death of someone other than the grantee.

PROFIT A PRENDRE: A license to remove minerals or other produce from land.

VOIR DIRE: Process of questioning jurors as to their predispositions about the case or parties to a proceeding in order to identify those jurors displaying bias or prejudice.